1870 CENSUS

CABELL COUNTY WEST VIRGINIA

Carrie Eldridge

Heritage Books
2024

HERITAGE BOOKS

AN IMPRINT OF HERITAGE BOOKS, INC.

Books, CDs, and more—Worldwide

For our listing of thousands of titles see our website
at
www.HeritageBooks.com

A Facsimile Reprint
Published 2024 by
HERITAGE BOOKS, INC.
Publishing Division
5810 Ruatan Street
Berwyn Heights, MD 20740

Heritage Books by the author:

1860 Census, Cabell County, West Virginia

1870 Census, Cabell County, West Virginia

An Atlas of Appalachian Trails to the Ohio River

An Atlas of German Migration and America

An Atlas of Northern Trails Westward from New England

An Atlas of Settlement between the Appalachian Mountains and the Mississippi/Missouri Valleys: 1760–1880

An Atlas of the Southern Trails to the Mississippi

An Atlas of Trails West of the Mississippi River

Cabell County's Empire for Freedom

Cabell County, Virginia/West Virginia, Superior Court Records, 1843–1848

Etna Iron Works: Ledger Book - Expense Records, 1876–1878 (Final Ledger), Lawrence County, Ohio

Looking at the Personal Diaries of William F. Dusenberry of Bloomingdale, (Cabell County), Virginia/West Virginia, 1855 and 1856, Plus Parts of 1862, 1869, 1870, and 1871

Minute Books: Cabell County, [West] Virginia Minute Book 1, 1809–1815

Miscellaneous Cabell County, West Virginia Records: Order Book Overseers of the Poor, 1814–1861; Fee Book, 1826–1839; 1857–1859 (Rule Book); Cabell Land for Tax Purposes, 1861–1865

Nicholas County, Kentucky Property Tax Lists, 1800–1811 with Indexes to Deed Books A & B (2), and C

Nicholas County, Kentucky Records: Stray Book 1, 1805–1811; Stray Book 2, 1813–1819; Stray Book 3, 1820–1870; and Execution Book A, 1801–1878

On the Frontier of Virginia and North Carolina

Owen County, Kentucky Stray Books 1 & 2: 1819–1830, 1830–1864

Torn Apart: How Cabell Countians Fought the Civil War

— Publisher's Notice —
In reprints such as this, it is often not possible to remove blemishes from the original. We feel the contents of this book warrant its reissue despite these blemishes and hope you will agree and read it with pleasure.

International Standard Book Number
Paperbound: 978-0-7884-2776-3

1870 CENSUS

CABELL COUNTY, WEST VIRGINIA

11

	sq.mi.	1809	1842	1867
CABELL	232			
Lincoln	439			721
Wayne	508		1229	
Logan	456	2109		
Mingo	424			

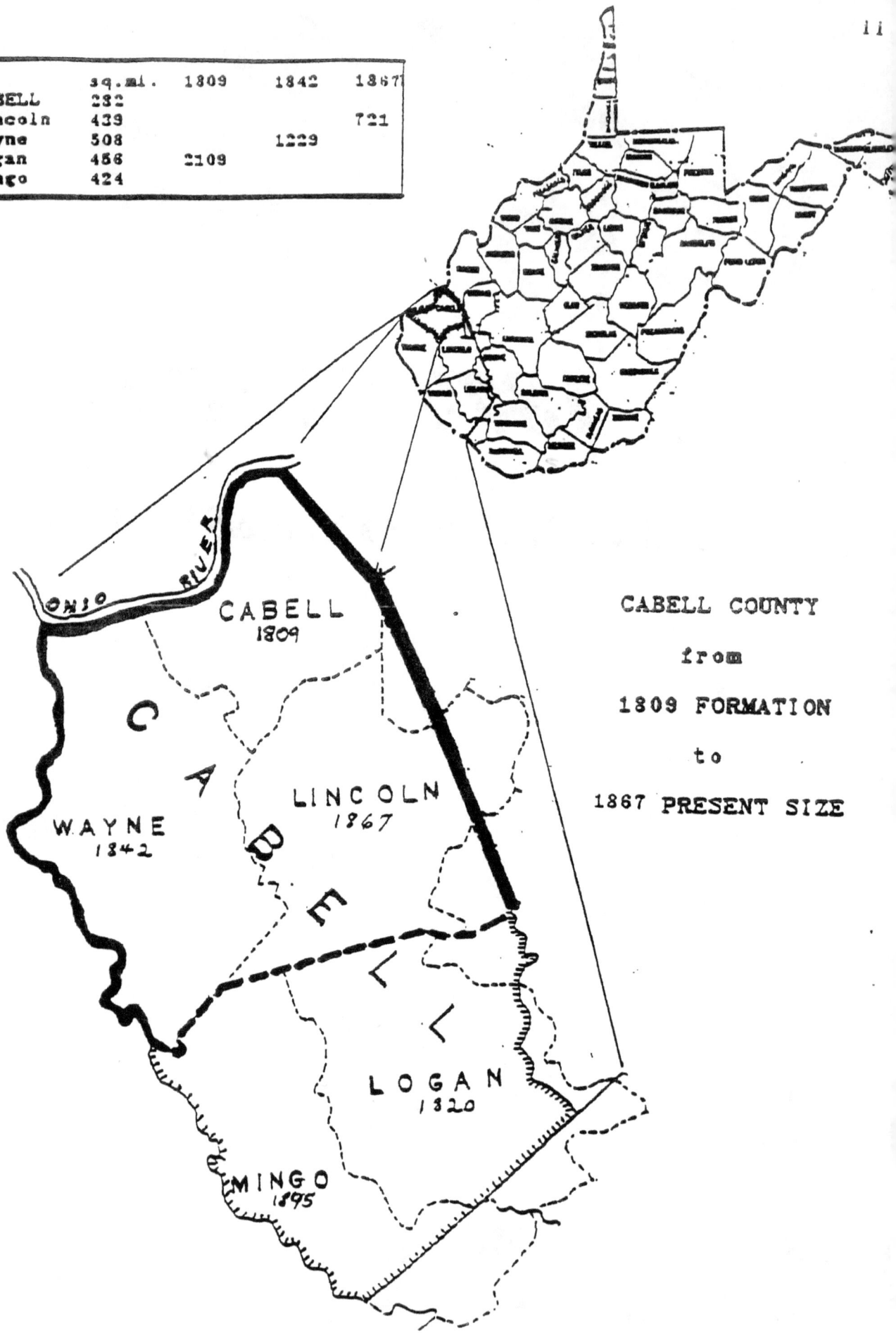

CABELL

1809

CABELL COUNTY

from

1809 FORMATION

to

1867 PRESENT SIZE

OHIO RIVER

WAYNE
1842

LINCOLN
1867

C A B E L L

LOGAN
1320

MINGO
1895

This book is dedicated to Betty Jamison who passed away the same day this book was completed.

TABLE OF CONTENTS

ILLUSTRATIONS

A Census Introduction

The United States Population Census is the primary tool for anyone doing historical or genelogical research. The U.S.Census, begun in 1790 in order to get an idea of how many people lived in the new nation, can provide much information about an area's residents. The first census was a simple list of the heads of the household and their taxable property. Each census taken since that date has added more information and given us a greater research tool. The census should be your first research material after you have organized information from family sources. If you have a name or location then your family is before you; if you have no idea where to look then a family name can be located by searching different census. Like "footsteps in the sand" the trail may be indistinct, but it will lead someplace.

Every census has it's own value; something that makes it different from all the rest. 1870's value comes from the information which can be gleaned about the Civil War. Are the sons missing ? Too many widows ? Not enough married women ? The War casued many changes in America and sent many families west for a new begining. Much about these displaced families appears in the 1870 Census if the researcher just has the patience to dig into the material.

Remember, there is more to the census than a name. Look at neighbors for interrelationships, and location for origin or destination (often groups traveled from one area to another and most often they had family ties). Although most nineteenth century occupations read "farmer", it certainly is not the only listed occupation. Sometimes occupation can even indicate place of origin and it definitely tells to you look in a town if the person is a merchant, doctor or lawyer.

Census records can be a real piece of information and if you find one relative many more may be close at hand. I, personally, have returned to the same page and two adjacent pages of one small county for five great-great families. Hopefully, you will also have that feeling up your spine when all your cousins are there on the page in front of you.

HOW TO READ A CENSUS ENTRY

```
                                              age      birth place
                                              sex         ocupation
household number
                         #94-93
head of household        Dundass,James      33m WV farmer    (1)
    wife                    Eliza           29f WV
                            Mary J.          8f WV
    children                Betty            6f WV
                            Charles          4m WV
                            Sallie           2f WV
    wife's parents       Seamonds,William   62m VA farmer    (2)
                         Seamonds,Nancy      60f VA
    wife's brother       Seamonds,Paton     28m WV laborer
```

(1) James Dundas married Eliza Seamonds-------
(2) William Seamonds m Nancy Harshbarger 2 mar 1829 Cabell Co.

NUMBER - most census give each house in a district a separate number(even empty houses). Sometimes, if there are two families in the same house, each family is numbered created the dual number 94-93.

This particular census does not use continuous numbers for the whole county, but numbers each district separate. Confusion.

```
        170-174
        Kyle,Tennessey      27f WV housekeeper
          Justice,Jennetta  5f
```

(?? widow with child by first marriage??)

```
        151-146
        Shaver,John         26m VA farmer
          Luella            23f
          Mary M            9/12f WV
 his brother  Shaver,Daniel 23m VA laborer
 & family     Shaver,Clore E. 18f WV
              Shaver,Emogene  1f OH
```

(2nd family husband b VA, wife b WV, child b OH)

NOTE: The State of West Virginia was created in 1863, so a person who says he was born in West Virginia before 1863 usually means in the western Virginia and usually in the Same county as being presently enumerated.(This place)

1

United States Census 1870 Cabell County, West Virginia

1-1 represents the house number given by U.S.Census
-places of birth are not repeated when same in household
-Persons in household w/different name---entered completely

----

abbreviations

B----Black(negro) after state (whites are not marked)

asse--assessor	press-pressman	AR-Arkansas
barb--barber	river-works on river	CT-Connecticut
blks--blacksmith	RR----Railroad	IA-Iowa
blksw-blacksmith worker	RR----RR worker	IL-Illinois
br----bridge	RRC---RR contractor	IN-Indiana
brclk-Bridge clerk	sadl--sadler	KY-Kentucky
brmn--brick mason	saw---sawmill worker	LA-Louisana
bsf---boat & shoe	sch---school	MD-Maryland
manufarture	sh----shop	ME-Maine
btbr--boat builder	spcar-ships carpenter	NC-North Carolina
butc--butcher	shoe--shoemaker	NH-New Hampshire
carp--carpenter	slsm--silversmith	NJ-New Jersey
clk---clerk in store	tan---works tanyard	NY-New York
coop--cooper	tavern-tavern owner	OH-Ohio
dom---domestice servant	tayl--tailor	PA-Pennsylvania
dray--drayman	teach-teacher	SC-South Carolina
drt---drives team	team--teamster	TN-Tennessee
drug--druggist	timdl-timber dealer	VA-Virginia
eng---engineer	timr--timber merchant	VT-Vermont
farm--farmer	tin---tinner	WI-Wisconsin
flor--works flour mill	tobm--tobacco manufactor	WV-West Virginia
fur---furrier	tunn--builds tunnels	
groc--grocier	wgmk--wagon maker	
hack--hack driver	wgsh--wagon shop	
hotl--hotel	whfclk-wharfboat clerk	
jail--jailor	VINEYARD	Aus-Austria
kph---keeping house		Can-Canada
lab---laborer		Eng-England
law---lawyer		Fra-France
lnag--land agent		German States
lrmr--leather manufactor		Baden
lrst--livery stable		Bav-Bavaria
lvsk--livestock dealer		Ger-Germania
mail--mail carrier		Han-Hanover
man---manager		Hes-Hesse Durmstand
mer---merchant		Num-Numlomburg
min-- minister		Pru-Prussia
mlrt--millright		Radon
pau---pauper		Sax-Saxony
phy---physician		Wur-Wurlonburg
pilot-riverboat pilot		Hol-Holland
plst--plaster		Ire-Ireland
pntr--painter		Sct-Scotland
PO----Post Office		Swe-Sweden

page 1(p539) Barboursville Twp   9 jul 1870   PO Cabell Court House

1-1
Workman,Ambrose   27m VA farm
   Susan   27f WV
   James N.   3m
   Lizzie V.   1f
   John E. 3/12m

2-2

Hoback,Lorenzo   39m WV farm
   Martha   32f
   Mary S.   12m
   Hannah   10f
   Franklin   4m
   Ida   2f
Davis,Margaret   6f
Blankenship,Jefferson 22m lab
Blankenship,John   24m   lab

3-3
Nite,Wayne   32m WV farm
   Elizabeth   28f
   Nancy A.   7f
   John L.   6m OH
   Adalade   1/12f WV

4-4
Dillon,Benjamin   38m WV farm
   Catherine   26f
   Stephen D.   7m
   William J.   5m
   Nannie   2f
   Claudius   8/12m

5-5
Hughs,Lorenzo D. 25m WV farm
   Electir   26f
   Beverly   3m
   Mary   8/12f

6-6
Hughs,Ralph   23m WV farm
   Margaret V.   32f VA
   Mary E.   27f WV

7-7
Mather,John   37m KY lab
   Sarah A.   37f KY
   James A.   13m WV lab
   Jacob   7m
   Nancy   3f

7-7 (con't)
Mather--
   John   4m WV
   Mahala   1f

p539a
8-8
Smith,Ralph   47m WV farm
   Mahala   41f
   Talethia   15f   school
   Allen   10m
   Roda   9f
   Ann   6f
   Ellison 3/12m
Smith,William   69m   labor

9-9
Bryant,Marion   24m WV farmer
   Isabella   18f
   James   1m

10-10
Nite,Mathew   61m KY farmer
   Nancy   60f WV
   Mary   29f
   Alvin S.   2om   labor
Cook,James   13m

11-11
Dillon,Reece P.   35m VA farm
   Adalade   26f WV
   Sarah E.   12f
   Thomas J.   8m
   Charles   6m
   John M.   5m
   Susan   3f
Boland,Thomas   11m

12-12
Dillon,John L.   49m VA farmer
   Ruth A.   43f WV
   Julius   15m   labor
   Orenda J.   13f
   Mary A.   11f
   John R.   9m
Shy,Edward   84m VA
Shy,Elizabeth   75f VA

13-13
Patton,Erastus   34m OH farmer
   Sabina   23f WV
   Emma M.   1f OH

13-13 (con't)	Patton			
Yates,John W.	17m	WV	lab	
Yates,Sarah E.	10f			

14-14				
Edens,Edward	59m	VA	farm	
p540 Mary I.	57f			
Lucy A.	31f			
Martha J.	27f			
Sarah F.	18f	WV		
Benjamin	16m		lab	
Mary E.	14f			
Samuel H.	11m			
Edward	9m			

15-15				
Dunkle,Henry C.	31m	WV	teacher	
Catherine	27f	WV		
William H.	9m	WV		
John A.	7m			
James A.	4m			
Minnie	1f			

16-16				
Cook.Abner	71m	VA	farm	
Mary	65f	WV		
Mary	30f			
Catherine	24f		dm sv	
Eliza A.	22f		dm sv	
Martha A.	20f			
Henry L.	17m		labor	
George A.	15m		labor	

17-17				
McCartie,John L.	45m	VA	lab	
Ford,Nancy	65f			
McCartie,Francis	18m			

18-18				
Laywell,James	36m	VA	farm	
Cristina	36f			

19-19				
Hale,Samuel	32m	VA	farm	
Nancy J.	26f	WV		
Mary J.	9f	VA		
Robert H.	7/12m	WV		

20-20				
Thornburg,John W.	37m	WV	farm	
Emily H.	37f			
Mary S.	16f			
Willie F.	15m			

20-20 (con't)	Thornburg			
Claudius	13m	WV		
Gerturde	8f			
James L.	7m			
John M.	4m			
Blankenship,James	18	m		

21-21				
Hensley,Samuel	70m	VA	farmer	
p540a Thona	65f	NC		
Lucy	22f	WV		
George W.	39m		labor	
Prise,Albert	20m		labor	

22-22				
Hensley,John L.	43m	WV	labor	
Catherine	40f	VA		
Charles L.	12m	WV		
George B.	5m			
Marengo	4f			
Clark,Angelia	10f			

23-23				
Morrison,Patrick	39m	WV	farmer	
Malinda	38f	IL		
Charles	13m	WV	labor	
Franklin	12m			
Elizabeth	11f			
Eugenia	9f			
William	7m			
Patrick H.	6m			
Nannie W.	5f			
Thomas W.	2m			
Malinda	1/12f			

24-24				
Hensley,Bird	60m	VA	farmer	
Nancy	59f	KY		
Mary A.	28f	IL		
Sarah	25f	IL		
Columbus	23m	WV	labor	
Fannie	19f		school	
Allice	14f		school	
Willie	8m			

25-25				
Keller,Samuel	36m	VA	farmer	
Elizabeth	35f	IL		
Nancy E.	8f	WV		
Jasper	7m			
Allice	5f			
Adam	3m			
William S.	1m			

4

26-26

Hensley, James 34m WV farm
Ann 36f
Julius 8m
p541 Thornburg, Caroline 44f
Thornburg, Sarah W. 16f sch
Thornburg, Elizabeth 15f sch
Thornburg, Charles 4m
*(27-27)Thornburg, Moses 75m WV (out of position on census)

27-27

Hensley, James A. 6m WV
Mary F. 5f
Willie A. 4m
Ida May 2f
Davis, Edna 13f

28-28

Chapman, Willie 33m WV lab
Missouri 28f
Albert 8m
Fannie 6f
Mary 1f

29-29

Walker, Harvey 48m VA farm
Adelia 44f OH
Martha V. 18f WV
James A. 22m VA lab
Sarah J. 15f WV sch
Henry W. 12m
Adelia 10f
Anna M. 9f
Sidney B. 8m
Richard E. 6m
Franklin 4m
Elizabeth G. 1f
Elisha C. 1m

30-30

Herold, William 75m TN farm
Nancy J. 48f VA

31-31

France, Benjamin 25m WV farm
James 36m farm
Viley 37f
Lidea 6f
William 4m
Henry L. 2m
Roxey 1f

32-32

Smith, Elizabeth 44f WV house
Jefferson 20m lab

32-32 (Con't)

Smith----
Ela C. 17f
Burrel 15m lab
James 13m lab
p541a James
Anjalina 10f
Jacob F. 11m
Marenda J. 7f

33-33

Adkins, John S. 60m VA farmer
Nancy 60f VA
John 26m KY lab
Mary 25f WV
Olaver 1m

34-34

Davis, Alven 35m WV farmer
Adaline 30f
Milton J. 10m
William B. 9m
Francis 7f
Jefferson 5m
Abreham 4m
Randolph 1m
Prichard, Sarah 23f

35-35

Childers, William 42m WV farmer
Ann 29f

36-36

Parson, John H. 27m WV farmer
Julia 19f
Edward 17m lab
Lorenzo D. 15m lab
*27-27 (out of position on cen)
Thornburg, Moses 75m WV lab

37-37

Bensen, John L. 31m WV farmer
Hester A. 30f
Laura W. 8f
Hugh B. 6m
William 3m

38-38

Davis, Valentine 24m WV farmer
Cintha 22f
Walter 4m
Otis 2m
Alfred 10m

```
39-39                                     48-48
   Elmore,William    37m WV farm          Childers,Samuel   53m WV farmer
            Jeanna   25f                          Cathrine   51f
            Roddie   14f     sch                  Sarah E.   29f
            Edwin    12m                          Patrick H. 24m     teacher
            Jefferson 10m                         John M.    22m     Blksmth
            Sarah    6f                           Phillip M. 20m     lab
p542        Bennett  5m                           Charles F. 19m     lab
            Pascal   2m                           James M.   16m     lab
                                                  Samuel     15m     lab
40-40                               p542a         Newton     13m
   Elmore,Edward     72m WV farm                  Rufus,J.   13m
            Roddie   64f                           Anna B.   10f
40-41                                             Benjamin   8m
   Blankenship,Aranna 20f WV        49-49
                                       Morris,Benjamin 32m B WV lab
41-42                                           Mahaley    28f B
   Bishop,John       22m WV farm                Ann         8f B
            Martha   19 f                       Moses       6m B
            James S.  3m                        Charles     4m B
            Elizabeth 3/12f                     Mary        2f B
                                                William   4/12m B
42-43
   Ghear,Acy         42m WV farm     50-50
            Nancy    35f OH             Nicely,Dudley    41m VA farm
            Acy M.    3m PA                      Susan     29f
            Liddie J. 1f WV                      Zach      14m
                                                 Sarah     13f
43-44                                            John      10m
   Dudley,John       66m VA farm                 William    8m
            Pollie   60f VA                      Charles    5m
            Julia A. 30f WV                      Mary     11/12m WV
            Elizabeth 30f
44-        John      26m    lab       51-51
            Margaret 22f                 Jenkins,Phillip E.31m VA farm
            Mahaly   27f                         Mary J.       37f
                                                 Jackson       6m
45-45                                            Medina B.     4f WV
   Adkins,Riley      25m WV lab                  Ida E.      6/12f
            Frances  21f
            Martha    2f               52-52
            James   4/12m                 Baumgardiner,Jas.62m VA farm
                                                 Margaret    22f WV
46-46                                            John        23m     lab
   Bruce,John        51m OH board                Welcom      18m
            Rebecca  35f PA                      Valentine    6m
            Riley    14m OH                      Grant        3m
47-47                                            Phillip      1m
   Prise,John        36m Eng boar     53-53
            Emma     30f Eng             Booth,William     25m WV farm
            William  10m Eng                     Mary        27f
            John O.   6m Eng                     Emily J.     2f
```

```
54-54
   Waugh,Charley      39m OH farm
      Lemary          32f WV
      Hiram           10m
      Susan S.         8f
      Nancy            4f
      Patrick          2m
p543
   Cremeans,James     13m
   Cremeans,Sarah A. 10f
   Cremeans,Susan      8f
55-55
   Childers,William S.27m WV far
      Victoria        21f
      Sarah A.         1f
   Joy,Sarah          28f

56-56
   Childers,George W.25m WV farm
      Virginia        23f
      John A.          2m
      Mary             1f

57-57
   Willey,Joseph L.   32m WV farm
      Arametta        28f
      William F.       3m

58-58
   Herrenkohl,Albert 40m Sweden
      Louisa          39f WV
      Hellena         75f Prussia
      Charles         12m WV
      Milinka         10f
      Envil            7m
      Albert           5m

59-59
   Baumgardiner,Wm.   21m WV farm
      Sarah           19f
60-60
   Collins,Aaron      23m WV farm
      Susan           26f

61-61
   Wentz,Lewis M.     29m WV farm
      Sarah E.        22f
      Arnetta       9/12f
      Ienetta       9/12f
      John            38m    lab
```

```
62-62
   Ferguson,William 54m WV lab
      Polley        63f VA
      Lenard        15m WV lab

63-63
   Wood,George H.   23m WV farm
      Susan         27f OH
      Millroy        8m OH
      Lucy           3f WV
      Anetta         1f

64-64
   Derton,Henry     29m WV saw
      Henrietta     31f
p543a Sarah F.       6f
      Mary E.        4f
      Albert A.      2m

65-65
   Collins,William  86m VA farm
      Zilpha        61f NY
      Enoch         18m WV

66-66
   Bias,Beny        44m VA farm
      Sarah         35f VA
      Lewis         17f WV lab
      Andersen      15m    lab
      Emaline       13f
      Mary          11f
      Leandir        9m
      Hestir Ann     6f
      Nancy          4f
      John           2m
   Bias,James       76m VA lab

67-67
   Mealing,Charles  23m Numlomburg
      Matilda       22f WV
      Elizabeth      2f
      John           1m
68-
69-68
   Fulks,James J.   26m OH farm
      Mary A.       26f OH
      Luhatta        1f OH

70-69
   Meeling,Charles F.54m Baden
      Catherine     57f Wurlonburg
      John          16m OH
```

70-69 (con't)				
Payne,Henry	16m	OH	lab	
Kelly,Mary	27f	WV		
Kelly,Stephen	4m			

71-70				
Bowen,Dyke	36m	WV	farm	
Sarah A.	31f			
Hensen H.	14m			
Isadira	12f			
Wayne P.	8m			
Garland	5m			
Edward	3m			
Morris	8/12m			

72-71				
McCune,Benjamin	34m	WV	carp	
p544 Sarah	39f			
Julia	20f			
John	19m		carp	
Frank	16m		carp	
Charles	14m			
Lawrence	12m			
Bailey	10m			
Mary E.	7f			
Henry	4m			
Salem	6m			
George	1m			

73-72				
Cox,John A.	39m	WV	farm	
Adelia	39f	OH		
William L.	16m	OH	sch	
Saka	15f	OH	sch	
Albert E.	10m	WV		
Harris M.	6m			
Edward	4m			

74-73				
Cox,Joseph	31m	WV	farm	
Mariah	29f	OH		
Sarah	74f	VA		
Eugene L.	1m	WV		

75-74				
Knight,Henry	62m	NC	farm	
Margaret	57f	WV		
Laffyett	25m	WV	lab	
Lucy A.	21f	OH		
Sarah M.	20f	WV		
Henrietta	13f			
Amacetta	13f			
Sheff,Albert	1m			
Knight,Fannie	1f	OH		

76-75				
Jefferson,Henry	50m	WV	lab	
Mary A.	41f			
Samuel	19m		lab	
William	17m		lab	
America E.	15f		sch	
Malinda	13f		sch	
Marenda	11f			
John W.	10m			
Louisa E.	6f			
p544a Charles	4m			
Lucetta	2f			

77-76				
Floyd,James	20m	WV	coop	
Elizabeth	19			
Editha	60f			
Margaret	17f			
Rossey	18m		lab	
Finley	21m		coop	

78-77				
Sheppard,James	50m	VA	lab	
Elizabeth	52f			
Charles	18m			
George	16m			
William	1m	WV		

79-78				
Ash,Daniel	50m	WV	farm	
Mary M.	49			
Sarah C.	18f			
Stephen C.	14m			
Peter D.	12m			
Hudly B.	10f			
Marshall	7m			
Levory	4f			
Margaret	9/12f			
Morgan,John	60m	WV	farm	

80-79				
Johnston,Wilson	24m	WV	farm	
Martha	33f	VA		
Charles R.	4m			
Clemintine	2f			
James L.	7/12m			
Burkley,Charles	50m	VA		
Burkley,Eliza	47f	VA		

81-80				
Clark,Taylor	21m	WV	farm	
Catherine	19f	NY		
Mary M.	3/12f	WV		

82-81			
Howerd,Aaron	46m	VA	farm
Lydia	47f	VA	
Hugh	15m	OH	lab
Ellen	20f	OH	
David	13m	OH	
Margaret	10f	WV	
Louisa	9f	WV	
Lucy A.	5f	OH	

p545

83-82			
Chapman,William	53m	VA	lab
Eliza	50f	WV	
William	17m	OH	lab
James	15m	OH	lab
Lucy M.	12f	KY	
Thomas	9m	Ky	

84-83			
Pulley,John	28m	KY	lab
Mary	23f	WV	
Malissa	23f	KY	dom

85-84			
Winters,Hannah	39f	WV	
Telitha	15f		

86-85			
Perry,Melcher A.	36m	WV	farm
Rebecca	24f		
John L.	1m		

87-86			
Kyle,Peter	33m	WV	lab
Margaret	26f	KY	
Peter	14m	WV	lab
John E.	8m		
James J.	6m		
Catherine A.	1f		

88-87			
France,Isaac	25m	OH	lab
Nancy	24f	WV	
Pheby J.	5f		
Patience	2f		
Isabel	5/12f		

89-88			
France,Henry	50m	OH	farm
Patience	51f	OH	
Nancy A.	16f		sch
Matilda	15f		sch
George	14m		lab
Adaline	11f		
Thomas	9m		

89-88			
France (con't)			
James G.	7m	WV	
Harvey	5m		

90-89			
Sandridge,Benjamin	46m	VA	far
Lucy	44f	WV	
Sarah E.	21f		
John	19m		lab
Virginia	17f		
p545a Allice	13f		
Amacetta	10f		

91-90			
Holdroyd,Sarah	70f	VA	
Elizabeth	48f	WV	
Harrison,William	36m	TN	stm
Harrison,Sarah V.	25f	WV	
Harrison,John A.	3m	WV	
Harrison,Sarah Q.	2f		
Harrison,Luvenia	8/12f		

92-91			
Wilson,Acy L.	55m	OH	farm
Mary A.	45f	WV	
Ellen	20f		
Malinda	15f		sch
Hettie	10f		
Maggie	8f		
Nipps,Morris	15m		lab
Poteet,James	9m		

93-92			
Reece,John B.	50m	WV	farm
Dianna	38f	VA	
Mary E.	2f	WV	
Hatfield,Allice C.	12f	WV	

94-93			
Dundass,James	33m	WV	farm
Eliza	29f		
Mary J.	8f		
Betty	6f		
Charles	4m		
Sallie	2f		
Seamonds,William	62m	VA	far
Seamonds,Nancy	60f		
Seamonds,Paton	28m	WV	lab

95-94			
Harshbarger,John	30m	WV	far
Ellen	24f	IN	
Elizabeth	8f	WV	

95-94 Harshbarger (con't)			
Mary F.	6f		
Ida	4f		
Dora M.	1f		

96-95				
Sexton,John	66m	WV	farm	
Horatio H.	25m		farm	
Henry B.	22m		lab	
p546 Mary	22f			
Ann	20f			
John A.	6m			
William	3m			
Frank	1m			

97-96				
Harshbarger,David	58m	WV	farm	
Mary	49f	VA		
Henry	24m	WV	lab	
George	19m		lab	
Edna A.	17f			
Mary F.	15f		sch	
Ira J.	10m		sch	
Josephine	8f			
Samuel	6m			

98-97				
Smallridge,James	28m	WV	farm	
Ellen E.	22f			

---98				
Granway,John	24m	VA	RR	
Mary A.	20f	TN		
Sarah A.	2f	VA		

99-99				
Bibb,Robert	51m	VA	RRC	
Margaret	46f			
Hellen	24f			
Virginia	22f			
Josephine	20f			
James	17m	TN		
Victoria	16f			
George	13m			
Clara	11f			
John	9m			
Hattie	5f			

100-100				
Crimens,John	52m	Ire	RR	
Henova	45f	Ire		
Mary A.	12f	Can		
Patrick	9m	Can		

101-101				
Clark,Charles	30m	OH	RR	
Nancy	45f	NC		
Carson,Caroline	21f			
Carson,Stephen	19m		RR	
Carson,Arkansas	16f			
Carson,George	13m			
Carson,Albey	10f			
p546a Carson,Allice	3f	TN		

102-102				
Boice,James	36m	NC	RR	
Matilda	23f			
Mary L.	4f			
Anna F.	2f	TN		

103-103				
McComas,John	29m	WV	farm	
Eliza	31f			
Lelia F.	10f			
Alexander	9m			
Roxey L.	8f			
Agnus	4f			
Kate R.	4f			
McComas,Oliver P.	16m	OH	lab	

104-104				
Summerson,Chas.H.	39m	VA	farm	
Emma	32f	WV		
Richard	10m			
Netta	8f			
Charles	7m	MD		
Ada	6f	VA		
Birdie	3f	WV		
George	2m			
McMahon,George	17m	WV	lab	

105-105				
Wilson,Ann V.	50f	VA		
Mary V.	30f	LA		
Peyton,Sofia	80f	VA		
Peyton,Thomas	19m	WV		
Peyton,Francis	17m	WV		
Price,Frances	23f	LA	dom	
Price,Joseph	3m	WV		

106-106				
Nelson,Allen E.	54m	WV	carp	
Catherine	53f			
Isabel	25f			
James W.	23m		carp	
Henry E.	20		lab	
Catherine	17f			
Sarah A.	13f			

107-107

	Seamonds,William	30m	WV	farm
	Sarah J.	28f		
	Randolph	8m		
p547	Mary M.	6f		
	Susan	3f		
	Helena	1f		

108-108

Farley,Elijah	47m	WV	farm
Anges	44f		
John	16m		lab
William	14m		
Thomas	12m		
Ann	10f		
Franklin	7m		
Sarah	5f		
Edwin	5m		
Fredrick	1m		

109-109

Newman,Morris	46m	WV	farm
Serena	30f		
William	18m		
Frances	16f		sch
Dora D.	13f		sch
Isabel	11f		
James S.	2m		

110-110

Turley,Jonathan	44m	WV	farm
Eliza A.	38f		
Fannie	16f		sch
Florence A.	14f		sch
Eliza	12f		
Douglas	9m		
Mary D.	7f		
Anna	3f		
Sofia	10/12f		

111-111

Seamonds,Andrew	40m	WV	farm
Mary	41f		
Henrietta	17f		sch
Albert G.	12m		
John L.	10m		
Charles W.	8m		
James D.	8m		
Frank P.	7/12m		
Mann,Catherine	45f	OH	

112-112

	Newman,Winston	40m	WV	lab
	Sarah	39f		
	Emily E.	12f		
p547a	Ulysses	8m	WV	
	Robert M.	6m	OH	
	Winston S.	2m	WV	

113-113

Herd,William	53m	NJ	saw
Sarah	43f	TN	
Carrie	18f	WV	sch
Ella	15f		
Willie	13f		
Melia	8f		

114-114

Wentz,Elizabeth	46f	WV	
William	19m		lab

115-115

Woodyard,Manly	40m	WV	farm
Eliza	35f		
William	13m		
James F.	8m		
George H.	6m		
Abraham	3m		
John W.	2/12m		

116-116

Woodyard,Amos	28m	WV	farm
Rebecca	24f		
Barthena	8f		
Charles	6m		
Jasper	4m		
Susan	2f		

117-117

Dundass,John	42m	WV	farm
Mary	36f		
Kyle,Ann	18f		sch

118-118

Buck,Anthony	45m	Ire	RR
Briget	45f	Ire	
James	13m	MD	
Thomas	8m	KY	
John	3m		
Mollie	1f		
Kennedy,Patrick	36m	Ire	RR
Maghee,Lucinda	30f	WV	dom
Maghee,Harriet	6f		
Maghee,Mary B.	1f		

119-119
```
    McDermont,James      27m  WV  RR
          Elvira          22f
p548  George M.            2m
          Leslie         7/12f
    McDermont,Mary        24f
    McDermont,Geo.R.      23m       team
```

----120
```
    Shelton,Walter        20m  WV  RR
          Mary Y.         20f
```

120-121
```
    Joy,Thomas            64m  VA  farm
          Nancy           44f  WV
     Barnett,Martha E.     8f
     Barnett,John F.       4m
```

121-122
```
    Joy,Thomas            23m  WV  farm
          Anna            22f
          Josafine         1f
```

122-123
```
    Sheff,William P.      67m  VA  flr
          Olevia          50f  WV
```

123-124
```
    Stroops,William       78m  WV  farm
          Sarah F.        78f
          William         12m
          John H.         10m
     Adams,Nancy          53f  VA  dom
     Adams,George         19m  WV  lab
```

124-125
```
    Adams,James F.        26   WV  farm
          Emma E.         23f
          Charles S.       3m
          Minnie         3/12f
```

125-126
```
    Hodge,Margaret        46   WV
          Charles A.       8m
     Lusher,James M.       25       lab
     Lusher,Tolaver S.     21       lab
     Lusher,Mathew E.      17       lab
```

126-127
```
    Thompson,Isaac        34m  VA  lab
          Sarah           40f  VA
     Lucas,Cintha         13f  WV
     Thompson,James        7m
     Thompson,Almeda       4f
```

127-128
```
    Sturgeon,Robert       21m  KY  RR
          Mary A.         20f  WV
```

128-129
```
    Fetters,Henry         40m  NC  sadl
          Louisa          40f
          Ada S.          11f  WV
          Willie B.        8m
p548a  Flora F.            5f  IN
          Carrie F.        5f  IN
          Eli R.           3m  WV
          Nettie D.      9/12f  WV
```

129-130
```
    Merrett,Melchi        60m  WV  farm
          Mary            64f
          Thomas          26m       lab
          Martha          20f
```

130-131
```
    Merrett,Joseph        36m  WV
          Olevy           14f
          Cassie          11f
          Joseph          10m
          Emma             8f
          Willie           6m
```

131-132
```
    Dodds,John            51m  VA  farm
          Thomas          25m  OH  lab
          Harriet V.      20f  WV
          Charles E.      17m       lab
          Margaret        10f
          Rebecca J.       7f
```

132-133
```
    Blake,Sarah           67f  VA
     Salmon,Lucy           2f
    (Salmon)Catherine     15f  B
```

133-134
```
    Butcher,James         44m  WV  farm
          Margery         34f  Ire
          Rachael         10f  WV
          William H.       8m
          Reuben L.        2m
```

134-135
```
    Vess,Mathew           38m  VA  farm
          Mary E.         34f
          Mary J.         21f
          William         17m       lab
          Filande         15m
```

p134-135	Vess(con't)					
	Huldy	13f	VA			
	Sallie	10f				
	Oliver	9m				
	Missouri	4f				
	James	2m				

135-136					
	Morris,Charles K.	51m	VA	farm	
	Martha	50f			
p549	Ellen L.	28f	WV		
	Edna E.	20f			
	Iva V.	15f		sch	
	Chas.R.	11m		sch	
	(Morris)Rose	15f		B	dom

----137				
	Morris,John A.	25m	WV	farm
	Emily	25f		
	Mary E.	3f		

136-138				
	Roffe,Charles L.	61m	WV	farm
	Mary E.	41f		
	Ida	14f		
	Ann	12f		
	Augusta	9f		
	Susan	5f		
	Kate	4f		
	Charles	2m		

137-139					
	Morris,Samuel	85m	VA	B	lab
	Louisa	28f		B	
	Ester	30f		B	
	Henry	22m		B	
	Anderson,Wm.	18m		W	
	Anderson,Fannie	19f		W	
	Anderson,Clarence	16m		W	

138-140				
	Adkins,Edward	37m	WV	farm
	Susan	30f		
	Emily J.	9f		
	Mary E.	7f		
	Anna	5f		
	Sidney	2m		

139-141				
	Adkins,Sylvester	25m	WV	lab
	Ann E.	23f		
	William	4m		
	Cordelia	2f		

140-142					
	Fulwiler,George	46m	VA	carp	
	Matilda	36f	WV		
	John	20m		RR	
	George	17m		lab	
	Kate	11f			
	Mary	10f			
	Ella	3f			
p549a	William	3m			

----143				
	Lenard,John	41m	OH	fur
	Hester	36f		
	Franklin	15m		sch
	Harvey S.	10m		

141-144				
	Farrell,Francis M.	43m	VA	tay
	Elizabeth	38	WV	
	William	18m		pntr
	Mary S.	17f		
	Lawrence	12m		
	Isaac	5f		

142-145					
	Nelson,Anderson	39m	SC	B	dray
	Jane	38f	WV	M	

----146					
	Marshall,Lewis	26m	VA	B	barb
	Lucy	32f	KY	B	

143-147					
	Allen,Robert B.	47m	Sct	W	groc
	Frances L.	44f	WV		
	Jennie B.	23f	IN		
	Lemaster,John	10m	WV		

144-148			
	Prise,Sophia	27f	WV
	Minnie	1f	

145-149				
	Cockings,Thomas	46m	Eng	hotel
	Mariah	37f		
	Joseph	22m		
	Anna M.	18f		
	Thomas	15m		
	Carrie L.	6f		

146-150				
	Hatfield,John L.	38m	WV	hotel
	Malind	41f		hotel
	Effie A.	14f		sch

146-150 Hatfield(con't)			
Millard	11m	WV	
Maggie A.	10f		
Sedam,Abraham	35m	VA	law
Schmidt,Ludwick	37m	Sax	saw
Schmidt,Antonio	40f	Sax	

147-151			
Miller,George	40m	Ire	Lab
Mary	40f	Ire	

148-152			
Mather,Oscar W.	47m	WV	Asse
Augusta G.	42f		
Valcolon W.	23m		clk
p550 George H.	16m		sch
Sidney	5m		
Sumner	2m		
Prise,George	21m		
Prise,Rochy	19f		

149-152			
Thornburg,Thomas	52m	WV	mer
George E.	24m		clk
Thomas H.	20m		clk
Nannie A.	23f		
Mary S.	31f		
Maggie	13f		

150-153			
Bryan,Whitfield	64m	SC	shoe
Elizabeth	58f	WV	
Morris,Eliza	16f	M WV	

151-154			
Bright,Rodrick D.	30m	OH	drug
Emma D.	18f	WV	

152-144			
Leist,Vallentine	37m	Radon	far
Nannie	25f	TN	
Walton	10m	OH	
Catherine	8f	WV	
Flora	4f		
Philip	2m		

153-156			
Dyer,James R.	58m	VA	far
Rowena	51f		
Ann L.	26f		
Margaret M.	24f		
Rebecca	21f		
John W.	19m		RR
Morgan H.	14m		

153-156 Dyer (con't)			
James E.	11m	VA	

154-157			
Poteet,Henry C.	40m	WV	mer
Maggie A.	38f	KY	
Fannie	14f	WV	
Albert	12m		

155-158			
Eggers,Joseph	28m	WV	shoe
Elizabeth	24f		
Eggers,William	63m	KY	shoe
Eggers,Elizabeth	60f	WV	
Eggers,Wilbert	10m		
Eggers,John	2m		

page 550a

156-159			
Thornburg,Moses	40m	WV	
Mary L.	36f		
Samuels,Mary E.	11f		

157-160			
Samuels,Henry J.	45m	WV	farm
Rebecca A.	43f	PA	
Ceres B.	17m	WV	
Nettie D.	11f		
Hamlin,Sallie	15f	B	dom

158-161			
Miller,William C.	61m	OH	farm
Eliza	55f	WV	
Joseph	21m		clk/court
John W.	25m		
Anna	22f	KY	
Frank	4m		
William C.	2m		
Charles H.	30m	WV	lum mer
Adams,Bettie	14f		

159-162			
Salmon,Joel K.	40m	NY	mer
Martha	33f	WV	
Albert E.	13m		sch
Edward B.	7m		
Mary L.	4f		
Lucy	2f		
Blake,Edna	21f		

160-163			
Shelton,Thomas	40m	WV	carp
Eliza	36f		
Charles	16m		sch

160-163 Shelton (con't)

Name	Age/Sex	Birthplace	Occupation
Robert	13m	WV	sch
Frank	11m		
Emma	5f		
Mattie	4m		
Gains	3/12m		

161-164

Name	Age/Sex	Birthplace	Occupation
Shelton, James	34m	WV	RR
America	26f		
Albert	13m		
Fannie	9f		
Willie	6m		
Mary	3f		
Shelton, Margaret	52f	VA	
Shelton, Anthony	77m	VA	

page 551
162-165

Name	Age/Sex	Birthplace	Occupation
Adams, William	34m	WV	farm p551a
Sarah M.	27f	MO	
Sarah L.	6f	MO	
Nancy J.	4m	OH	
Sophia E.	1f	WV	

----166

Name	Age/Sex	Birthplace	Occupation
Witcher, Stephen	70m	B VA	lab
Anna	90f	M	
Stewart, Harriet	38f	B	dom
Stewart, Mary	7f	B WV	
Stewart, Charles	2m	M	
Stewart, Edward	2m	M	

163-167

Name	Age/Sex	Birthplace	Occupation
Harrison, Greenville	52m	VA	Blks
Ellen	35f	WV	
Mary	40f	VA	
Ellen	17f	WV	
Thomas	2m	WV	

164-168

Name	Age/Sex	Birthplace	Occupation
Miller, John	52m	WV	coop
Mary M.	54f	MD	
William	30m	WV	farm
John O.	26m		
Maxium	20f		

165-169

Name	Age/Sex	Birthplace	Occupation
Thornburg, John W.	42m	MD	farm
Sarah	31f	WV	
Georgie	4f		
Henry	1m		
McGinnis, Eliza	65f		

166-170

Name	Age/Sex	Birthplace	Occupation
Crooks, John C.	45m	KY	min
Virginia H.	30f		
Ann E.	20m		
William H.	15m		sch
Mary W.	12f		sch
John W.	7m		
Lucy E.	5f		
Robert E.	3m		

167-171

Name	Age/Sex	Birthplace	Occupation
Moss, Randolph	42m	VA	phy
Mary	31f	WV	

168-172

Name	Age/Sex	Birthplace	Occupation
Merrett, William	57m	WV	clk cour
Debera	54f		
Tennessey	24f		
Walter	18m		lab
Thadeus	15m		
Davis, Permilla	50f	B VA	

169-173

Name	Age/Sex	Birthplace	Occupation
Pinnell, Perry G.	44m	WV	
Mary E.	38f		
Thomas N.	15m	OH	sch
Mary V.	13f	OH	
Alma L.	12f	WV	
Clara L.	10f		
Witten H.	6m		
Perry	1m		
Estetta M.	2f		

170-174

Name	Age/Sex	Birthplace	Occupation
Kyle, Tennessey	27f	WV	
Justice, Jennetta	5f		

171-175

Name	Age/Sex	Birthplace	Occupation
Shipe, Charles	41m	VA	jail
Ellen	41f	WV	
William A.	14m		
Mary E.	11f		
Robert A.	4m		
Hellen	1f		
Gibb, William	35m	B WV	lab

172-176

Name	Age/Sex	Birthplace	Occupation
Samuels, Laffayett	42m	WV	farm
Fannie	38f	OH	
Mary E.	11f		
John E.	14m		
Verona	8f		
Willie R.	3m		
Minnie	5/12f		

15

172-176 Samuels(con't)
Lusher,Mary E.	21f	WV	

173-177
Moore,Mary	78f	VA	
George	15m	WV	

174-178
Keenan,Patrick H.	31m	WV	hotel
Mary A.	26f	VA	
John C.	10m	WV	
Andrew	8m		
Kate E.	5f		
Henry P.	3m		
Missouri	1/12f		
Dorman----------	35m	KY	phy
Church,Archibald	37m	VA	butc
Brooks,Fredrick	50m	VA	

p552
Walker,Leland	25m	VA	lab

175-179
Martin,Andrew	50m	WV	saw
Eliza	46f	VA	
Fannie	18f	WV	
William	16m		
John	14m		
Ida	11f		
Earnest	9m		
Turner,Alice	6f		
Sheff,Carolina	44f	VA	

176-180
Miller,George F.	52m	WV	RRC
Mary	44f		
Hannah	23f		
George M.	21m		
William	14m		
Mary	12f		

177-181
Martin,George	25m	WV	hack
Emaline	22f		
Sirus,Emma	6f		

178-182
Derton,William	40m	WV	saw
Mary	36f		
William	10m		
George	7m		
Joseph	5m		
Dundass,Lucy	25f		

179-183
Derton,Harrison	48m	WV	carp
Ann	34f	VA	
Mary A.	18f	WV	
Isabel	12f		
Elmore F.	9m		
Maggie	4f		

180-184
Condon,Michael	23m	WV	stm
Catherine	19f	VA	
John	8/12m	TN	

181-185
Newberger,Harriet	69f	Saxony

182-186
Scott,Harvey M.	26m	WV	editor
Delphine	27f		
Harvey	10/12m		
Bailey,Harvey	18m		pntr

183-187
Laidley,Albert	48m	WV	Ld ag
p552a Vesta	48f		
Alberta	23f		
John B.	20m		sch
Price,Clarence	12m	B	

184-188
Thackston,Benjamin	34m	VA	teach
Eugenia	33f	WV	
Mary W.	8f		
William C.	6m		
James A.	3m		
Kate K.	1f		

185-189
Lloyd,John E.	57m	VA	shoe
Urania	46f	OH	
Jerry,Anna M.	16f		sch

186-190
Stentson,Anthony	52m	Baden	lab
Laura	52f	Baden	
Henry	12m	WV	

187-191
Dean,Patsey	33f	WV
Wheatfield,Fredk.	16m	
Miller,Marcelles	13m	
Miller,Susan	8f	
Wheatfield,Henry	7m	
Miller,Charles	5m	

187-191 Dean (con't)
Dean,Arabella   2f

188-192
Simon,Fredrick   58m Pru wg mk
  Bena   46f Pru
  Henry   16m OH wg sh
  Catherine   14f WV sch

189-193
Swan,Benjamin   37m WV blks
  Louisa J.   38f
  Francis M.   17m   blks sh
  Emily J.   14f   sch
  Charlotte   11f   sch
  Lizzie K.   7f
  Nettie   2f

190-194
Kline,Thomas B.   28m WV Law
  Jacob A.   23m   mer

191-195
Blume,Evan W.   47m NC sadl
  Evaline   37f VA
  George   16m WV mail
  Ida A.   14f   sch
p553 Albert   12m
  William   9m
  Henry C.   7m
  Luke   2m

192-196
Dick,Andrew   39m WV hack
  Mary V.   34f
  Lena E.   3f
  Ida A.   1f

193-197
Baumgardner,John B. 46m VA farm
  Louisa   42f WV
  Alonzo F.   20m   lab
  William L.   20m   lab
  Charles A.   17m   lab
  Cora V.   13f

194-198
Lallance,Charles N. 33m OH pntr
  Martha E.   29f
  Harry H.   5m WV
  Henrietta   3f
  Anna   1f

----199
Creel,George A.   23m WV pntr
  Lizzie A.   24f

195-200
Merrett,John   45m WV milr
  Frances   33f
  George   18m

195-200 Merrett (con't)
  Virginia   16f
  Susan   14f
  John   13m
  Sarah   8f
  Lucy   4f
  Thomas   2m
  Baker,John   23m Can lab

196-201
Lusher,Johnston   50m WV lab
  Lucy   39f
  Winfield S.   23m   lab
  Henry J.   10m
  Lucy F.   7f
  Mary E.   4f

197----

198-202
Ferguson,James H.   53m VA law
  Elizabeth   38f
p553a Ong,Margaret 72f
  Ong,Joseph   10m WV

199-203
Anderson,Baxter   39m VA hotel
  Harriet   28f WV hotel
  Camey   1m
Morgan,John   24m NY eng
Dalmer,James   28m Ire stm
Joel,James   45m Ire stm
Kief,Charles   34m Ire stm
Mattson,Avel G.   28m Swe stm
    (James reversed ??)

200-204
Flinn,Thomas   45m Ire lab
  Brown,William   22m VA RR
  Brown,Mary O.   20f
  Mooney,James W.   23m   RR

201-205
Cochran,Andrew   27m WV RR
  Mary   22f
  Ella D.   3f
  Thomas   2m
  Vallentine   9m

202-206
Derton,John   52m WV lab
  Louisa   50f
  William Z.   24m   lab
  Louisa A.   17f
  John T.   14m

17

```
202-206 Derton (con't)              207-212 McComas (con't)
      Henry J.       12m                  June          8f KY
   Brown,William     26m      lab         George        5m VA
   Brown,Eliza       26f                  Margaret      3f WV
   Derton,Elizabeth  86f                  Martha        1f

203-207
   Miller,John G.    62m Wur far
      Evvie V.       38f WV                  End Cabell Court House Dist.
      Frances        22f                         at Barboursville
      George R.      19m      lab
      Claudius       15m      lab
      Alexander       8m
      Eliza           6f
      Fredrick S.     5m
      Levna A.        1f
      Leo G.          1m
   Miller,Sigman     64m Wur far
204-208
   Baumgardener,John 60m VA farm
p554  Malinda        48f WV
      Worth          23m      lab
      Fredrick       21m      lab
      Enery          16f
      Margaret       15f
      Frank          12m
      Motire          7m

205-209
   Creig,William     43m VA lab
      Mary J.        36f
      Martha E.      19f      dom
      John H.        16m      lab
      Mary I.        15f
      Sarah          11f
      Anna A.         7f
      Lorena F.       5m
      William R.      2m WV
      Thomas A.    9/12m

206-210
   Bellemy,Henry C.  33m KY farm
      Sarah T.       30f WV
      Georgie E.      5f KY
      Mary            3f WV

207-211
   Hall,Charles      33m OH teach
      Harriet M.     30f WV
      William T.     11m OH

208-212
   McComas,Jefferson 33m WV farm
      Martha         33f KY
```

17 A

Map labels:

Howell's Mill · Doolittle Mill · Cox · WM. P. YATES · POOR'S HILL · SARAH EUBERTT · HOWELL'S MILL · FUDGE'S CK · HOLDRYDE · BLUE SULPHUR · HARVEY NEWMAN · JOHN DUNDAS · CYRUS CK · MATHEW LUSHER · HENRY CHAPMAN · TURNPIKE · LOWER TOM'S · ROAD · CALVARY SWAN · (LOGAN RD) · JOHN DAYTON · ANDREW HATFIELD · MOSES HATFIELD · SARAH HATFIELD · MCHA... · SMICK · KOUST · MERRITT'S · COLLINS · JOE J. WINTZ · ARON · MERRITT'S · STROOP MILL · BARBOURSVILLE · SARAH BLAKE · JAMES NEWMAN · IRVIN LUSHER · CHARLES ROFFO · DUSENBERRY MILL · THOMPSON · McCOMAS · RIVER · WILLIAM MORRIS · GUYANDOTTE · JOHN MERRITT · DAUNGARDNER · MOSES THORNBURG · ELISHA McCOMAS · JAMES · GUYANDOTTE RIVER · JOHN THORNBURG · EDWARD EDENS · DAVIS CK · SHELTON · DIDOW · JOHN DEBOW · JAMES WILSON · ABNER COOK · SYLVESTER FULLER · EDWARD SHY · JOHN GRIFFITH · RUSSELL CK · POTECT · DIETZ · JOHN EUBERTT · GUYANDOTTE

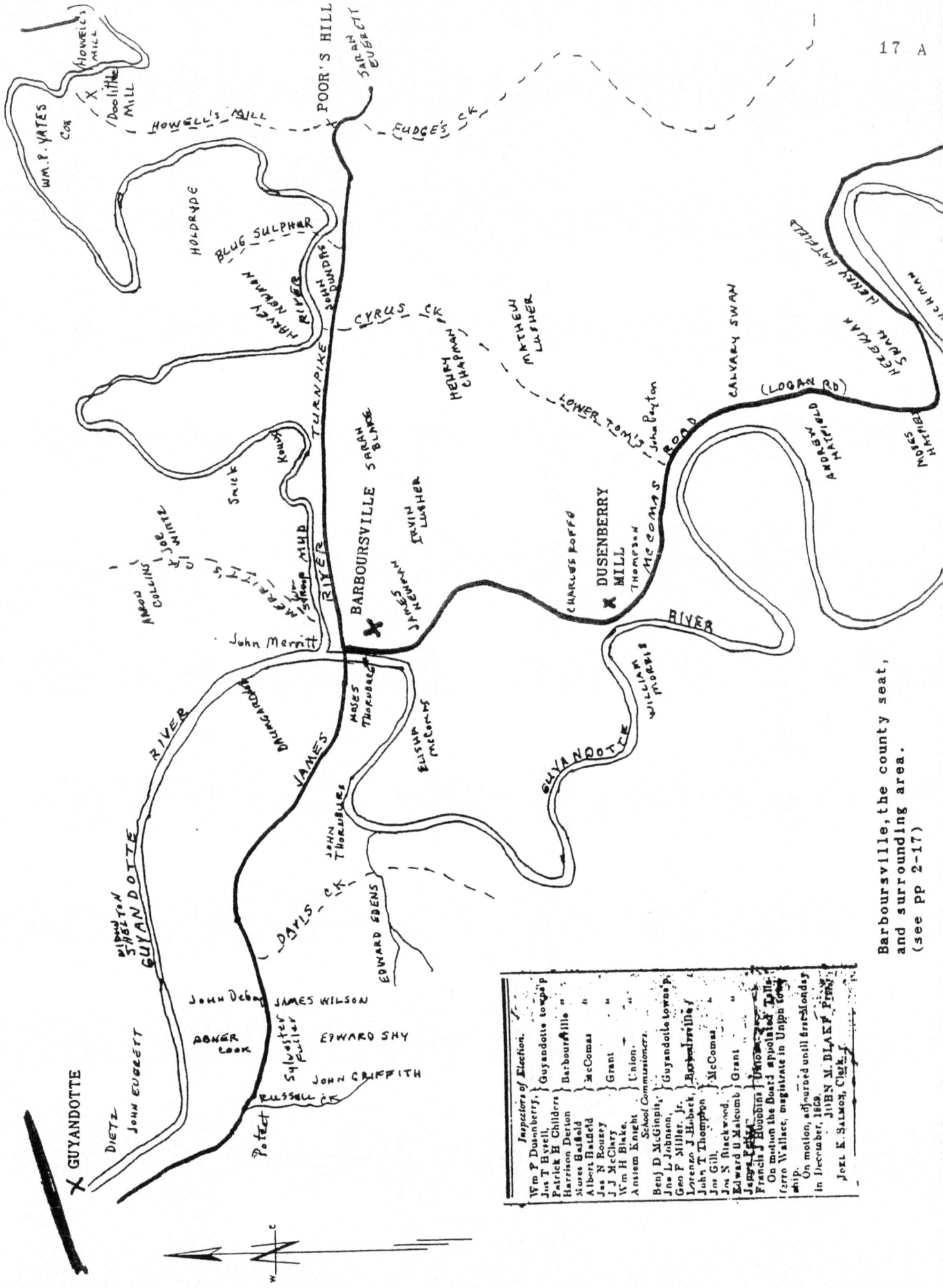

Inspectors of Election.
Wm P Dusenberry, } Guyandotte town'p.
Jos T Hyvell,
Patrick H Childers } Barboursville "
Harrison Derion
Stuses Hatfield } McComas "
Albert Hatfield
Jas N Rousey } Grant "
J J McClary
Wm H Blake, } Union.
Anstem Knight
School Commissioners.
Benj D McGinpis, } Guyandotte town'p.
Jno L Johnson,
Geo F Miller, Jr. } Barboursville "
Lorenzo J Hulbert,
John T Thompson } McComas "
Jno Gill,
Jno N Blackwood, } Grant "
Edward U Malcomb,
Jams Petty, } Union "
Francis J Robbins
On motion the Board appointed Lorenzo Wallace, magistrate in Union town-ship.
On motion, adjourned until first Monday in December, 1859.
Joel K Salmon, Clerk.

Barboursville, the county seat,
and surrounding area.
(see pp 2-17)

17 B

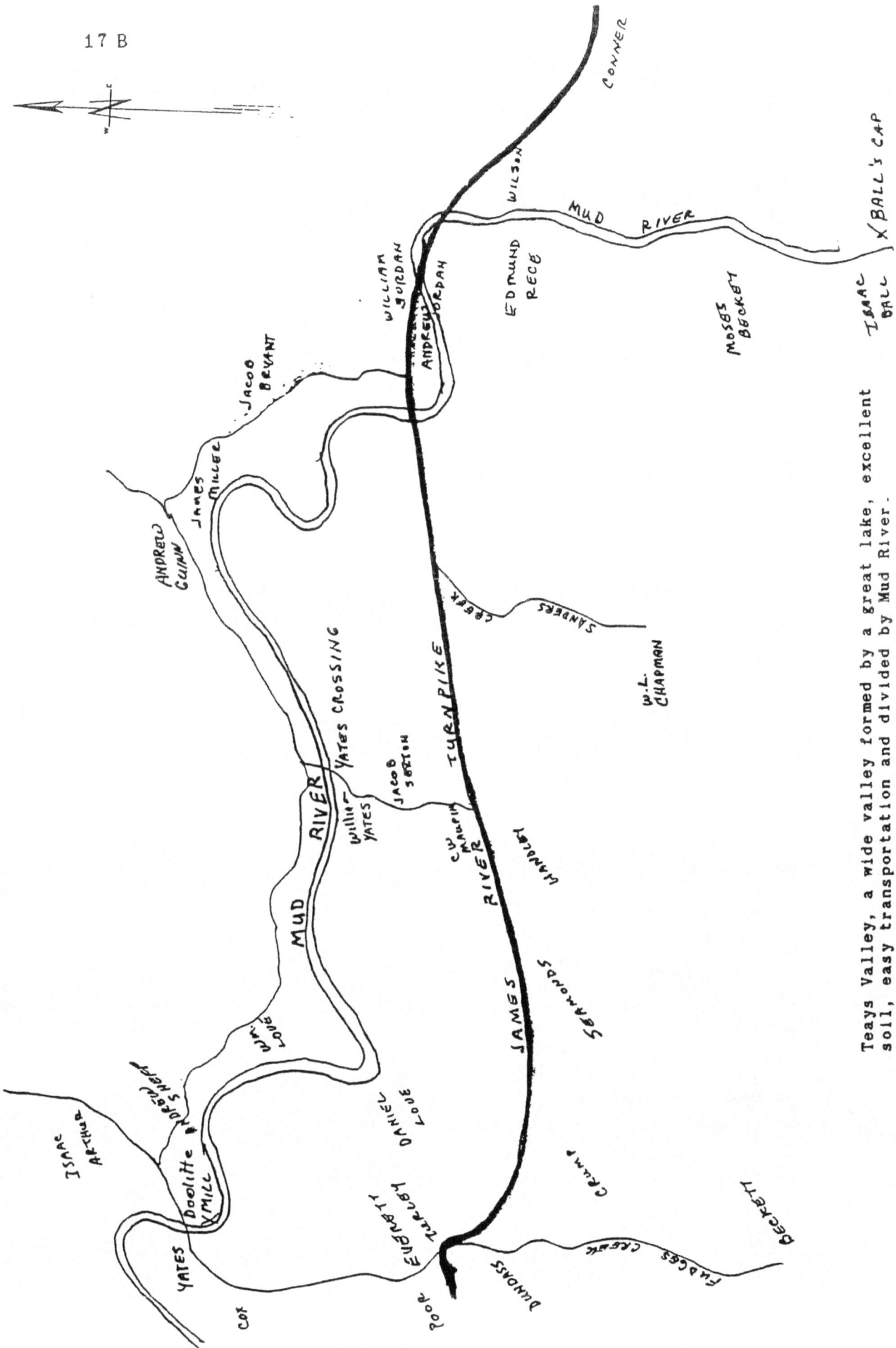

Teays Valley, a wide valley formed by a great lake, excellent
soil, easy transportation and divided by Mud River.
(see pp 18-26)(44-46)

CONNER

WILSON

MUD RIVER

X BALL'S GAP

ISAAC BALL

EDMUND RECE

MOSES BECKET

WILLIAM JORDAN

ANDREW JORDAN

JACOB BRYANT

JAMES MILLER

ANDREW GUINN

SANDERS CREEK

W.L. CHAPMAN

YATES CROSSING

MUD RIVER

WILLIAM YATES

JACOB SEXTON

TURNPIKE

C.W. MAUPIN

HANDLEY

JAMES RIVER

SEAMONDS

JOHN LOVE

ISAAC ARTHUR

DOOLITTE MILL

DREWETT

YATES

DANIEL LOVE

POOR TURNPIKE

EVERNEY

GRAND CREEK

DUNNAS

FLAGGS CREEK

BECKETT

COX

p555 GRANT DISTRICT-THORNDYKE P.O.   p555a

1-1
```
    Herndon,James L.      58m VA farm

          Mary A.         54f
          James F.        18m WV lab
          Mortica V.      16m
          Charles S.      12m
          Susan E.        10f
    Smith,Martha          39f      dom

2-2
    Burdett,James R.      42m WV farm
          Eizabeth        38f
          William          8m
          Jeneva C.        6f
          Frank L.         3m
          Mary E.          9f
    Yates,William P.      83m VA lab
    Yates,Elizabeth       75f VA

3-3
    Wilson,John T.        24m WV RR
          Ammacetta       19f
          Mary S.       8/12f
4-4
    McCorkle,Ellen S.     49f VA kph
          Effie M.        17f
          Ida S.          14f
          George          12m
          Arthur          10m
    Hanly,Samuel          21m

5-5
    Cox,James O.          45m WV mer
          Margaret        42f
          Jennie C.       19f
          Georgie         16f
          Alvin H.        10m
          Frank L.         4m

6-6
    White,Peter           44m Hol carp
          Mary            41f VA
          Emily           14f WV sch
    Blackwood,Mary         3f

7-7
    Switzer,Ellen         43f OH kph
          Rufus           15m WV sch
          Clymer          13m      sch
          Vara            10f
          Virginia         6f
    Jourden,Rosa          47f B
```

8-8
```
    Brown,Thomas          31m WV blks
          Cintha          27f
          Morris G.       10m
          Edgar S.         5m
          Levina A.        4f
          Lenvita          1f
    Lafter,Morgan         22m VA lab
    Lafter,Elizabeth      25f WV
    Lafter,Malina J.7/12f
    Brown,Sarah M.        14f      sch

9-9
    Hoges,Preston         51m VA groc
          Sarah           28f WV
          Ellen           18f
          Leah            14f

10-10
    Poar,Alford           30m WV farm
          Mary J.         23f
          Frank M.         2m
    Poar,Elias            20m      lab
    Poar,Allen            18m      Lab
  ---11
    Howell,Armsted B.     59m VA man
          Fannie          60f
          John            30m      farm
          Alice           16f WV
    Grass,George          12m

11-12
    Thomas,Nelson C.      35m VA man
          Mary S.         24f WV
          William         11m
          Legalia          9f
          Martha A.        6f
          Fannie           5f
          Julia A.         2f

12-12
    Hanley,Charles        38m WV farm
          Elizabeth       36f
          Marion L.       12m
          Frank W.        10m
          Ona              8f
          Leondas          6m
    Lucas,Adaline         13f

13-14
    Wall,John             41m Ire RRC
          Zernah          41f NY
```

13-14 Wall (con't)
p556 Clark,Franklin C.17m IN RR
    Clark,Elizabeth 14f IN sch

14-15
  Ronoe,Daniel 28m IN RR
    Adelia 31f
    Micheal 5m CT
    Henird 4f PA
    John 2m KY
    Margaret 5/12 f IN
  Keheff,William 28m Ire RR

15-16
  Blag,Joseph 37m OH blks
    Hannah 33f IN
    Mary A. 12f
    John 11m
    Ella B. 8f
    Eli A. 7m
    Laley 6f
    Loley 2f

16-17
  Campbell,William 52m KY carp
    Harriet 47f OH
    William 17m IN
  Frey,William 20m Ire RRC

17-18
  Doland,Thomas 45m Ire BH
    Briget 40f
    Briget 13f IN sch
    Mary 3f IN
  McGown,James 22m Ire lab
  Tiche,Martin 22m lab
  Gaven,William 50m lab
  Higgins,Patrick 28m lab
  Gaven,Micheal 40m lab
  Murrey,Thomas 30m lab
  Phinetta,Patrick 30m lab

18-19
  Hanley,Cornelius 40m Ire lab
    Ann 45f
    Ellen 19f NY
  Collins,John 19m Ire lab
  Conner,John 23m lab
  Gibbons,Paul 40m lab
  Bailey,Andrew 40m lab

19-20
  Woolwine,Henry 33m WV lab

19-20 Woolwine (con't)
p556a Mary 26f WV
    Nancy 4f
    William 2m
    Charles 4/12m
  Mooney,Edward 22m WV RR
  Mooney,Elizabeth 24f

20-21
  McClary,Alexander 65m VA farm
    Lucretia 57f
    Joseph A. 31f farm
    Isaac W. 25m lab
    Mary L. 22f
    Catherine 18f
    Charles L. 16m WV
  Hill,Mary J. 8f

21-22
  Love,Daniel 72m VA farm
    Cintha 69f KY
    Shelby J. 31m WV
    Alphonso 24m
    Mary H. 24f VA
    Cintha A. 2f WV
    Charles 9/12m

22-23
  Cunningham,John M.47m NY farm
    Mary 44f
    Mary J. 7f
    Johnathan 5m
    Lucy H. 4f
    Harry C. 3m
  Marshall,Allen 32m lab
  Smith,Fredrick 20m lab
  Cunningham,Amanda17f

23-24
  Christy,William 25m Ire RR
    Martha 21f
    John M. 75m
    Agnes 70f
    Jane 3f PA
    John 1m WV

24-25
  Mechesly,John 45m Ire farm
    Ellen 43f
    Agnis 13f WV
    Ellen 11f
p557 Susanna 8f
    Elizabeth 6f

```
25-26
   Bowen,Strother        50m VA RRC       31-32
      Mary E.            44f MD               Black,Camel         39m WV farm
      Henry L.           20m VA sch              Elizabeth        39f OH
      Strother           18m                     Allice           17f WV
      Grovener           16m                     Ametha           15f
      Susan              13f                     Lovle            11m OH
      Flora A.            9f                     Theodore         10m MO
      Georgie J.          4f                     McCellen          8m WV
   Coalman,Margaret      27f     dom             Jane              6f
   Coalman,William       30m     RR
   Coalman,Loucilla       2f              32-33
   Coalman,Mary E.        1f                  Woods,William       40m Ire lab
                                                 Mary             35f
26-27                                            James            10m PA
   Murphy,Francis        41m KY phy              Briget            5f
      Julia              35f                      Ellen            1f IL
      Mary N.            14f     sch
      Allice M.          10f WV          33-34
      James M.            7m                  Rece,Abia           86m VA farm
      Paul                5m                  Johnston,Agnes      78f
      Ella E.             3f                  Jarrett,Martha      75f
   Harrsion,Margaret     38f KY            Morrison,David      60m

27-28                                     34-35
   McDowney,James        35m PA man           Burton,William      50m VA farm
      Mary               33f WV                  Mary             50f WV
      William C.         13m                     John             23m     lab
      Charles            10m                     Morris           18m
      Henry               8m                     Victoria         14f
      James B.         7/12m                     Andrew           12m
   Maupin,Ada R.         25f                     America          11f
                                                 Allice            5f
28-29                                         Bread,James          7m
   Black,William         51m WV farm
      Virginia           45f              35-36
      Isabel             26f                  Reece,Warren P.     48m WV farm
      Ezra               19m     lab             Ella             28f VA
      John               16m                     Medora S.        25f WV
      Cintha             14f                     Lizzie H.        15f
      Ida                 6f                     Frankie S.        3m
                                              Benam,John A.       24m VA lab
29-30
   Stevenson,Everman     60m WV farm       36-37
      Mary C.            59f                  Reece,Joseph A.     42m WV farm
      William H.         20m                     Permilla         35f
   Smith,Sarah           32f                     Leanora          12f
p557a "  David           12m           p558
   Smith,William          8m              37-38
   Smith,Ellinor          3f                  Wheeler,Adison      42m WV farm
                                                 Sarah            35f
31-30                                            Robert J.        16m
   Mullen,Michael        50m Ire RR              Joseph           15m
      Mary               40f Ire                 Edna J.          13f
                                                 William          10m
```

21

```
37-38 Wheeler (con't)
      Jefferson           8m
      John M.             4m
      James               2m

38-39
   Reece,Edmond C.        59m WV  car
      Sophia              55f
      Jennie L.           10f
   Reece,James A.         26m
   Reece,Alice L.         25f
   Sheff,William          11m

39-40
   Sulliven,Jerry         53m Ire lab
      Mary                46f
      Mary                19f NH
      Julia               14f NY  sch
      Briget               8f PA
      John                13m
      James                6m

40-41
   Beckley,William        29m VA  groc
      Henrietta           21f WV
      Rodrick              2m
      Charles              1m

41-42
   Blackwood,Joseph       38m VA  farm
      Charles W.          13m WV
      James H.            11m
      Joel H.              9m
      Robert E.            6m
   Anderson,John D.       33m VA  farm
   Anderson,Peter         19m     lab
   Anderson,David         16m     lab
   Anderson,Melcina       21f WV
   Anderson,Julia S.7/12f

42-43
   Morris,Joseph W.       21m WV  farm
      Fannie              24f
      Albert               2m
      Charles              1m
p558a
43-44
   Gillen,John            29m VA  farm
      Sarah               26f
      Milten               3m WV
44-45
   Bryan,Lucy             58f WV
      Francis             24m     farm
      Chapman             21m     farm
```

```
45-46
   Ball,Isaac             60m WV  farm
      Susan               29f
      Calvary             14m
      Conwelsa            12m
      George              10m
      Allice               7f
      Isaac                5m
      Bell                 2f
      Willie             7/12f

46-47
   Rousey,James           56m VA  farm
      Mary                58f
      John                14m WV

47-48
   Irvin,Mathew           44 WV   farm
      Nancy               44f
      Delia M.            16f
      David               15m
      Elizabeth           13f
      Mary E.             11f
      Hannah               8f
      Edward               6m
      Napeleon             4m
   Rousey,James S.        20 VA   lab

48-49
   Crowder,Henry          52m VA  farm
      Sarah A.            48f
      Sarah M.            25f WV
      David               18m
      Mirum               15f
      John J.              8m

49-50
   Wallace,Henry          34m WV  farm
      Edna                34f
      Georgia             11f
      Emily                8f
      Isaac                6m
      Jenetta              4f
p559  Luvena               2f

50-51
   Lunsford,Joshua        56m WV  farm
      Sallie              50f
      Mary E.             25f WV
      John                18m     lab
      Peter               15m     lab
      Hughy               10m
      James F.             8m
```

```
51-52                                  57-58 Carpenter (con't)
   Peyton,Alexander    44m WV farm        Mahaley          11f
      Palina           35f VA             Matilda S.        8f
      Isabel           12f WV
      Fianna           10f             58-59
      Mary E.           9f                Irvin,Amanda      27f WV
      Alzira            7f                   Nancy J.        7f
      Allen             5m                   John H.         5m
      Luvada            4f                   Virginia        3f
      William           3m
      Viola M.        4/12f            59-60
   Albert,Benjamin     17m VA             Runnels,Griffin   70m VA carp
                                             Elizabeth      72f
52-53
   Hodges,Stephen      43m WV farm     60-61
      Mary J.          41f                Deal,Henry H.     55m WV
      Lewis            19m                   Ruth           54f
      Peter            15m                   Cad.C.         27m
      William          13m                   Elenyey        36m
      John             11m
      Mary E.           8f             61-62
      Edgar L.          5m                Wallace,Thona     55f VA
                                             Margaret,      26f WV
53-53                                        Tabitha        24f
   Bias,William        29m WV farm
      Martha R.        24f             62-63
      David A.          3m                Adams,Joshua A.   37m VA lab
      James A.          2m                   Sarah F.       27f WV
      Riley M.          1m                   Mary F.        11f
                                             Sarah          10f
54-55                                        John H.         9m
   Wallace,Jessey      45m VA farm          Agnis            7f
      Letta            80f                   William         4m
   Johnston,Henry      17m WV lab           Allen L.         1m

55-56                                  63-64
   Wallace,Hughy       38m VA farm        Conner,Adison     38m WV farm
      Harriet          42f WV               Emeretta        29f
      Uriah             9m                   John M.         9m
      Ida               6f                   Joseph          8m
      Ada               3f
p559a                                  64-65
   Johnston,Nancy      12f MO             Currey,William    27m WV farm
                                             Martha         31f VA
56-57                                        John C.         8m WV
   Davis,Thomas        27m WV farm          James F.        7m
      Susan            24f                   Ida M.         5f
      Mary E.           2f        p560      Bennett         2m
      Lunetta           1f
                                       65-66
57-58                                     Thomas,Samuel     44m VA carp
   Carpenter,John      68m WV blks          Jane            40f
      Frances          51f                   Henry          19m   lab
      Fannie           14f                   Burton         15m   lab
```

23

65-66 Thomas (con't)			
Cora	11f		
Flora	10f		
Nora	8f		
Viola	6f		
Samuel	2m		

66-67			
Parish,James	55m	VA	farm
Julia	54f		
Elizabeth	16f	WV	
Julia A.	15f		
Malard	13m		
Smith,Barlery	53f		
Smith,Virginia	18f		
Smith,Isadora	16f		

67-68			
Lytes,Isaac	42m	MD	shoe
Matilda	46f	VA	
Mary E.	12f	WV	
Joseph	9m		
Howard	6m		
Sarah J.	3f		

68-69			
Watters,George	25m	WV	lab
Jane	21f		
Mary	21f		

69-70			
Summers,George	45m	WV	farm
Sarah	48f		
Thomas	22m		sch
Edgar	24m		teach
Lyra	20m		lab
Mathew	18m		lab
McNeely,Mary	21f		dom

70-71			
Summers,Sylvester	32m	WV	farm
Margaret	21f	VA	
Julia	1f	WV	
Holt,Flora	6f		

71-72			
Jordan,John L.	60m	WV	farm
Harriet	41f		
p460a Henry C.	13m		
Emily C.	11f		
Jorden,Christopher	28m	WV	Carp

72-73			
Jorden,Thomas	28m	WV	lab
Eliza F.	28f		
Carena F.	9f		
Lora B.	6f		
Sarah	4f		
Alkendrew	2m		
James	1m		

73-74			
Chapman,Eli	44m	WV	farm
Milda	35f		
Jenetta	16f		
Charles	15m		
Henry	11m		
Everman	8m		
Ira	6m		
Randolph	4m		
Luana	3f		
Ezra	4/12 m		

---75			
Chapman,Jerman	40m	WV	lab
Ellen	30f		
Charles	12m		
John	10m		
Jennie	6f		
Luella	2f		

74-76			
Smith,Daniel	64m	VA	farm
Catherine	23f	WV	
Elijah	19m		
John	14m		
Anderson,James	26m	VA	clk
Anderson,Perlina	18f	WV	

75-77			
Neal,Andrew	31m	WV	farm
Malinda	30f		
Charles H.	12m		
Eliza A.	11f		
John M.	9m		
Adison G.	6m		
George	2m		

76-78			
Harshbarger,Henry	25m	WV	farm
p561 Edna	20f		
Gracy	4m		
Drucilla	2m		

```
77-79
  Gwinn,Andrew          75m  VA farm
     Rachel             63f
     Jefferson          22m  WV
     Esherman,Edward     7m
     Esherman,Ida        5f
78-80
  Guinn,Andrew          33m  WV farm
     Harriet            35f
     James              15m
     Charles            12m
     William             9m
     Jefferson           8m

79-81
  Reece,Allen W.        30m  WV farm
     Louisa             28f
     Albert S.           3m

80-82
  Runnels,John D.       37m  WV farm
     Cassie             33f
     George             14m
     Frances            11f
     Charles T.         10m
     John E.             9m
     Benjamin            5m
     Joseph              2m
     Elijah           9/12m

81-83
  Newman,Meltin         24m  WV farm
     Emma               20f
     Albert G.           1m
     Hettie F.        8/12f

82-84
  Branam,Catherine      36f  Ire kph
     Michael            17m  WV
     Mary               16f
     John               14m
     Peter              12m
     Elizabeth          10f
     William             9m
     George              7m

83-85
  Newman,Adison         33m  WV farm
     Amanda             32f
p561a
     Estus,Elizabeth    44f
     Estus,John         12m
     Estus,Mary E.       8f
```

```
83-85 Newman (con't)
     Estus,James         5m  OH
     Smith,James        40m  VA blks
     Smith,Eliza        33f  WV
     Smith,Mary          3f  IN
     Smith,William       1m  WV
84-86
  Reece,James           57m  WV farm
     Rebecca            50f
     Thomas             23m
     Rebecca A.         21f
     Mary C.            15f

85-87
  Killgore,Thomas W.    48m  WV farm
     Mary J.            41f
     Joseph C.          22m      lab
     John E.            20m
     Charles            15m
     Galiten             9m
     Netta               5f
     Bennett             2m

86-88
  Chapman,Henry         48m  WV ;ab
     Julia A.           33f
     William            21m
     Linnie             18f
     Henrietta          15f
     Charles            10m
     Isa                 5f
     Thomas              3m

87-89
  Reece,James T.        28m  WV farm
     Martha E.          29f
     Charles             2m
     Walter              1m
  Miller,Palina         19f      dom

88-90
  Howkins,Thomas        47m  VA farm
     Ann                50f
     Mary               15f  WV sch
     Martin             14m      sch
     Thomas             12m      sch
     William            10m
p562
89-91
  Ball,Jeremiah         34m  WV farm
     Jennie             24f  KY
     Albert              5m  WV
     Louisa              3f
```

89-91 Ball (con't)
Mary   1f

90-92
Hackworth,George   32m KY mer
  Hetti   30f WV
  Robert   8m
  Thomas   6m
  Annie   5f
  Georgie   2f
  Randolph   5/12 m

91-93
Bench,James   58m VA farm
  Sarah   49f
  Mary   27f WV
  John   21m WV
  Eliza J.   18f
  Elizabeth   15f
  Sallie   13f
  James R.   12m

92-94
Bench,William   24m WV farm
  Margaret   20f
  William   2m
  Carolina   1f

93-95
Chapman,William   40m WV farm
  Thersey(?)   27f
  Mary A.   9f
  William   7m
  Albert   3m
  John S.   1m

94-96
Malcum,Edward   46m WV farm
  Virginia   45f
  Edward   13m
  Francis   12m
  Wilard   9m
  Mary V.   7f
  Margaret   1f

95-97
Gwinn,George   42m WV farm
  Marietta   38f
  Elizabeth   20f
p562a Sampson   18m   lab
  Conwelsa   16m   lab
  Charles   13m   lab
  Thomas   12m   lab
  Robert E.   8m

95-97 Gwinn (con't)
  Mary   4f
  Margaret   1f

96-98
Vinson,Bennett   30m TN phy
  Mary F.   29f WV
  Gracy   7f MO
  Charles   4m WV
  William   2m

97-99
Legg,Thomas   32m WV farm
  Elizabeth   23f
  Allen   14m
Legg,James   65m   lab
Legg,Violetta   60f

98-100
Reece,John M.   56m WV farm
  Mirem   43f
  Mary   13f

99-101
Camard,George   30m WV farm
  Mary   27f
  Frank   2m

---102
Everett,James   47m WV mer
  Elizabeth   15f

100-103
Jorden,William   55m WV farm
  Esther   55f
  John   22m   RR
  Henry N.   21m   RR
  Harriet   17f
  Moris F.   16m
  Abreham   13m

101-104
Chapman,Green   55m WV farm
  Lucy   55f VA
  Charles   13m WV
Devore,Susan   30f
Devore,Fannie   1f

102-105
Harshbarger,Elizabeth 60f WV
  Charles   18m
  William   13m
p563 George   11m

```
102-105 Harshbarger(con't)              111-114
  Woodard,Henrietta 69f VA                Nicely,Roland        43m VA farm
  Woodard,John       17m WV                 Martha             42f
                                  p563a     Morgan             18m    lab
103-106                                     Mary L.            16f    sch
  Sunderlin,Charlotte 32f VA                William            14m    sch
    William            11m WV               Anna J.            12f    sch
    John H.             9m                  Nancy              11f
                                            Palina             11f
104-107                                     Zacheriah           9m WV
  Eggers,Nancy         66f VA               Robert              9m
    Fleming            30m    lab           Elizabeth           7f
    Mary               37f                  Charles R.          3m
    Adaline            26f           112-115
    Samuel             24m    lab     Hanly,Harrison           51m WV farm
                                            Sarah              45f VA
105-108                                     Eliza              17f WV sch
  Laidley,James H.     32m WV farm          John W.            14m    sch
    Laura A.           26f KY               Sarah E.            9f
                                            Jefferson           7m
106-109                                     Jackson             6m
  Morris,James R.      41m WV farm          Martha              3f
    Hellen             41f                  Nancy               1f
    Walter             15m               Frasier,Alfred        23m    lab
    Sallie             13f                  Mary J.            24f
    Fannie             12f                  Effie               1f
    Eugene             10m
    Buregard            8m          113-116
    Ferdenan            4m            Killgore,William         36m WV farm
  Morris,Mary          79f WV               Rachael            32f
                                            George S.          14m
107-110                                     Eliza N.           13f
  Conner,John M.       23m WV farm          James M.           10m
    Harriet            23f                  Sarah               9f
    Randolph            1m                  Mary F.             7f
  Canard,Ephram        35m    lab           Rufus C.            5m
                                            John W.             2m
108-111
  Wiley,Robert         60m WV farm   114-117
    Elizabeth          51f PA          Harmon,Thomas          44m WV far
    Lucinda            22f WV teach        Amey F.            35f KY
    Frances            18f                 Indson             15m
    Martha             17f                 Leonadas           12m WV
    Henry              12m                 Victoria            9f
    Jesse              11m                 Virginia            4f
    James               8m            Lunsford,Lewis          7m
                                      Bell,Marion            26m IN RR
109-112
  Wiley,William        27m WV farm   115-118
    Anna               21f VA          Conner,James          64m VA fa
                                 p564    Luvina              58f WV
110-113                                  Everman             17m    la
  Conner,Joseph        24m WV farm    Conner,Lewis           35m    la
    Martha             23f
```

116-119			
Woodard, Hezekiah	30m	WV	farm
Sarah	59f	VA	
Sarah	17f		
Anjaline	13f		
John W.	12m		
Mary	11f		
117-120			
Seashols, John	64m	PA	farm
Lucretia	49f	VA	
Lucretia	12f	WV	
Ematine	10f		
Luster, Ellen	11f		
118-121			
Morris, Sarah A.	47f	WV	kph
Hellen J.	20f		sch
James T.	8m		
Joseph W.	7m		
119-122			
Canard, Howard	64m	VA	lab
Nancy	59f	WV	
Joseph	24m		lab
Sarah A.	17f		
Mary M.	17f		
120-123			
Duding, John	62m	WV	farm
Casandia	58f		
Alfred	16m		lab
Madlem	21f		
Foster, Ellen	28f		dom
Foster, Arno	1m		
Thompson, Frances	68f		
121-124			
Dunsford, William	24m	Ire	lab
Mary J.	41f	VA	
122-125			
McCollister Olevia	60f	WV	
Eliza	40f		
Hamilton	19m		lab
John	17m		
Patrick	14m		
Nancy	12f		
William	8m		
Elizabeth	4f		

p564a			
123-126			
Roberts, Elizabeth	64f	VA	kph
124-127			
McKinney, William	28m	WV	farm
Sallie	67f	VA	
Estaline	22f	WV	
William	4m		
George	3m		
125-128			
Woods, Elsly	32f	VA	kph
Mary F.	15f		
Margaret	12f		
Luanna	9f		
126-129			
Miller, Henry	60m	WV	farm
Sarah	54f	VA	
Lewis T.	31m	WV	lab
Alvin N.	26m		
Manerva	17f		
Cornelia	14f		
127-130			
Woods, Lyda	64f	VA	kph
128-131			
Ashworth, William	42m	VA	farm
Harriet	36f		
Martha	12f		
Elizabeth	6f	WV	
Jane	7f		
William	2m		
Taylor	1m		
129-132			
Janney, John	52	VA	farm
Elizabeth	46f		
Michael	15m		lab
Viley A.	10f		
Mary L.	9f	WV	
Anna L.	6f		
Manerva	4/12f		
130-133			
Smith William	30m	Va	carp
Malinda	30f		
Anna L.	2f		
Lee	2/12m		

131-134			
Long,William	50m	VA	farm
Emily J.	46f		
James S.	19m		lab
Bettie A.	15f		
Sarah B.	13f		
p565 William	9m	WV	
Adaline	6f		

132-135			
Becket,Emesly	35m		farm
Mary S.	32f		
John H.	14m		
Louisa	12f		
Rebecca	10f		
George	7m		
Adaline	4f		
Fannie	2f		
Arvilla	5/12f		

133-136			
Woodard,Madison	22m	VA	farm
Adaline	24f		
Elizabeth	5f	WV	
Harriet	3f		

134-137			
Becket,Moses	69m	VA	farm
Mary	56f	WV	
Isiah O.	18m		lab
Susan J.	15f		
William C.	13m		

135-138			
Smith,Charles	39m	WV	teach
Julia	19f		
Bennett	2m		

136-139			
Payne,Charles	39m	WV	teach
Sarah	18f		
William	13m		
Ella	10f		
Sidney B.	1m		

137-140			
Conner,Conwelsa	27m	WV	farm
Sarah E.	21f		
Virginia	1f		

138-141			
Comer,William	44m	WV	farm
Susanna	54f		
Elizabeth	26f		

138-140 Comer (con't)			
America	17f		
Virginia	17f		
Carpenter,Savina	60f		

139-142			
Connor,Andrew	63m	WV	far
Milley	63f		
Mary	14f		

p565a

140-143			
Commer,William	33m	WV	far
Eliza	30f		
Charles	12m		
John	11m		
James	9m		
Andrew	3m		
Ball,Virginia	9f		

141-144			
Keaton,Calvary	33m	WV	far
Emily	30f		
Jefferson	7m		
William	8/12m		

142-145			
Keaton,John	25m	WV	far
Sarah F.	26f		
Mary E.	4f		
Albert	2m		
Henry	1m		

143-146			
Johnson,Warren M.	23m	WV	far
Ammasetta	25f		
Bennett	2m		
Ada C.	10/12f		

144-147			
Becket,Charles	35m	WV	fa
Martha A.	26f		
Rebecca M.	3f		
Cora	2f		

145-148			
Keaton,Rilen	65m	WV	fa
Lucinda	61f		
Amanda	21f		
Jefferson,Louisa	15f		

146-149			
Keaton,Preston	30m	WV	fa
Almeda	29f		

29

146-149 (con't)

Keaton,Rosali	3f	WV	
Leele A.	1f		

147-150

White,Zacheriah	64m	VA	farm
Lucy	65f		
Dave	30m		
Mary	30f		
Octava	10f	WV	

148-151

Ball,Henry	72m	KY	farm
Telitha	40f	WV	
John C.	19m		
p566 Henry	18m	WV	lab
Edna	14f		sch
Hezekiah	10m		
Mediva	8f		
Parilla	6f		
Bennett	7/12m		
Luella	4f		
Clark,Nancy	72f	KY	

149-152

Ray,Cathorine	42f	WV	kph
Ulysses	11m		
Jennie	3f		

150-153

McCollister,Alexander	47m	WV	farm
Hellen	47f		
Albert	18m		lab
Evaline	17f		
Louisa	14f		
Joseph	11m		
Mary E.	9f		
Letha	6f		
Martin	22m		lab

151-154

McCoy,Lawrence	24m	WV	lab
Emily	23f		
William H.	4m		
Semantha	3f		

152-155

McCoy,Elizabeth	28f	WV	kph
Charles L.	12m		
Catherine	10f		
Rutha	6f		

153-156

Sidebottom,John C.	24m	WV	farm
Elizabeth	24f		
George	1m		
Jennings,Mary	59f	Eng	

154-157

Davis,Jesse	36m	OH	farm
Jane	25f		
Cora	5f		
Henry L.	3m		

155-158

Davis,Thomas J.	28m	OH	farm
Lucinda	25f	WV	
Jesse M.	4m		
Manerva	2f		
p566a William	1f	OH	

156-159

McCollistor,Preston	43m	WV	farm
America	37f		
Mary A.	21f		
Isabel	18f		
James	16m		lab
Lafyette	13f		
Wilmothe	9f		
Manuel	6m		
Elizabeth	5f		

157-160

Becket,Charles W.	43m	WV	farm
Susanna	41f		
James	18m		lab
Samuel	16m	AR	lab
Julia A.	14f		
John L.	12m	WV	
Lucinda	8f		

158-161

Becket,Andrew L.	46m	WV	farm
Emily S.	45f		
Henry	19m		lab
Oliver	9m		

159-162

Chapman,William	58m	VA	farm
Elizabeth	54f	KY	
Henry G.	26m	WV	lab
John G.	25m		lab
Elijah	24m		lab
Sarah H.	22f		
Elen	17f		
Oliva	14f		

```
159-162  Chapman(con't)
        Edna S.       12f  WV
        Matilda         10f
        Verina           8f

160-163
     Tasson,John      42m  Hol  farm
        Cintha A.     33f  WV
        Rebecca H.    16f
        Mary          14f
        Ona A.         1f

161-164
     Meyers,Charles   40m  Ger  farm
        Julia         43f  WV
        Mary A.       15f
p567 Charles          14m
        Ellen         10f
        Milton         6m

162-165
     Dundass,Thomas   36m  WV  farm
        Martha        35f
        Virginia      11f
        Croney         2m

163-166
     McCallister,Boniah 45m VA  farm
        Harriet       42f  WV
        Martha J.     21f
        Eliza S.      19f
        John H.       16m        lab
        Joseph        14m        lab
        George        11m
        Annie          8f
        Emma           6f
        Ada            3f

164-167
     McClary,John J.  27m  Va  farm
        Mary          32f  WV
        Ida M.         4f
```

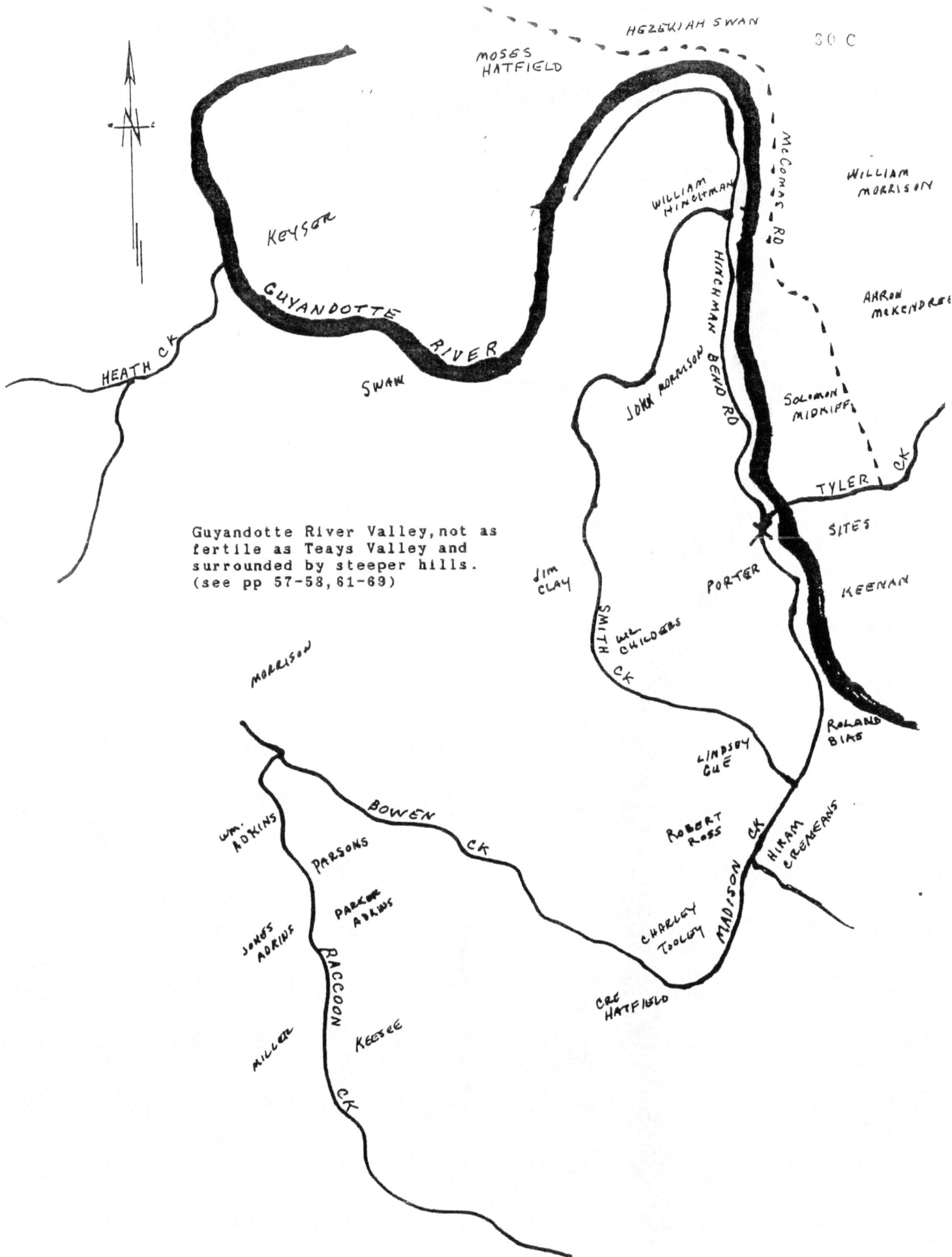

Guyandotte River Valley, not as
fertile as Teays Valley and
surrounded by steeper hills.
(see pp 57-58, 61-69)

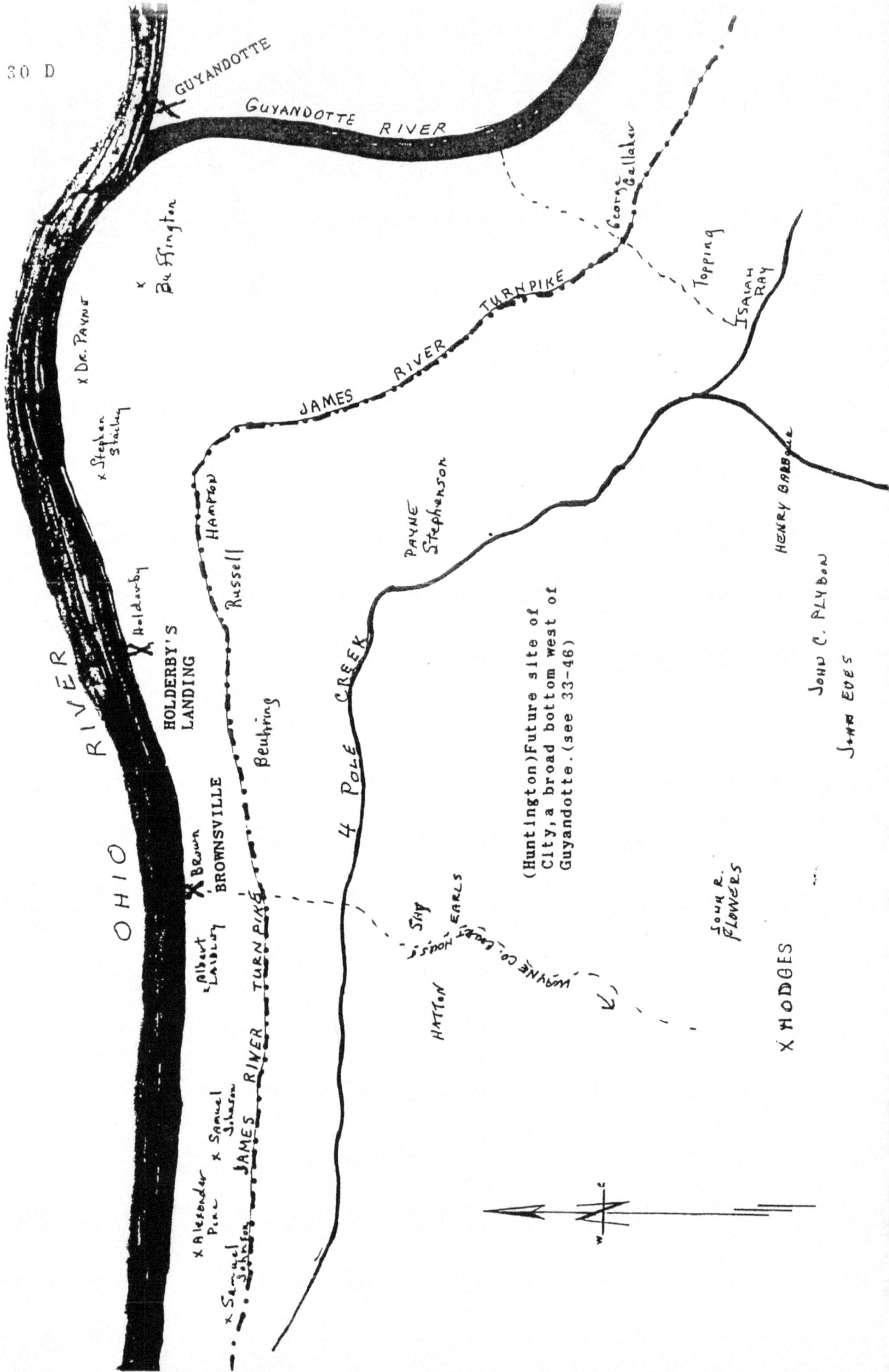

GUYANDOTTE

GUYANDOTTE RIVER

OHIO RIVER

Buffington

x Dr. Payne

x Stephen Stailey

Hampton

Russell

x Holderby

HOLDERBY'S LANDING

x Brown

BROWNSVILLE

x Albert Laidley

Beuhring

JAMES RIVER TURNPIKE

x Alexander Pirc

x Samuel Johnson

x Samuel Johnson

JAMES RIVER TURNPIKE

George Gallaher

Topping

Isaiah Ray

HENRY BARBOUR

JOHN C. PLYBON

JOHN EVES

Payne Stephenson

4 POLE CREEK

(Huntington)Future site of
City, a broad bottom west of
Guyandotte.(see 33-46)

WAYNE CO. EARLS HOUSE

Shy

Hatton

EARLS

JOHN R. FLOWERS

x HODGES

31

p569   Gyandotte Township Guyandotte Post Office 13 jun 1870

1-1			
Meadows,James	40m	VA	farm
America	30f		
James	14m	WV	
Henry	12m		
John A.	6m		
Thomas	3m		
Anna B.	1f		
2-2			
Keller,Adam	65m	Bad	farm
Nancy	55f	WV	
Thomas	29m		lab
Edward	22m		lab
Henry	20m		lab
Lucretia	23f		
Matta	14f		
Ray,Marion	4m		
3-3			
Carter,James	38m	WV	farm
Eliza	47f		
Jennie	13f		
Thornton	11m		
]4-4			
Davis,Harrison	57m	WV	farm
Louisa	40f		
Henderson	21m		lab
Paul	19m		lab
William W.	17m		
Ulysses	5m		
Drucilla	14f		
Missouria	11f		
Flora	9f		
Mary	7f		
5-5			
Topping,Levi	47m	OH	farm
Catherine	36f	WV	
Cassus	14m		
Virgel	9m		
Femanda	7f		
Medley	6/12m		
Fenton	17m		
Nancy	4f		
6-6			
Turner,Nathaniel	46m	WV	
Zerilda	44f		
Henry B.	12m		
p569a Allice	9f		

7-7			
Keller,Albert	37m	WV	farm
Adaline	35f		
Jefferson	9m		
John	3m		
James	10/12m		
Virginia	8f		
Elizabeth	7f		
Davis,Mary	80f	KY	
Davis,Cortis	12m	WV	
8-8			
Crooks,Morran	26m	WV	farm
Lucy H.	22f		
William	2m		
Crooks,Mitchell	19m		lab
9-9			
Toppings,Elinda	60f	VA	kph
10-10			
Droun,Rufus	44m	WV	farm
Sarah	33f		
Newton	15m		lab
John P.	13m		lab
Leat	11m		
David	6m		
Hellen	3f		
Elby	10/12m		
11-11			
McCorkle,James	50m	OH	farm
Sarah	50f	KY	
James	17m	WV	lab
Benjamin	15m		lab
Arena	12f		
Oliva V.	9f		
Jefferson	7m		
Lee Jackson	4m		
12-12			
Brown,James	40m	VA	lab
Amasetta	40f	WV	
Adaline	15f		
Jane	10f		
Kitty	6f		
Permilla	5f		
Ammasetta	3f		
Josephine	11/12f		
William W.	14m		lab
p570 Labon L.	11m		

```
13-13                              20-19 Dodson (con't)
    Dillion,William  50m WV farm       Henry            10m
    Julia A.         41f OH            Albert G.         4m
    Elizabeth        19f WV        Dodson,Nancy         73f

14-14                              21-20
    Martin,James     24m NC            Heath,George A.  33m MD lab
    Nancy            26f VA            Mary A.          22f WV
    Olivia            2f WV            Lucetta           4f
    Sallie         6/12f              Edward            2m
                                      Tom Kline      4/12m
15-15
    Bates,Nancy      80f KY kph    22-21
    Susan A.         32f WV            Blankenship,Henry 27m WV far
    Farelander       30f               Margaret         33f VA
    Susan            13f               Rosalie           3f WV
    Mary E.          11f               Mary F.           1f VA
    Martha         4/12f               Charles E.        5m

16-16                              23-22
    Bates,Andrew     38m WV farm       Sullavin,Jacob   39m KY far
    Olive E.         25f               Amanda           33f WV
    Lucy E.           9f               Harriet        3/12f
    Thomas            7m               David            11m
    Manoah            5m               Andrew            9m
    Willis R.         2m               William           7m
                                      Jacob             2m
17-17
    Stephenson,Samuel 28m WV farm  24-23
    Amanda           27f               Sullavin,Anna    42f KY

    William          73m MD lab        Ellen            70f VA
18---Mary E.         70f WV            Ellen            14f WV
    Manera            1f               Parvilla         12f OH
    Georgie F.        7f               John             10m WV
    Sylvester J.      5m
    McHerston         3m           25-24
                                      Plybon,James     35m VA far
19-18                                 Emily            34f OH
    Stephenson,William 38m WV farm     William          10m WV
    Martha           32f               James L.          8m
    Addison          12m               Jacob M.          7m
    Elby             10m               Lewis G.          5m
    Allen             8m               Sherman           3m
    Lucian            7m               Sheriden          1m
    Sidney            6m
    William E.        1m           26-25
    Evaline           4f               Insco,Joseph     24m VA lab
                                      Sarah            20f WV
20-19                                 Amasetta          1f
    Dodson,Jesse B.  45m VA farm
    Lucetta          42f WV        27-26
    Amanda           17f               Plybon,John      56m WV fa
p570a  Ida            2f               Irene            41f
    Edgar            19m    lab   p571  Lucinda         18f
```

27-26 Plybon (con't)

Elizabeth	18f		
Victoria	8f		
Isabel	5f		
Simeon	2m		

28-27

Jarrell,Ambrose	39m	KY	farm
Mary E.	32f	WV	
Irby,John	5m		

29-28

Wilks,Burwell	54m	OH	farm
Barbery	53f	VA	
Alexander	21m	WV	lab
Albert	15m		
Henry	12m		
America	10f		

30-29

Aams,Elijah	46m	WV	farm
Jane	44f	VA	
Mark L.	18m	KY	
Famian	14m		
Mary J.	12f	WV	
Martha A.	10f		
Eliza	8f		
Crooks,Everman	14m		lab

31-30

Owens,James M.	31m	WV	farm
Mary A.	22f		
Martha	4f		
Elizabeth	2f		
James	8m		
John L.	3m		

32-31

Plybon,John C.	24m	WV	farm
Eliza E.	24f		
Cintha V.	9/12f		
Isaac N.	1m		

33-32

Owens,Salinda	66f	VA	kph
Edward	25m	WV	farm
Mary B.	12f		sch

34-33

Estep,John	52m	KY	farm
Mary	46f		
Elizabeth	11f	WV	
Susan A.	5f		
Nancy	2f		

-34-33 Estep (con't)

George	16m	WV	
Harrison	14m		
Corbon L.	19m		

35-34

Barbour,Henry	63m	VA	farm
Susan	55f	WV	
Elisha	29m		lab
Jacob D.	21m		lab
Henry E.	17m		lab
Samuel	14m		lab
Sarah J.	27f		
Martha	24f		

36-35

Herd,Isriel	24m	IL	farm
America	24f	WV	

37-36

McElavy,David	54m	PA	farm
Mary	40f		
Barbery	18f	WV	
Alich	12m		

38-37

Ray,Isiah	32m	WV	farm
Catherine	30f		
Mary E.	11f		
William	9m		
Albert	7m		
Sarah F.	5f		
Isriel	1m		

39-38

Ray,William	54m	WV	farm
Emily	55f		
Virginia	22f		
Jefferson	19m		lab
Marcillaus	15m		

40-39

Ray,Lemuel	28m	WV	farm
Lucetta	24f		
Georgie	6f		
Alonzo	5m		
Marion	3m		
Lemuel	1m		

41-40

Weeman,Otto	37m	Pru	man
Omillian H.	2m	OH	
Henry E.	1m	WV	
Meiller,Dwies	65f		

40-41
Eves,John   32m VA farm
p572   Mary A.   17f WV kph

        Thomas   70m MD lab
        Sarah   19f WV
        Eliza   59f VA

43-42
  Eves,Thomas M.   35m VA farm
    Eliza E.   24f WV
    Elizabeth   13f   sch
    James F.   10m
    Sulvira   7f
    Mary E.   4f
    Thomas A.   8/12m

44-43
  Irby,Samuel T.   48m VA farm
    Nancy E.   38f
    Sarah   17f   sch
    Marg.A.   15f
    Edward   9m WV
    Charles   6m
    Robert A.   2m
  Irby,George   81m VA lab

45-44
  Irby,Lacheriah   44m VA lab
    Sarah A.   30f
    Berry   8m
    George   4m
    Mary E.   3f
    Julia   1f WV

46-45
  Carter,Lemuel   37m WV farm
    Louisa   32f
    Benjamin   16m   lab
    George H.   11m
    Matilda F.   12f   sch

47-46
  Chatterton,George   56m Eng farm
    Roxey   44f WV
    Mary   19f
    Amanada   12f
    Edna   10f
    Richard   17m   lab

48-47
  Newcomb,George   21m TN lab
    Louisa   22f WV
    Lemuel P.   7/12m

49-48
  Flowers,John R.   52m VA far
p572a   Fildred   49f (Mildr

         Hermina   18m WV
         John A.   15m
         James L.   13m
         Amasetta   11f
         Daniel C.   9m
         Lorenzo   4m
         Sadler R.   1m

50-49
  Flowers,George   29m WV far
    Julia   30f VA
    Henry L.   5m WV
    Gerard   2m

51-50
  Flowers,Fredrick   27m WV RR
    Martha   20f
    Frances   2f

52-51
  Hodges,John   27m VA lab
    Allice A.   24f WV

53-52
  Ray,Lucy   49f WV kph
    Joseph   27m   lab
    Elijah   17m   lab
    Millard   15m   lab
    Sarah R.   13f
    Anna H.   10f

54-53
  Ray,Benjamin   24m WV
    Mary   23f KY
    Cato   3f WV
    Oley   1f

55-54
  Grayham,Marion   30m WV fa
    Mary E.   30f
    Aratitum   6m
    Phillips.Robert   22m VA sc

56-55
  Stephenson,Mary   48f WV kp
    Georgianna   23f
    Charles   22m   la
    William P.   20m   la
    Thomas   16m   la
    Medora   14f   sc
    Sidney A.   12m

56-55 Stephenson (con't)
    Ella M.   10f
  Stephenson,Mark   75m VA lab
p573
57-56
  Neuman,Warren   19m WV lab
    Pernellia   20f OH
  Henckly,Jacob   36m VA lab
  Henckly,Lois   28f OH
  Henckly,John L.   3m
  Henckly,Bell   1f WV

58-57
  Grayham,Jonas   63m VA farm
    Mary   59f OH
  Smith,Thomas   45m OH

59-58
  Riggs,James   37m WV lab
    Amanda   32f OH
    Greenville   12m WV
    Mary   10f
    Larrah   8f
    James   6m
    Effe   4f
    Nancy   4f
    Hatty   2f

60-59
  Thacker,Gerard   24m OH lab
    Elizabeth   21f
    Louisa   2f
    Benjamin   10/12m
  Thacker,Clarissey 48f WV

61-60
  Grayham,Jefferson 30m WV farm
    Mary   26f
    William J.   7m
    Ivda   4f
    Georgie   2f

62-61
  Ray,William E.   35m WV farm
    Sophia   25f
    Cornetta   10/12f

63---
  Ray,James F.   27m WV lab

64-62
  Harrison,William   66m VA farm
    Sina   60f
    Catherine   31f

64-62 Harrison (con't)
    Selina R.   18f WV
65-63
  Roberts,Patterson 46m VA lab
    Jaunetta   39f
    Salicia   18f WV
    John   16m
p573a Selvana   14f   sch
    James H.   12m
    Benjamin   8m
    Jeremiah   6m
    George A.   3m
  Harris,Netta   1f

66-64
  Burks,William   60m KY farm
    Mary   60f
    John   15m WV

67-65
  Burks,Jesse   29m KY lab
    Elizabeth   28f
    William   4m OH
    Sarah   2f WV
  Gibson,John L.   11m KY

68-66
  Sullavin,Henry   47m WV farm
    Catherine   40f
    Alonzo C.   20m   lab
    Daniel C.   19m   lab
    Mary J.   18f
    Malissey   17f
    Martha S.   15f
    Elizabeth   13f
    Henry M.   11m
    George   9m
    Sarah E.   6f
    Emma   4f
    Alven   10/12m

69-67
  Hatton,Solomon   64m VA farm
    Mary A.   44f
    William   19m WV
    Edmond   17m
    Perlows   15m
    Sanford   12m
    Elizabeth   9f
    Lincoln   7m

70-68				
Roberts,Neuman	39m	VA RR		
Mary A.	11f	WV		
Booten,Elizabeth	80f	VA		

71-69			
Simmonds,Joseph	34m	WV lab	
Lussa J.	24f	WV	
p574 (Seamonds)			
John W.	4m		
Fannie	2f		
Lucy E.	5/12f		

72-70		
Seamonds,Aaron	67m	VA farm
Delia	58f	
Nathaniel	23m	WV lab
Richard	22m	
Burks,Georgie	9f	

73-71		
Cardwell,Manoah	48m	WV farm
Sarah	48f	
Semantha	20f	
William	18m	lab
Melvil	16m	lab
Henry	14m	lab
Susan	9f	sch
Hollenback,Ellen	78f	VA

74-72		
McVickers,Hilvery	39m	VA lab
Vianna	35f	WV
Archebald	10m	OH
Mary	11f	
Nancy	13f	
Malinda	5f	WV
James	5/12m	
Johnson,Amasetta	10f	
Johnson,Jenetta	5f	
Johnson,Sarah J.	14f	

75-73		
Edwards,Sarah	40f	KY kph
Turner,Mary	18f	WV
Porter,Alonzo	22m	
Turner,Columbia	2f	

76-74		
Benchfield,John	52m	NC lab
Martha	39f	VA
Manerva	18f	
Harriet	16f	
Susana	15f	

76-74	Benchfield (con't)		
	Wader H.	9m	WV
	James C.	8m	
	Levisa J.	6m	
	Samuel	4m	
	William	4m	
p574a	Margaret	3f	
	Henry	2/12m	

77-75		
Beuhring,Fredrick	42	WV farm
Francis E.	32f	
Henry H.	10m	
Fredrick	5m	
Frances E.	12f	
Virginia E.	8f	
Mary L.	7f	
Lee D.	3m	
Nora B.	2f	

78-76		
Cassell,John W.	32m	VA lab
Mary	22f	
Margret	3f (5)	
Lura B.	1f	WV

79---	

80-77		
Ruatin,David	23m	VA lab
Eliza	21f	
Marion	2m	KY
Jesse S.	5/12m	

81-78		
Adams,Jeremiah	44m	VA far
Elizabeth	33f	OH
Asden	17m	WV
Thomas	14m	
Samuel	7m	
Fannie	4f	
Emma	11/12f	

82-79		
Elkins,Dudley	31m	IN lab
Celey	26f	WV
James M.	10m	
Sarah E.	8f	
Mary E.	6f	
Charles H.	2m	

83---	

84-80		
Gallaher,Edward	49	PA farm

85-81		
Sullvin,Alonzo	21	WV farm

```
86-82                                              93-89
   Thompson,Gilbert   36m WV lab         Allen,Reynolds    32m  WV lab
      Lucinda          37f                    Martha        25f
      William          10m                    John          5m KY
      Lucy C.           8f           p575a    Robert        4m WV
p575  James             5m                    Ida           2f
      Sarah J.          3f
      Richard           2m           94-90
      Ora               5f              Ratcliff,Virginia  42f OH kph
                                          John             27m WV lab
87-83                                     Matilda          24f
   Seamonds,Robert    30m WV lab          Ephram           22m IA lab
      Mary             22f                 Squire           18m    lab
      James A.          5m                 William          16m    lab
      Robert        11/12m                 Allice           15f
                                           George            9m
88-84
   Sullaven,James     50m WV farm      95-91
      Elizabeth        51f KY             Ross,David P.     45m VA farm
      Topping,Andrew   47m VA lab            Jane          40f
                                             William D.    19m OH lab
89-85                                        Amacetta      15f
   Harrison,William   34m WV lab            Isaac         11m WV
      Lucy A.          35f VA               Cela J.        8f
      Henry H.          3m WV               George         4m
      Phenton           1f
      Robert         6/12m               96-92
                                            Allen,John W.    73m VA farm
90-86                                          Nancy         66f
   Erls,David         35m KY farm            Virginia      14f WV
      Cela             35f VA               Samuel        15m    lab
      Charles H.       10m WV
      William R.        9m               97-93
      David             7m                  Allen,James      42m OH farm
      George            4m                     Elizabeth    42f VA
      Lucien E.         3m                     Ellen        16f WV sch
      Columbia       1/12f                     Willie       11f    sch
                                               James        10m
91-87                                          Sarah         6f
   Carson,John        23m OH lab              Dexter         3m
      Mary             18f WV                 Minnie      3/12f
      James         11/12m
                                         98-94
92-88                                       Allen,Samuel     35m OH lab
   Marre,Joseph       57m VA lab               Eliza         30f WV
      Nancy            47f WV               Hunter,John      48m Ire fai
      Daniel           22m    lab          Hunter,Julia  A. 38f VA
      Amanda           24f                 Hunter,Nancy L.  16f WV sch
      Wesley           16m VA lab          Hunter,Mary      14f    sch
      Edward           15m    lab          Hunter,Eliza     11f
      Louisa           13f KY              Hunter,Charles    7m
   Williams,Lucinda     3f                 Hunter,Emma       2f
   Williams,John A.3/12m WV                Hunter,Jessie   5/12f
```

p576
100-96
Adkins, Sarah	41f	WV	kph
George	19m		lab
Peter	16m		
William	12m		
Frances	1f		

101-97
Huxham, Henry	40m	Eng	farm
Sarah	38f		
Elizabeth	16f		sch
Charles H.	14m	WV	
Florence	10f		
Victoria	7f		
Harry	5/12m		

102-98
Oley, John	40m	VA	blks
Elizabeth	29f	WV	
Eliza C.	11f		
Martha	10f		
Luticia	8f		
John	7m		
Julius	5m		
Emma	4f		
Alberta	11/12f		

103-99
Insco, William	42m	WV	farm
Eliza J.	33f	VA	
Martha	11f	WV	
William	8m		
George	6m		
Olive C.	1f		

104-100
Huffman, Andrew	24m	WV	lab
Matilda	22f		
Meteoni	1f		

105-101
Hall, Nancy	60f	WV	
Christofer	15m		lab
French, Henry	7m		
French, John	5m		

106-102
Williams, Samuel	24m	Eng	farm
Sarah E.	19f	WV	
Mary	1f		
Lilley B.	2/12f		
Tacket, Minerva	21f		dom

107-103
Thornburg, Hezakiah	37m	WV	far
p576a Barbery	39f		
Walter	15m		lab
Bentin	12m		
Thomas	9m		
Reynolds, Solomon	63m		lab

108-104
Hughs, Richard	44m	VA	lab
Julia A.	41f	WV	
Ora S.	19f		sc
James	14m	OH	
Isadora	9f	WV	

109-105
Townson, William	34m	NJ	far
Amanda	33f	VA	
Hagan	9/12m	WV	

110-106
Legrand, James	58m	VA	lab
Mary	18f		
William	15m		lab
Robert	8m		
Bowden, Susan	22f		
Bowden, Baxter	4m	WV	
Bowden, Mary E.	1f		

111-107
Stark, John	45m	Pru	v
Emily	27f	WV	
James	15m		l
John	12m		
Mary V.	10f		
Charena	8f		
Lerona	8f		
George	6m		
Emily	3f		
Fannie	6/12f		
Hensley, Ann	18f		

112-108
Harrison, Henry	30m	WV	fa
Francis	23f	VA	
Arianna	7f	WV	
Lucy A.	6f		
Frances	3f		
Mary V.	1f		

113-109
Shy, Franklin	38m	WV	
Abigal	38f	VA	
Dudley	15m	WV	
p577 Marcellus	14m		

113-109 Shy (con't)

Name	Age/Sex	Birthplace	Occupation
Frank	13m		
Clarona	10f		
Jackson	9m		
Melvina	8f		
William	5m		
Gerard	3m		
Robert	2m		
Albina	3/12f		

114-110

Name	Age/Sex	Birthplace	Occupation
Everett,Samuel	50m	WV	lab
Temperana	30f		
Peter	14m		
George	7m		
Kate	2f		
Lucy F.	7/12f		

115-111

Name	Age/Sex	Birthplace	Occupation
Marten,William	47m	OH	farm
Harriet	38f		
Benjamin	19m		lab
John F.	15m		lab
Josephine	13f		
Ella	11f		
Clementine	9f		
Amanda	6f		
Charles	4m		
George	8/12m		

116-112

Name	Age/Sex	Birthplace	Occupation
Noell,Larkin	49m	VA	farm
Polley	48f		
Arthur	18m		lab
Queen V.	15f		
James	12m		

117-113

Name	Age/Sex	Birthplace	Occupation
McConnell,William	52m	VA	lab
Mary A.	41f		
Eliza	14f	WV	
Albert	12m		
James K.	10m		
George	6m		
Clarona	3f		
Lerona	3f		

118-114

Name	Age/Sex	Birthplace	Occupation
Mores,Henry	26m	VA	farm
Mary E.	23f		
p577a George M.	2m	WV	
Edward	1m		

119-115

Name	Age/Sex	Birthplace	Occupation
Ellis,Preston	53m	VA	lab
Ellen	50f	OH	
Addison	33m		lab
Siles	18m		lab
Lewis	21m		lab
Mores,Anna	32f		
Mores,William	7m		
Mores,Cratin	5m	WV	
Mores,Robert	2m		

120-116

Name	Age/Sex	Birthplace	Occupation
Bates,Lee	40m	KY	lab
Julia A.	40f	WV	
Georgie	17f		
Peter	15m		lab
Eliza	10f		
Martha	7f		
John	5m		
Cook,Henry	15m		

121-117

Name	Age/Sex	Birthplace	Occupation
Wilks,James	31m	WV	lab
Levila	26f	IN	
Barbery	6f	WV	
Josephine	4f		
America	2f		
James	1m		
Adams,John	77m	VA	
Adams,Sarah A.	53f	IN	
Hackworth,Pleasent	26m	OH	lab
Hackworth,Eliza	20f		
Hackworth,George	1m	WV	
Hackworth,Martha	1/12f		

122-118

Name	Age/Sex	Birthplace	Occupation
Wentz,William	61m	WV	farm
Matilda	56f		
Henry C.	22m		lab
Alexander	21m		lab
William	18m		lab
Louisa F.	23f		

123-119

Name	Age/Sex	Birthplace	Occupation
Wentz,John P.	35m	WV	lab
Mary E.	30f		
Cora	12f		
p578 Nora E.	9f		
Matilda	8f		
John W.	5m		
Morris	4m		
xxxxAnthony	1/12m	xxxxx	

p578
124-120

Stephenson, Joseph	36m	WV	lab	
Amanda	35f			
Etna C.	13f			
Joseph M.	11m			
St.Luke	11m			
William	9m			
Lucy	7f			
Robert	5m			
John M.	3m			
Susan	2f			
Charles	8/12m			

125-121

Bryant, Dennis	53m	VA	farm

126-

Mary A.	22f	WV	
Thomas	20m		lab
Lebert	18m		lab
Virginia	16f		
John R.	12m		
Lucy F.	10f		
Andrew	8m		

127-122

Nite, William	24m	WV	farm
Jane	25f		
Allen	3/12m		

128-123

Hall, Andrew H.	52m	VA	farm
Elizabeth	44f		
Samuel	17m		lab
Luticia	13f		
Martha	11f		
Henry	10m		

129-124

Arthur, Sanders	52m	WV	farm
Elizabeth	53f		
Thomas	19m		lab
Ann	16f		
Eliza	14f		
Ella	12f		
Josephine	8f		

p578a
130-125

Cook, Peter	54m	WV	lab
Sarah	81f	VA	
John	24m	WV	
Elizabeth	18f		

131-126

Poteet, Clements	36m	WV	farm
America	30f		
George	7m		

132-127

Ricketts, Virginia	44f	WV	farm
Edwin	18m		lab
Girard	14m		lab
Charles	13m		lab
Ella	11f		sch

133-128

Bowden, Cintha	45f	WV	kph
Columbus	19m		RR
John E.	16m		lab
Stewart	12m		
Evaline J.	21 f		

134-129

Farrist, James	39m	B VA	fa
Julia R.	35f	B	
Anna E.	17f	B	
Lurena	15f	B	
Francis	14f	B	
Dorenda	12f	B	
Lewis	9m	B	
Jugley	5f	M	
Lucy A.	3f	M WV	
Elijah	1m	M	

135-130

Wyett, Ralph	70m	B VA	la
Rhoda	74f	B NC	
Joseph	23m	B WV	la
Sarah	28f	B	
Douglas	13m	B	

136-131

Bowden, James	23m	WV	farm
Elizabeth	30f	OH	
Boyer, Philip	8m	WV	
Hatrly, Isabel	65f		

137-132

Arthur, Lewis	76m	VA	farm
Lucy	73f		
Ferguson, William	30m	WV	farm
Ferguson, Leanora	28f		
Ferguson, Levera	8f		
Ferguson, Rebecca	7f		
Ferguson, Julius	5m	MO	

p579

138-133
  Plybon,Jacob   72m VA farm
    Mary   67f WV
    Eliza   26f
    Elizabeth   23f

139-134
  Shy,Harvey W.   37m WV farm
    Josephine   30f
    Edna   11f
    Georgie E.   7f
    Waldo J.   4m
    Jefferson   2m

140-135
  Crump,George W.   33m KY farm
    Susan A.   24f WV
    Nettie   9/12f

141-136
  Sanders,Francis   46m VA farm
    Margaret   28f WV
    John H.   10m
    Malinda   8f

    Catherine   6f
    Robert L.   4m
    William F.   2m

142-137
  Ferguson,John   51m VA blks
    Julia A.   48f
    Samuel   17m WV lab
    Charles   12m
    William   8m
    Elias   7m
    Lucien C.   4m
    George   1m
  Roberts,John   23m
  Roberts,Susan   15f---aug
  Roberts,Sanford 1/12m

143-138
  Vanatta,William   29m WV lablks
    Lucy   24f
    Robert   3m
    John J.   1m

144-139
  Ferguson,John   19m WV lab
    Lucy   19f----aug
p579a John A.   2/12m

145-140
  Mores,Eton   65m VA farm
    Lucy   44f
    George   21m   lab
  Taylor,Edward   14m
  Warren,Bluford   30m VA farm
  Warren,Sarah   19f
  Warren,Elizabeth 2f WV
  Warren,Anna   9/12f

146-141
  Coffman,Noah   35m WV farm
    Lucy   32f
    Athen J.   9m
    Elizabeth   6f
    Alfred   4m
    James   1m

147-142
  Spicer,Henry   37m OH farm
    Lucella   25f WV
    Lee   4m
    Medora   3f
    Nicholas   2m
  Mores,Nancy   55f VA

148-143
  Fowler,Harrison   24m OH lab
    Frances   23f WV
    Gray   1/12m

149-144
  Cook,James   49m OH lab
    Clarinda   49f
    General   8m WV
    Emily J.   7f

150-145
  Ellis,Addison   31m OH farm
    Sarah A.   22f VA
    Albert   4m WV
    Gilbert   1m OH

151-146
  Shaver,John   26m VA farm
    Luella   23f
    Mary M.   9/12f WV
  Shaver,Daniel   23m VA lab
  Shaver,Clore E.   18f WV
  Shaver,Emogene   1f OH

152-147
  Arthur,William   35m VA farm
    Emily   28f WV
p580   Jenna   7f

152-147 Arthur (con't)   p580a
   John L.   6m WV   160-154
   Lucy F.   5f   Donthit,John L.   27m WV groc
   Clara B.   1f   Elizabeth   20f
                                       Gracy   3f

153-148   161-155
  Roberts,Absolum   53m VA farm   Donthit,William   60m WV mer
   Lubecia   29f WV   Charlott   49f
   Lutrecia   9f   Edward   21m
   Mary E.   5f   Richard H.   16m
   Viola E.   1f   Clara   12f
                                       Lecky,Henry   25m OH mill
154-149   Lecky,Columbia   18f WV
  Shultz,Jacob   24m Fra farm   Wilson,William   3m
   Mary   23f WV
   Charles   4m   162-156
   James E.   2m   Thompson,Henry   40m WV tav
                                       Elizabeth   56f VA tav
155-150   Albers,John   50m   shoe(
  Turner,Thomas   52m WV farm   Ward,Mortica   3m WV
   Susan   52f OH
   Victor A.   23m WV lab
   Lymon   20m   lab   163-157
   Leanera   17f   Wood,Horatio H.   54m WV lab
156- Mary J.   17f KY   Margaret   43f
                                       Fannie   21f
157-151   Mary E.   17f
  Stephenson,Lafyett 45m WV lab   Laura   10f
   Nancy   40f   William   3m
   Charles   16m   lab
   Hutaka   14f   164-158
   Preston   12m   Johnson,Irvin   30m WV carp
   Amasetta   10f   Martha   29f PA
   John H.   8m   Mary E.   1f
   Vinson,W.   6m
   Anna   4f   165-159
   Jefferson   6/12m   Claughton,Richard   64m VA jwlr
  Arthur,William   4m   Susan   64f WV
                                       166-160
158-152   Hysell,Joseph L.   29m OH mer
  Wolford,James   43m VA lab   Elizabeth   27f WV
   Cintha   32f WV   Nannie   1f
   Amanda   10f
   Jennie   6f   167-161
   David   4m   Wilson,James   58m VA farm
   William   2m   Sarah A.   57f WV
                                       James   18m
159-153   John   14m
  Clark,William   36m VA lab   Thornburg,Nannie   23f
   Martha   27f WV   Nicholas,Sela   38f B   dom
   John B.   2m
   Thomas   1/12m

43

168-162
  Mitchell,Elizabeth 54m VA kph
    William 16m WV RR
    Nancy 14f
    Ella 9f
    Schankes,Lucy 18f
page581
169-163
  Baker,John C. 52m VA carp
    Leanora 22f WV

170-164
  Bonner,John W. 41m NJ swml
    Isaac N. 14m OH
    Amelia 34f VT

---165
  Mossgrove,Thomas 40m PA tayl
    Mariah 40f OH

171-166
  Letulle,Nancy 59f WV kph
    Leanera 31f
    Sarah 27f
    Lewis P. 25m Plas
    Josephine 22f

172-167
  Hayslip,James L. 35m OH groc
    Victoria 29f WV
    Minnie 6f
    George 3m

173-168
  Scott,Sanford W. 32m VA blks
    Mary J. 36f WV
    William H. 11m
    James 9m
    Abbia 7f
    Charles 8/12m
    Scott,Charles 20m blksj
    Jones,Robert J. 27m VA blksj

174-169
  Neal,Abreham 46m PA wgmk
    Salina 34f KY
    Mary E. 14f PA
    Graf,Caroline 16f PA

175-170
  Carroll,Thomas 59m Ire BH
    Mary 35f Ire BH
    Augustis 18m WV team
    Margaret 20f MD

175-170 Carroll (con't)
    Ellen 12f WV
    Kate V. 12f WV
    Charles 7m
    Mary 3f

176-171
  Keenan,Samuel 26m WV sdlmk
    Frances 26f

177-172
  Blankenship,E.D. 48m KY groc
    Louisa L. 44f WV
p581a   Charlott 20f
    Gerald 19m
    Mary V. 14f
    Sarah 13f
  Lovejoy,John 62m groc

178-173
  Roberts,James M. 57m WV wgmk
    Sarah L. 42f VA
    John W. 22m
    William 18m
    Emma J. 14f

179-174
  Douthit,William H. 29m groc WV
    Jane A. 19f
    Frank W. 7/12m

180-175
  Butcher,Worden 59m WV mer
    Ann F. 57f VA
    Sarah M. 23f WV

181-176
  Wright,William O. 33m WV mer
    Sallie E. 23f VA
    Edward E. 6m WV
    Ada -f

182-177
  Lecky,William 59m WV groc
    Susan 49f OH
    Ana B. 17f
  McMahon,Wayne 53m Bridge c
  Watton,Emma 15 M OH dom
----178
  Cochran,Jacob 28m OH WfB c
    Amelia C. 26f WV
    Ida A. 1f KY
    Abey J. 2/12f WV

```
----179
   Campbell,Henry C.    33m OH carp
   Leinta               31f WV
   Henry J.             9m  OH
   Clayton              7m  OH

183-180
   Smith,Persivel       73m OH mer
   Mary E.              62f VA
   Persivel             34m WV
   Lucas,Fannie         17f    dom

184-181
   Mather,John N.       28m WV clk
   Emma                 22f
   Carrie B.            3/12f
page 582
185-182
   McGinnis Benj.D.     44m WV law
   Sarah                28f
   Eva                  3f

186-183
   Ong,Susan            46f VA kph
   Ernest M.            23m WV carp
   Isaac B.             16m

187-184
   Clark,Silas M.       49m MD team
   Martha               38f VA
   Robert               17m WV drtm
   Alexander            15m
   Thomas               10m
   Mary E.              4f
   McCorkle,Pheba       36f OH

----185
   Pollard,John         30m KY farm
   Frances              25f WV
   George E.            4m
   Ida C.               2f

188-186
   Clark,William L.     54m VT stm
   Julia A.             42f MD
   Fredrick             17m WV
   Elizabeth            13f
   Emily                6f
   Minnie               1f
   Lorenzo              9m

189-187
   Hite,John B.         65m VA lmanf
   Elizabeth            53f Can
```

```
189-187 Hite (con't)
   Eliza                59f VA
   John                 14m WV sch
   Maretta              11f

190-188
   Hite,William         62m VA tany
   Mary                 50f
   Malinda              28f WV
   Womeldorff,Daniel    24m OH carp
   Womel- ",Virginia    22f WV

191-189
   Ward,Adaline         47f WV kph
   William              21m    plst
   Foster,John          29m    dtean
   Foster,Lizzie        20f
   Foster,Walden        4m

192-190
   Maupin,America       44f WV kph
p582a   Allen F.        19m    lab
   Sarah A.             12f
   Ira J.               11m

193-191
   Reed,Mary A.         40f WV kph
   Ida                  11f
   John                 9m
   Vinson               8m
   Charles L.           5m
   Marmaduke,James      35m
   Vance,Elizabeth      31f    dom

194-192
   Gross,George W.      65m VA sdl
   Martha               40f MD
   Theadore             22m WV RR
   Grant                5m
   William              8/12m

195-193
   Everett,John         82m VA farm
   Hannah               60f NY
   Woodrum,Sarah        16f WV dom

196-194
   Worden,William       28m WV stm
   Hatta B.             28f
   Charles M.           3m
   George               1m
   Ida                  1/12f
```

197-195			
Smith,Edward A.	39m	WV	mer
Josia G.	35f		
Mary P.	13f		
Edward S.	10m		
Lucas,Hamit	20f		dom

198-196			
Womeldroff,James	48m	OH	farm
Anna E.	41f		
Harriet E.	19f		
Henry C.	18m		
Robert E.	14m		
Augustes	12m		
Jennie L.	7/12f	WV	

199-197			
Rider,Charles W.	55m	VA	farm
Mary J.	54f		
Elizabeth	21f	Il	
Sarah	17f	WV	
Martha	15f		

page 583

Thompson,Samuel	46m	PA	teach
Thompson,Lucy	40f		
Thompson,Mary	4f		

200-198			
White,Albert G.	40m	WV	mer
Mary L.	35f		
Atta A.	20f		
Susan G.	11f		
James G.	7m		
Sallie M.	5f		
Skitter,Anna	4f		

201-199			
Dietz,Hugo	45m	Hes	carp
Charlott	15f	WV	
George	10m		
Hugo	7m		
*Magnus,Johanetta	65f	Hes	

202-200			
Wright,James H.	37m	VA	carp
Fannie	36f		

203-201			
Butcher,Getmont	36m	WV	clk
Clementine	36f		
Temima	14f		sch
William	10m		
Charles	7m		

* reversed on census

203-201 Butcher (con't)			
Jennie B.	5f		
Morton	2m		

204-202			
Laidley,George S.	28m	WV	clk
Mary V.	21f		

205-203			
Lauson,John(Lawson)	35m	VA	lab
Luemma	26f	KY	

----204			
Butcher,Edward	23m	WV	dray
Mattie E.	21f		

206-205			
Dusenberry,William	42m	mer	NY
Cintha	40f		
Caleb C.	17m		
Sarah K.	15f		
Jessie	12f		
Clark,Roland	27m	MD	
Clark,Susie	23f	NY	
Clark,Frank	1m	WV	

207-206			
Sedinger,James D.	31m	WV	plst
Agnes	29f		
p583a Henry L.	11m	WV	

208-207			
Hayslip,Thomas J.	62m	VA	CCR
Margery	62f	OH	
Cary B.	28m		pntr
Thomas J.	22m	WV	
Richard B.	18m		PO

209-208			
Russell,St.Mark	67m	VA	farm
Dollie	69f		
Allice	23f	WV	

210-209			
Peters,Lewis	43m	VA	pntr
Violet VA.	37f	WV	
Richard H.	18m		sch
Mary V.	16f		sch
Stonewall J.	7m		
John L.	1m		
Gardiner,Elizabeth	56f		

```
211-210
   Holderby,George W.    30m WV mer
      Addie C.           30f
      Jessie R.           3f
      Susie               1f

212-211
   Weed,Isaac            42m CT carp
      Sarah A.           32f
      Dora F.            13f
      Aldie F.           12m
      Flora J.           11f
      Gennie             10f
      Howerd              5m
      Addus S.            3f
      Bula             6/12f

----212
   Poindexter,James      33m WV pres
      Nannie             23f
      Charles             2m PA

213-213
   Flowers,Alford C.     60m WV mlrt
      Sarah              60f KY
      Alonzo             21m WV
      James F.           16m
      Esra               28m OH carp
      Nancy              19f
      Oscar            9/12m WV

----214
   Tucker,William        28m WV farm
p584  Malissa            26f OH

214-215
   Flowers,Thadeus       30m OH mlrt
      Emily              22f WV
      Edgar               1m

215-216
   Joseph,John           43m WV swml
      Hellen M.          39f KY
      Francis M.         19m WV
      Alford L.          18m
      William E.         16m KY
      James L.           15m WV
      Nathaniel          13m
      Charles W.         10m OH
      Sarah M.            8f
      Ezara S.            6m KY
      Emma R.             1f WV

216-217
   Gasner,George         35m Hes tan
      Mary               45f Eng
      Victoria           16 WV
      Henry              14m
      Stella             11f

217-218
   Hayslip,Samuel D.     30m OH clk
      Nancy L.           25f
      Charles H.          6m
      Rubie K.            4f WV
      Okey K.             2m

218-219
   Fruitell,Julius       44m Pru lvs
      Sophia M.          45f
      Christian          18m PA lab
      Mary C.            16f
      Henry A.           14m WV
      William            12m
      Alexander          10m

219-220
   Prise,Joseph          55m WV tobn
      Minerva            45f KY

220-221
   Russell,Albert G.     44m WV pilc
      Olivia M.          23f KY
      Laura J.           15f WV
      Edward T.          11m
      Mary M.             1f
p584a
221-222
   Thornburg,David       56m MD tean
      Joanna             43f VA
      Rachel             17f WV sch
      David B.            9m
      Moses M.            8m

222-223
   Hysell,James H.       32m OH phy
      Mary L.            25f WV
      Fitz H.             4m

223-224
   White,John H.         38m WV gro
      Drucilla E.        33f VA
      Martha M.          14f    sch
      Mary V.            12f
      Eugenia            10f
      Anna R.             7f
```

47

224-225				
Smith,Austin	45m	OH	team	
Lucy A.	54f	VA		
Luella	15f	WV		
Henry S.	11m			

225-226				
Hoops,Isiah	53m	VA	shoe	
Mary	44f			

226-227				
Serange,George	38m	VA	hotel	
Rebecca	31f	OH	hotel	
Thacker,William	35m	WV	timdl	
Thacker,America L.	24f			

227-228				
Witcher,John S.	31m	WV	MC ?	
Mahaly F.	27f			
Valera	8f			
William V.	7m			
T.Sheriden	5m			
John T.	3m			

228-229				
Holdroyd,Peter	40m	WV	carp	
Susan E.	37f			
Anna M.	14f		sch	
Robert	12m			
Maggie	9f			
George	6m			

229-230				
Shinburg,John	40m	Fra	carp	
Mary E.	49f	Eng		
George	18m	WV	sch	

230-231				
Hyder,Henry	70m	B VA	lab	
p585 Virginia	58f	B VA		
Federal	9m	B WV		

231-232				
Shultz,Rosey	60f	Fra		
William	20m		lab	

232-233				
McGinnis Allen	42m	WV	phy	
Sarah E.	30f			
Jennie	10f			
Maggie	6f			

233-234				
Cook,Thomas	46m	WV	team	
Louisa	46f	NC		
Martha	17f	WV	sch	

234-235				
Laidley,John	37m	WV	mer	
Sarah E.	32f	VA		
Mary L.	11f	WV		
Charles	9m	KY		
Anna L.	7f	WV		

235-236				
Ferguson,Sarah	47f	WV	kph	
Mary A.	25f			
Areanna	8f			
Ardel	6f			
Sarah S.	6/12f			

236-237				
Arthur,William	43m	WV	carp	
Martha	35f	OH		
Lucetta	17f	WV		
Virginia	15f			
Bradford	13m			
Martha	11f			
Catherine	9f			
Elizabeth	7f			
Georgie	2f			

237-238				
Smith,Dudly D.	67m	OH	mer	
Eloner	57f			
Mary A.	30f	WV		
Dudly J.	28m		mer	
Abraham	26m		clk	
Pease,Josaphine	14f	OH	sch	

238-239				
Tucker,Fulton	24m	OH	lab	
Georgie	21f	WV		
Aber S.	3m			

p585a

239-240				
Dusenberry,Chas O.	38	NY	slsm	
Anna F.	24f			
William C.	11m	WV		
Nellie B.	8f			
Dusenberry,Nancy	62f	NY		

240-241				
Hanly,Benjamin	25m	WV	lvrst	
Augusta	20f			
Susie	6/12f			

```
241-242
  Brammer,Clark K.    39m OH BSF
    Sarah P.          33f WV
    Sarah V.          14f OH
    George L.          9m WV
    Willie V.          6f

242-243
  Bukey,Rudolph       44m WV tav
    Evaline           48f
    Rebecca           17f
    Preston M.        13m

243-244
  Keenan,Andrew J.    50m WV mer
    Rebecca           40f
    Sanford           17m    clk
    Sallie            14f    sch
  Spurlock,Joseph     19m    sch

244-245
  Hiltbruner,Jacob    49m PA tin
    Mary              47f
    Stephen C.        28m    tin
    William P.        20m WV lab
    Martha V.         15f    sch
    Isiah             14m
    Hiram             12m
    Maggie R.          9f
    Anna               2f

245-246
  Newcomb,William     32m WV carp
    Margaret          25f
    Edgar J.           3m
    Labon T.           1m

246-247
  Wellington,Nodiah   42m WV carp
    Elizabeth         38f VA
    Taylor            23m WV clk
    Charlott          14f    sch
    Sarah V.          11f    sch
p586 Mary L.           6f
    Albina F.          3f
    Nathaniel         12m
    John               8m
  Wellington,Charlott 68f CT

247-248
  Dusenberry,Justin T.52m NY mer
    Louisa            42f WV
    Francis L.        18m    sch
    Theadore W.       16m    sch
```

```
247-248  Dusenberry (con't)
    James B.          14m WV sch
    George             3m
    Mary E.           11f
    Louisa             9f

248-249
  Dietz,Rudolph       53m Hes Shc
    Mariah            39f MA
    Iola              17f WV
    Allen G.          10m
    William            7m
    Edgar              6m
  Jewel,Daniel        26m NY blks
  Jewel,Mary E.       20f WV
  Jewel,Emma       1/12f

249-250
  Hite,Frances        50m WV shoe
    Mary              39f OH
    Edward            19m WV sch
    Gerturde          14f
    Henry C.          12m
    Charles           10m
    William            3m

250-251
  Everett,Talton      49m WV farm
    Elizabeth         46f
    Clayton           20m KY lab
    George S.         18m    lab
    Mary T.           16f    sch
    Emma C.           16f    sch
    Labon T.          14m
  Brown,William       21m MS

251-252
  Stewart,Mariah      46f OH kph
    Hamilton          22m WV brms
    Daniel E.         17m    lab
p586a Viola           15f    sch
    Fletcher          11m
    Sarah B.           9f
  Baker,Henry P.      24m TN
  Baker,Mary O.       19f WV

252-253
  Venatta,Jackson     24m WV farm
    Mary J.           19f OH

253----
254-254
  Cook,Abner          33m WV farm
    Nancy             22f
```

49

254-254 Cook (con't)			
Florena	3f		
255- Mary F.	1f		

256-255			
Rogers,William C.	40m	NY	farm
Emmetta	34f	WV	
Kate V.	14f		sch
Susie L.	12f		
James	9m		
Charles M.	7m		
Nannie	1f		

257-256			
Richards,Hezekiah	42m	VA	farm
Ann	40f		

258-257			
Ward,David Y.	38m	WV	lab

259-258			
Stephenson,Henry	40m	WV	farm
Ellena J.	37f	VA	
Edna	14f	WV	sch
Allin B.	11m		
Fredrick	9m		
Stonwall J.	7m		
Willie A.	5f		
John L.	3m		
Hensley,Rufus	20m		
Hensley,Eugenia	16f		

260-259			
Thornburg,Miller	29m	WV	farm
Mary F.	29f		
Mariah	5f		
Joseph	2m		
Griffin,Elizabeth	53f		
Griffin,Cora A.	13f		
Griffin,James W.	18m		teach
Nucel,James	37m	VA	phy
p587 Nucel,Sallie	17f	WV	
Nucel,Cora	2f		

261-260			
Smith,Charles	35m	Ger	far
Elizabeth	37f	WV	
William	15m		lab
Sarah A.	11f		
Chas.F.	10m		
Mary E.	5f		
Robert	1m		

262-261			
Fuller,John W.	33m	WV	farm
Sarah A.	25f		
Rosalie	10f		
Lillie B.	8f		
William	4m		
Ida M.	2f		
Sarah A.	7/12f		
Fuller,Elizabeth	54f		

263-262			
Hall,Andrew J.	36m	VA	farm
Eliza A.	30f	WV	
Martha J.	1f		
Filora	8f		
James J.	7m		

264-263			
Poteet,Skelton	64m	VA	farm
Martha	60f	WV	
John	22m		lab

265-264			
Gates,William W.	45m	OH	farm
Alvira	42f		
Ella A.	14f		
Laura	12f		
William	8m		
Edward S.	5m		
John M.	3m		
Hatta A.	1f		
McDowell,John	23m	WV	farm
Miller,George	23m		farm
Moses, Massie	25m	OH	farm
Moses,Martha	20f		

266-265			
Carver,James A.	39m	VA	BH-RR
Elmira	17f		
James J.	8/12m	KY	
p587a Burks,Thomas	46m	Ire	RR
Walker,Charles	35m	Ire	RR
Sides,Vincent	52m	OH	RR
Clemonds,Henry	33m	Ire	RR
Kelley,Martin	26m	Ire	RR

267-266			
Christian,William	43m	VA	farm
Mary	33f	KY	
James	1m	VA	
Low,George W.	21m		

```
268-267
  Clark,Able H.        44m ME farm
    Sarah              35f OH
    Alma               15f WV sch
    William            13m
    James L.           11m
    Edward             9m
    Hanner             6f
    John R.            3m

269-268
  Wilson,Thomas        25m WV lab
    Virginia           22f
    Georgianna         4f
    Ellen E.           2f
    James A.           1/12m

270-269
  Johnson,James        28m VA farm
    Mary               23f WV
    Florence           2f
    Emogene            1f

271-270
  Shelton,Chas.        36m WV farm
    Henry W.           23m    lab
    Nancy G.           44f
    Susan              74f

272-271
  Clark,Harvey         33m VA farm
    Emaline            33f WV
    John A.            4m
    Mirtie             2f

273-272
  Johnson,William      26m WV farm
    Eliza V.           27f
    Minnie L.          3f
    George H.          1m
    Shelton,Mary M.    12f
    Shelton,William    9m
p588  Shelton,Susie    6f

274-273
  Wilson,Jemy          74m VA farm
    Ellen              56f WV
    Albert             18m    lab
    Thurston           16m    lab
    Ella               11f
    Olliver            34m
```

```
275-274
  Harvey,Calvery       47m WV lab
    America            46f
    John W.            22m    lab
    Mary E.            12f
    Octava             12f
    Florence           11f
    Henry L.           9m
    Elizabeth          8f
    William            7m

276-275
  Boggs,John G.        58m VA farm
    Eliza              54f
    John A.            28m    riv
    Ulysses W.         25m WV riv
    Sarah              19f OH
    Lorenzo            17m WV lab
    James H.           16m OH lab
    Kate               12f
    Josephine          11f

277-276
  Ward,John            46m WV farm
    Joanna             41f
    Fannie             18f
    Eliza              16f
    William            14m
    Elizabeth          12f
    Henry              10m
    Phillip            9m
    James              7m
    Charles            5m
    John               2m

278-277
  Stewart,Robert       66m VA farm
    Martha             53f
    Mary F.            17f WV sch
    Emma               15f    sch
p588a  Ella F.         13f    sch
    Norris,Richard     16m B lab

279-278
  Diamond,Obadiah      64m VA farm
    Isabel             50f
    Susan              25f
    Isabella           17f
    Emma               12f
    William T.         7m
    James              18m
    Barger,William     36m    la
    Barger,Elizabeth   23f
```

51

280-279				
Taylor,Henry M.	31m	WV	farm	
Mary C.	30f	VA		
James W.	23m	WV	farm	
William R.	11m			
Henry P.	9m			
Sarah E.	5f			
Lotta B.	6/12f			
McComas,Rebecca	68f	VA		

281-280				
Adams,Amos	23m	OH	farm	
Emily J.	21f	WV		
Thomas	5m	OH		
Sarah	4f	WV		
Anna L,	1f			
Judy,Mary	22f	MD	dom	

282-281				
Webb,Theadorie	28m	WV	riv	
Arabella	24f			
Willie C.	7m			
Enoch G.	6m			
James D.	4m			
Arabella	1f			

283-282				
Deitz,Otto	52m	Hes	farm	
Rosanna	35f	WV		
Charles H.	14m			
Nonnan	10m			
Willie G.	3m			
Benjamin	1m			

284-283				
Lucas,John W.	34m	WV		
Sarah	23f			
Georgie	2f			

p589

285-284				
Everett,John S.	43m	WV	farm	
Emily	31f	OH		
Sarah	15f	WV	sch	
Peter	11m			
Fletcher	9m			
John H.	5m			
Emma	3f			

286-285				
Maupin,Beverly	61m	VA		
Julia A.	43f			
Virginia D.	8f	WV		
Lucy	7f			
Cintha	4f			
Chapman	2m			

287-286				
Burks,Beverly B.	59m	VA	farm	
Martha	45f	WV		
Martha E.	21f			
George	17m			
Elizabeth	15f			
Minnie L.	10f			
Burrel,Ashberry	10m	M		

288-287				
Buffington,John N.	37m	WV	farm	
Nancy	76f	NC		
Quinn,Margaret	41f	B	OH	dom

289-288				
Hagan,William H.	47m	WV	farm	
Mary J.	46f			
Nannie S.	19f		sch	
James W.	17m		sch	
Emogene	13f		sch	
Stella	8f			
Hugh A.	3m			
Blake,Louisa	15f	M		

290-289				
Warring,Clement	55m	KY	farm	
Rebecca J.	55f			
Susan P.	20f			
Elizabeth	17f		sch	
Chinn,John W.	12m	MO		
Stratton,Cezar	50m	B	KY	lab

291-290				
Pennybacker,James	38m	WV	farm	
Lucy	31f			
Florida	11f			
p589a Fannie	9f			
Braefton	6m			
William	4m			
Albert	2m			

292-291				
Tucker,Elijah	45m	B	VA	far
Virginia	30f	B		
Viney,Juptier	50m	B		lab
Viney,Virginia	50f	B		
Viney,Jupiter	16m	B	WV	lab
Viney,Leah	11f	B	VA	
Blake,Rose	12f	M	WV	
Blake,Henry	11m	B	VA	

293-292				
Spears,William	21m	OH	lab	
Mary J.	23f			

293-292 Spears (con't)

Albertia	1f	WV	
Spears,Margaret	50f		
Spears,Hulda J.	15f	OH	

294-293

Burks,Lewis H.	30m	WV	farm
Hellen M.	24f		
Eliza L.	2f		
Laidley,Mary S.	70f	NC	
Laidley,Ulisses	35m	WV	teach
Hite, Izza	40f		
Messinger,Marion	20m		lab
Hite,Sarah	87f	NC	

295-294

Harrison,Otis	43m	VA	lab
Ruth L.	37f	OH	
Luciene	15m	WV	sch
Eugenia	13f		
Orren B.	12m		
Mary V.	9f		
Charles O.	6m		
Flora A.	4f		
Ella	2f		
(clk uses w=u)			

296-295

Qwalk,Joseph	33m	PA	farm
Dorcas	27f		
Sarah E.	8f		
Kate	6f		
Willie	4f		
William	1m		

page 590

297-296

Wingo,Abner W.	50m	VA	car p590a
Sarah L.	45f		
Charles B.	16m	WV	sch
Henry L.	14m		sch
John T.	10m		
Samuel	4m		

298-297

Hord,William W.	58m	PA	farm
Sarah	58f		
Latta,William	26m		lab
Latta,Philena	24f		
Latta,Wiliam	1m		

299-298

Maupin,Chapman	59m	WV	farm
Matilda F.	45f	KY	
Fannie C.	23f	WV	
Lucy M.	20f		

299-298 Maupin (con't)

Albert	18m		
Mary A.	16f		sch
Shelby	13m		sch
William	9m		

300-299

Russell,William H.	40m	WV	farm
Susan	34f		
James C.	7m	VA	
John L.	5m	WV	

301-300

Buffington,Peter C.	55m	WV	farm
Sarah	28f	VA	
Garland	4m	WV	
Peter C.	1m		

302-301

Smith,Henry	50m	WV	farm
Sarah	47f		
Ann	26f		
John	16m		sch
Francis	14m		sch
Robert	8m		

----302

Wright,Henry	20m	OH	lab
Luticia	16f	WV	

303-303

Hoffman,William	60m	VA	farm
Catherine	54f		
Thomas	16m	WV	lab
Insco,James	32m	WV	lab
Insco,Ellen	32f	PA	
Insco,Mollie	6f	WV	
Insco,James	3m		
McConnell,Roddy	81m	PA	lab

304-304

Coe,Sheldon S.	50m	WV	farm
Mary	54f		
Lewis B.	23m		
John	19m		sch
Margaret	11f		
Williams,Ellen	10f		
Holderby,William	28m		farm
Holderby,James A.	34m		

305-305

Blake,Isaac	34m	WV	farm
Mary	33f		
Anna	13f		
Emma	11f		

305-305 Blake (con't)
```
    Ceraus                8f
    Virginia              5f
    Maggie                2f
```

306-306
```
    Poague,James H.      53m KY farm
    Sarah A.             43f WV
    Edgar                17m KY lab
    Bayless              14m
    Anna                 11f WV
    Sallie  K.            9f
    George H.             5m
    Robert C.            1m
    Gallaher,Sarah      76f PA
```

307-307
```
    Stewart,James        52m WV farm
    Sarah                49f KY
    Isaac F.             30m    brm
    Joseph               24m    phy
    Columbia             22f WV
    James B.             12m
    Henry H.              6m
    Allice               17f OH
    Kimble,Lara           8m
    Carter,Eliza         19f KY
    Everett,Rebecca J.  35f OH
    Everett,George F.   12m WV
    Everett,Kate M.       9f
p591 Wall,James O.      26m OH phy
    Everett,Sallie       75f WV
    Everett,Mary         54f
    Everett,Peter R.     47m
    Holderby,Edward      26m    farm
```

308----
309-308
```
    Shy,Benjamin         41m WV farm
    Mary                 36f
    Edgar F.             16m    lab
    Mary E.              11f
    Richard E.            9m
    Mary                  5f
    Benjamin              2m
```

310-309
```
    McVickers,Archibald  59m WV farm
    Permelia             59f
    James                22m OH lab
    Matilda              19f WV
    Bias,Martha          27f
    Bias,Linzy            8m
    Bias,Almedd           9f
```

311-310
```
    McVickers,John       25m OH lab
    Harriet              22f KY
    James F.            11/12m
```

312-311
```
    Mitchell,Elisha T.   55m VA mer
    Elizabeth            49f WV
    Arthur P.            29m    mer
    Martha V.            21f
    Isaac H.             22m    sch
    Samuel H.            19m    sch
    Fannie E.            11f OH
    Elisha S.             6m
```

313-312
```
    Johnson,Samuel       58m PA farm
    Eliza                45f WV
    Martha               22f
    Emily                20f
    Abner                18m
    Albert               11m
    Benjamin             14m
    Samuel               12m
    Daniel               10m
p591a(t) Robert          6m
    Thomas               4m
    Bell                 2f
```

314-313
```
    Penneybacker,John M. 34m WV farm
    Sallie H.            28f MD
    Mollie L.             8f WV
    Mason S.              6m
    Minnie M.             3f
    Tena L.              2m
    Collins,Millie J.    16f    dom
    Penneybacker,Wm.     31m
    Albers,John          50m Han clk
```

315-314
```
    Pettit,Hugh          54m VA coop
    Frances              59f
    Nodiah               27m    lab
    Ellen                19f
```

----315
```
    Pettit,William       29m VA coop
    Mary A.              30f
    Robert                6m WV
    James                 4m
    Fannie                4f
    George                1m
```

316-316			
Mayse,Parker	32m	OH	farm
Malissa	30f	WV	
Eliza	15f		
John	13m		
Mary A.	11f		
Sarah	9f		
America	7f		
Emily	2f		
317-317			
Johnston,Napoleon	28m	WV	farm
Sarah E.	25f		
Frank E.	3m		
Harry W.	1m		
318-318			
Johnson,William	48m	WV	farm
Susan L.	32f	OH	
Fredrick	21m	WV	brm
Marcelles	19m		lab
James E.	18m		lab
Mary M.	15f		sch
p592 Adda P.	9f		
Libba G.	7f		
Emma	5f		
Anna P.	5f		
Stephen	2m		
319-319			
Johnson,John L.	41m	WV	farm
Mary J.	36f	KY	
Sarah J.	45f	WV	
Martha C.	35f		
Pouge,Marcel A.	37f		
Pouge, Bertie E.	11m		
320-320			
Thompson,Thomas	31m	Wv	lab
Frances	22f		
Virginia	2f		
Mary L.	8/12m		
321-321			
Arthur,Pennel	51m	WV	lab
Virginia	41f	VA	
Lewis V.	20m	WV	
Morris S.	18m		
George W.	15m		
Marion	12m		
Thomas	9m		
Mary E.	6f		
James H.	4m		
Emma	9/12f		

322-322			
McCulloch,Patrick	53m	PA	farm
Fannie M.	36f	KY	
Emma F.	18f	WV	sch
Bob.C.	16m		
Frank F.	14m		
Georgie L.	9f		
Marshall,Sarah J.	24f	VA	dom
Holmes,Lucinda	26m B	VA	dor
Holmes,James L.	3m B	WV	
Holmes,John W.	1m B		
323-323			
Wolcott,Byron A.	27m	WV	farm
Clara A.	34f	OH	
Cora A.	3f	WV	
Missouri	1f		
Frampton,James	9m		
p592a Frampton,Albert	7m		
Frampton,David	5m		
324-324			
Williams,Arthur	32m	VA	farm
Harriet	32f		
----325			
Rider,John	23m	VA	farm
Isadore	27f	OH	
325-326			
William,John E.	62m	PA	farm
Ruth C.	52f	VA	
Lora E.	23f		
Mary M.	21f		teach
Phillip D.	18m	WV	
Herndon J.	11m		
326-327			
Kinser,John L.	24m	VA	lab
Mary J.	26f		
William	9/12m	WV	
327-328			
Smith,Samuel	32m	WV	farm
Fanney J.	28f	KY	
Mary J.	12f		
William	10m	WV	
John H.	8m	KY	
Ezra W.	6m		
James M.	3m		
Daniel G.	3m		
Viriginia	4/12f	WV	
Davis,Bradford	22m		
Walker,Eliza H.	16f		dom

328-329				
Wright,Bazel	47m	WV	farm	
Pheba	50f	VA		
James	21m	WV		
Benjamin	18m			
Thomas M.	14m			
Florida A.	12f			
Flora A.	10f			
Cora L.	8f			
Albert N.	4m			

329-330				
Thornburg,James M.	34m	WV	farm	
Virginia F.	31f			
Charles	11m			
Mary A.	7f			
Victoria	4f			
p593 Infant	8/12m			

330-331				
McGinnis,William	49m	WV	farm	
Allice B.	23f	OH		
Cora E.	5/12f	WV		

331-332				
Wolf,Reuben D.	46m	VA	farm	
Mary E.	31f	WV		
James M.	21m	VA	lab	
Martha J.	17f			
Julia E.	15f			
Emily F.	3f	WV		
Sannora E.	2f			
Fuller,Sarah F.	75f	VA		
Holt,Henrietta	10f	WV		
Holt,Sarah L.	8f			
Holt,Elizabeth	8f			
Holt,Eunice	6f			

332-333				
Woodrum,Ira	47m	WV	farm	
Catherine	45f			
John	18m		lab	
Sarah	16f			
Harriet	14f			
Mary A.	13f			
Lena	12f			
Lewis	7m			
Robert	6m			
Elizabeth	4f			
Anna	3f			
Cora	1/12f			

333-334				
Reece,John C.	53m	WV	farm	
Margaret	46f			
Andrew	13m			
Emma V.	10f			
Lewis	8m			
Radfort,Peter	19m	VA	lab	

334-335				
Bias,William	44m	VA	farm	
Elizabeth	39f	WV		
James L.	17m		lab	
Mary M.	15f		sch	
Andrew	13m		sch	
Lucinda	12f		sch	
p593a Wilbert	6m			
George H.	4m			
Martha F.	11/12f			

335-336				
Taylor,Gabriel	50m	VA	farm	
Isabella	45f			
Smith,Mary	48f			
Floyd,Allice	6f	WV		

336-337				
Tucker,Francis M.	24m	WV	farm	
Lucy	24f			
William M.	2m			
Wallard C.	5/12m			

337-338				
Blankenship,Marlin	26m	WV	farm	
Almeda	22f			
Gerturde	3f			
Charles A.	8/12m			
Bl'ship,Samuel D.	74m	VA	shoe	

338-339				
Angle,Peter	58m	VA	carp	
Elvira	57f	KY		
Calvin	16m	VA	lab	
Stephen	19m		lab	

339-340				
Davis,Greenville	52m	WV	lab	
Isabel	40f	OH		
Victor	20m	WV		
Lilla	18f			
Florence	16f			
Georgie	14f			
William	11m			
Mary	9f			
Ida	4f			

```
340-341                              346-347 McGinnis (con't)
   Toppings,John    47m WV farm         Grant            7m
      Colvia        41f VA              Minnie           4f
      Henry         20m WV lab
      Virginia      18f              347-348
      William T.    17m                 Russell,Malissa  33f MO kph
      Lucy          12f                    Charles A.    12m WV
      Lenard        10m                    Georgie       10f
      Albertie       7f                    Nannie         8f
      Susan          6f                    Robert E.      5m
      Emma           4f                    Olaver E.      2m
      John           2m
p594  Charles A.   7/12m            348-349
                                       Wright,Richard    31m WV tmmr
341-342                                   Mary E.        30f
   Miller,Henry     70m WV farm   p594a     Henry H.      4m
      Susan         65f                     Ethel         3f
      Abigal        40f OH
   Davis,Gallaton    9m WV         349-350
                                       Wright,Edward D.  59m VA farm
342-343                                   Elizabeth      55f WV
   Williams,John L. 27m VA blsm          James H.       29m    clk
      Nancy L.      20f WV               Sarah E.       23f
      Margaret     5/12m                 Lucy R.        20f
   Williams,Levery S.21m VA shoe         Albert         17m    lab
   Bryant,William   60m WV farm          Harriet E.     15f
   Bryant,Martha E. 55f VA            McGinnis,Amanda   50f

343-344                             350-351
   Hensley,John     59m WV farm        Galliher,John    30m WV lvsk
      Malinda       55f                  Drucilla       27f
      Elizabeth     26f                  Edward          8m KY
      David         23m    lab           Sarah           6f OH
      John W.       18m                  Elizabeth       4f WV
   Upton,John       21m VA              John            2m
   Upton,Missour1   28f WV              Lora          9/12f OH

344-345                             351-352
   Hensley,Bird     29m WV farm        Crump,Isaac      47m OH farm
      Hellana M.    34f                  Nancy          40f WV
      William G.     2m                  Mary           18f    teach
      Minnie H.    5/12f                 Martha         14f    sch
   Vass,John        27m    lab           Elizabeth      12f
                                         George          9m
345-346                                  Ella            7f
   Burks,Charles H. 27m WV mer           Isaac           5m
      Elizabeth     24f                  Nannie          1f
                                       Dunkle,Daniel    66m VA farm
346-347                                Dunkle,Eliza     52f WV
   McGinnis,Achilles 45m WV carp
      Miranne       33f             352-353
      Lucien        16m                Rose,Enoch       62m VA farm
      Benjamin      11m                  Elizabeth      52f WV
      Flavius        9m                  Charles H.     16m
```

352-353 Rose (con't)

Name	Age/Sex		
Eliza	13f		
John T.	9m		

353-354

Hall,William	25m	VA	farm
Amanda	27f		

354-355

Wyett,Davis	40m	B WV	lab

355-356

Childers,Louisa	35f	WV	
Oliver	10m		
Ada	4f		
Lane,Thomas	35m	Ire	tunn
p595 Lane,Ann	36f	Ire	
Lane,Mary E.	10f	KY	
Lane,Frances	7f	TN	

357-358

Bias,James F.	35m	VA	farm
Sarah A.	34f		
William	17m	WV	lab
George W.	10m		
Noel,Rodrick	23m	VA	lab

358-359

Medler,John	32m	Pru	farm
Eliza J.	29f	WV	
Emma E.	7f		
Henry C.	6m		
Ernest	4m	MO	
John G.	10/12m	WV	

359-360

Medler,Bruno F.	30m	Pru	man
Manerva	24f	WV	
Fannie	6f		
Henrietta	4f		
Julius	10/12m		

360-361

Smith,Percival	36m	OH	mer
Tamsey	28f	KY	
Charles	5m	IN	

---

page 597 McComas District - Ousley Gap PO

1-1

Rogers,William	55m	WV	farm
Isabel	45f		
Wilson	28m		btbr
Thomas	25m		btbr
William	15m		
Nancy	12f		
Jahive	9m		
Wentz,John T.	19m		lab
Swan,Martha A.	23f		

2-2

Dusenberry,Robert	32m	NY	farm
Mary A.	20f	WV	
Edwin M.	1m		

3-3

William,Samuel P.	50m	VA	blks
Martha	48f		
Mary E.	24f		sch
James A.	20m		lab
John W.	17m		lab
Charles E.	15m		
Lillie	13f		

3-3 Williams (con't)

Samuel L.	11m		
Andrew J.	10m		
Joseph H.	7m		
Robert E.	5m	WV	

4-4

Rogers,George	28m	WV	farm
Rodie	21f		

5-5

Francisco,Jacob	59m	VA	farm
Mary	52f		
Elisha	25m		lab
Elizabeth	23f		
Emily J.	14f		
Anetta A.	12f		
Nancy	24f		
Jacob	3m		
Floyd	1m	WV	

6-6

Morris,George	52m	WV B	lab
Nancy	55f	VA B	
Nancy A.	14f	WV B	
Peggy	41f	VA B	
Sallie	12f	WV B	
Margaret	2f	B	

7-7				
Lenard,Rufus	65m	VA	stm	
Mary E.	68f			
Dick,Anna E.	18f	WV		
Dick,Morris F.	15m			
Dick,Henry L.	13m			
8-8				
Dusenberry,Samuel	25m	NY	farm	
Sarah G.	21f			
Robert W.	2m	WV		
Flora F.	3/12f			
Epps,Harrison	36m		B lab	
Epps,Sophia	40f	VA	B dom	
Clement,Malinda	17f		B dom	
Stephenson,Thomas	21m		W lab	
Vess,Jacob C.	19m		lab	
9-9				
Wise,John	57m	VA	lab	
Jacob H.	16m	OH		
Hardin	12m			
Joseph L.	10m			
Maragret	8f			
Hester A.	6f			
John B.	5m			
Cerus J.	3f			
Wise,Nancy	25f			
Delantern,Elizabeth	52f			
Bird,Hannah	50f		dom	
10-10				
Lunsford,Richard	49m	OH	farm	
Nancy	41f	WV		
Mary	22f			
John H.	20m		lab	
Calvary	18m		lab	
Emily	16f			
Elijah	12m			
Eldrage	10m			
Nancy	4f			
Nora E.	3f			
Peyton,Mary J.	32f			
Peyton,Judy A.	3f			
11-11				
Peyton,Elisha	39m	WV	farm	
John	63m		lab	
Milla	49f			
p598 William	31m		lab	
Alvin	11m			
McComas,Pulina	17f		sch	

12-12				
McGhee,Benjamin	24	VA	farm	
Milda C.	24f	WV		
Eugenia	1f			
McGhee,George	21m	VA	lab	
13-13				
Thompson,William	54m	VA	farm	
Martha C.	49f	WV		
William	20m		lab	
Elizabeth	18f			
Stanhope	15m		sch	
James N.	13m		sch	
Lawson F.	10m			
Martha J.	8f			
14-14				
Hatfield,Moses	48m	WV	farm	
Peninah	49f			
Lucinda	23f			
Albert	21m			
Joseph M.	18m		lab	
James G.	13m		lab	
Hannah	7f			
15-15				
Payton,Archibald	51m	WV	farm	
Susan	32f	VA		
Sarah C.	18f	WV	sch	
Mary F.	14f		sch	
Emma	11f			
Kirby	5m			
16-16				
Aljoe,William	40m	KY	farm	
Ammacetta	28f	WV		
Bevely	11m			
William W.	9m			
Mary E.	8f	OH		
Rachel	6f			
Amacetta	4f	WV		
Augusta V.	1f			
17-17				
Howell,Sallie	65f	VA	kph	
Sarah	40f			
Josephine	12f	WV		
p598a				
18-18				
Swan,Isiah	74m	VA	farm	
Rachel	55f			
Beverly	27m	WV	farm	
George W.	19m		farm	
Joseph E.	17m		farm	

18-18 Swan (con't)		
Sarah	21f	
Vess,John	23f	VA
Vess,Cintha A.	24f	WV

19-19		
Swan,Calvary	50m	WV farm
Emily J.	51f	VA
Mary A.	22f	WV
Franklin	20m	lab
John T.	19m	lab
Edith	17f	sch
Richard	16m	sch
Daniel W.	13m	sch
Garrett J.	12m	MO sch

20-20		
Wilson,James	25m	VA farm
Margaret	30f	
Martha	22f	
Lorustus	2m	
George W.	1m	WV

21-21		
Wilson,James	60m	Ire farm
Sarah	50f	
Benjamin	17m	VA lab
Anna J.	16f	
George W.	15m	
Thomas	12m	
Alexander	10m	

22-22		
Osborn,Aaron	22m	OH farm
Jemima	24f	WV
Sarah C.	4f	OH
John T.	2m	WV

23-23		
Cain,Martin	53m	Ire farm
Mary	47f	
Ann	20f	sch
Thomas	17m	IN sch
Bryan	15m	WV sch
Michael	13m	WV
William T.	11m	
p599 Martin E.	9m	
Henry C.	3m	
Peter	5m	
Walter	7/12m	

24-24		
Hensley,Andrew J.	35m	WV farm
Amanda	25f	

24-24 Henlsey (con't)		
William	10m	
Mary E.	8f	
John F.	6m	
Olive	8/12f	

25-25		
Hinchman,Adam	27m	WV farm
Martha A.	25f	
Joseph A.	1m	

26-26		
Dick,Joseph	70m	WV farm
Catherine	46f	
Benjamin	18m	lab
Ballard	16m	lab
Casander	15m	lab
Margaret	13f	
Catherine	11f	
Henry J.	10m	
David H.	9m	

27-27		
Hensley,Ephram	23m	WV team
Sarah C.	18f	IL

28-28		
Edens,James A.	40m	VA farm
Harriet A.	35f	OH
William	14m	WV lab
Melvin E.	13m	
Emma J.	11f	
Mary V.	8f	
Willie E.	6f	
Jenevra	4f	
Benjamin F.	2m	
Sarah B.	1/12f	
Cook,Julius	20m	IN lab

29-29			
	Steel,Samuel E.	37m	PA farm
	Mary E.	36f	WV
	Wilmont L.	14m	PA lab
	Lyda L.	12f	WV
	Mary M.	10f	
p599a	Everett E.	7m	
	Emma E.	5f	

30-30		
Lawhorn,George W.	24m	KY farm
Pheba P.	23f	WV
Mary E.	1f	

```
31-31
  Lucas,George      70m VA farm
    Pheba J.        37f WV
  Webb,George        9m

32-32
  Diel,Elisha       46m WV farm
    Mary F.         32f
    Benjamin         5m
    Almeda           2f

33-33
  Hatfield,Andrew   55m WV farm
    Francis         51f
    America L.      20f
    Joseph N.       17m     lab
    Henry J.        13m     lab
    Thomas           7m

34-34
  Johnston,Columbus 23m WV farm
    Amanda A.       20f
    Everman          2m
    Martha J.      3/12f

35-35
  Hatfield, Henry M. 23m WV farm
    Martha J.       26f
    Eliza A.         2f
    Rufus A.      10/12m

36-36
  Hatfield,George   69m VA farm
    Eliza A.        52f WV
    Josaphine       28f
    Adam S.         25m     lab
    James A.        24m   teach
    John M.         19m     lab
    Margaret        14f     sch
    Charles F.      12m     sch
    Lucinda H.      10f
  Hatfield,Editha   35f

37-37
  Swan,Ballaard S.  42m WV farm
    Nancy           36f
    Patrick H.      12m
    Hezekiah         9m
p600 Anzonetta       5f
    Walter E.     11/12m
38-38
  Swan,Hezekiah     73m VA farm
    Catherine       67f
    Benjamin        77m farm


39-39
  Swan,Henley C.    35m WV farm
    Mary A.         29f
    Mary A.         12f
    Emeretta         9f
    Elizabeth        7f
    Isiah            5m
    Martha A.        3f
    Leanna           1f

40-40
  Knibb,Wilford     68m WV farm
    Rachel          58f VA

41-41
  Bledsew,William   34m VA farm
    Malissey        33f WV
    Waldon          11m
    Allice          10f
    Hannah           8f
    Grant            7m
    Francis          4f
    John             2m

42-42
  Roffe,Joseph W.   56m WV farm
    Rebecca         53f
    Charles P.      22m     lab
    Virginia        18f     sch
    Joseph W.       16m     sch
    Effie A.        15f     sch
    Callie D.       12f

43-43
  Morrison,Wesley   30m WV farm
    Sarah           29f
    Thomas J.       10m
    James A.         8m
    Marion W.        6m
    William          3m
    Mary M.          2f

44-44
  Carter,Salem      21m OH
    Algalena        21f WV
    Thomas          10m
p600a
45-45
  Peyton.Harrison   48m WV farm
    Elizabeth       43f
    Franklin        18m     lab
    Marietta        15f
    Emma M.         12f
    Evazetta        13f
```

61

45-45 Peyton (con't)
    Perlina F.   7f
    Martha J.   5f
    William K.   3m
    Rosco V.   6/12m
  Williams,John   28m   lab

46-46
  Sites,Godfrey   49m WV lab
    Mary A.   35f
    Cintha V.   13f
    Martha E.   12f
    Emily   9f
    Thomas J.   5m
    Carolina   4f
    Susan   2f

47-47
  McCallister,John   53m WV farm
    Mariah   44f
    Preston   24m   lab
    Malinda   21f
    Isaac H.   20m
    Susannah   18f
    Sarah A.   15f
    Harrison   12m
    Anis   10m
    Eliza   7f
    Leander   5m
    John   1m

48-48
  Irwin,William   26m WV farm
    Sarah A.   45f
    Sarah J.   22f
    James A.   18m
    Martha A.   14f
    Semintha   9f
    Mary A.   8f
    Mary E.   12f
    Eliza   6f
p601
49-49
  McCallister,Corydin 30m IN farm
    Betavia   19f WV

50-50
  Thompson, John L. 26m WV farm
    Emily S.   26f
    William   4m
    Walter   6/12m

51-51
  Morrison,Thompson 60m VA farm
    Annie   53f
    Calvin   24m WV lab
  Shankley,Annie   3f

52-52
  Hatfield,Henry   60m WV farm
    David J.   36m
    Nancy A.   30f
    Catherine   25f
    Emily C.   21f
    Eliza J.   19f   sch
    Isaac   11m

53-53
  Harrison,Thomas   30m WV farm
    Elizabeth   35f
    Henry B.   13m
    Thomas E.   11m
    Matilda   7f

54-54
  Yates,Peter A.   52m WV farm
    Sarah A.   41f
    Frances   21m   lab
    Virgel   19m   lab
    John W.   17m   lab
    William H.   15m   lab
    Nancy M.   13f
    Sarah E.   10f
    Clarke S.   7m
    Silas E.   4m OH
    James M.   2m

55-55
  Frye,Fleming   25m WV farm
    Frances   21f
    Randolph   1m

56-56
  Hinchman,Lewis   30m WV farm
    Eliza J.   23f
    George W.   1m
p601a
---57
  Hinchman,Wesley   25m WV farm
    Margaret   21f
    John W.   9/12m
  Hinchman,Elizabeth 58f
  Babcock,William   26m NY lab

```
57-58
   Perry,Silas          35m VA farm
      Affie J.          27f WV
      Cintha            15f     sch
      Charles C.        14m     sch
      Sarah J.          12f     sch
      Brevatta           9m
      Mary C.            5f
      Bailey S.       6/12m
   Adkins,Polley        17f

58-59
   Perry Mary A.        39f WV kph
      Mary E.           15f     sch
      William           14m     sch
      David L.          12m
      Randolph          10m

59-60
   Perry,Elijah         32m VA farm
      Cintha            28f WV
      Julia A.          11f
      James F.           8m
      John W.            6m
      Emily J.           4f
      Jackson            2m

60-61
   Jordan,Peter G.      56m Va farm
      Martha E.         84f
      Marshall          19m
      Charles R.        17m
      Peter G.          15m
      Potary F.         13f
      Sarah E.          10f WV
      John H.            8m
      Martha E.          6f VA

61-62
   Perry,Benjamin       27m VA farm
      Emily V.          24f WV
      America            2f
      Ira S.             8m
      Anna E.            6f
p602
62-63
   Bledsew,James A.     22m VA lab
      Rachel            25f WV

63-64
   McCoy,John L.        28m WV lab
      Mildred           23f VA
      William            4m WV
      Rachel F.          1f


64-65
   Midkiff,Gordon       28m WV farm
      Elizabeth         27f IL
      Harvey            18m WV lab
      Solomon           15m     lab
      Emily E.          13f     sch
      Eliza A.          11f
      Sarah             10f
      William A.         5m
      Veturi             3f
      Rachel S.          1f

65-66
   Bias,Roland          47m WV farm
      Martha            46f
      Mary A.           22f
      Elisha            18m     lab
      Sereptha          15f     sch
      Lucy A.           13m     sch
      Jacob B.          10m
      Pricilla           6f
      Roland S.      10/12m

66-67
   Rousey,Archibald R.24m VA farm
      Dicy              28f WV
      Andrew O.          4m

67-68
   Reynolds,Archibald 70m VA farm
      Susan H.          67f
   Holt,Elizabeth       21f WV dom
   Daulton,James W.     23m VA lab

68-69
   Roberts,Harrison     53m WV farm
      Susan             58f
      John              30m     lab
      America           21f

69-70
   Bledsew,Charles L.   25m VA farm
      Emily F.          19f WV

70-71
   Gibson,Job           70m Va farm
      Elizabeth         70f NC
p602a Joseph            45m     farm
      Lucetta           34f WV
      James             10m OH
      Malissey           7f WV
      Albert J.          4m
      Robert L.          2m
   Adkins,West          15m WV lab
```

63

70-71 Gibson (con't)			
Adkins,James	8m		
Gibson,Mary	12f		

71-72			
Johnson,Joseph	41m	VA	farm
Lucy	37f		
John W.	16m	WV	lab
Lucy A.	13f		
Joseph R.	11m		
Thomas R.	9m		
Jackson	7m		
Robert	5m		
Susan J.	1f		
Emily F.	12f		
Bradley	2m		

72-73			
Beckett,Lewis C.	42m	WV	farm
Susan	36f		
Charles M.	15m		lab
Francis M.	13m		lab
William L.	11m		
Mary S.	8f		
James R.	5m		
Hannah	3f		

73-74			
McKendree,Aaron F.	65m	VA	farm
Catherine	52f		
William P.	19m	WV	lab
Mary S.	16f		sch
Emma M.	15f		sch
Lydia	12f		
Retherford,Eliot	40m		pau
Cannon,Matilda	53f		pau
Jourdon,Matilda	26f		pau
Shumaker,Nancy	26f		pau
Shumaker,Lucy	1f		

p603

74-75			
Hill,William S.	32m	WV	mer
Susan S.	26f	VA	
Kaysar,John B.	13m	WV	sch

75-76			
Perry,James E.	41m	WV	blks
Mary C.	32f		
Ida A.	15f		blksw
Barbery	14m		
James	12m		
Manerva	6f		
Joseph	4m		

76-77			
Keyser.George	41m	WV	farm
Fannie	38f		
Ely B.	18m		lab
Mary M.	17f		
Charlott	15f		
John B.	12m		
Addie F.	10f		
Alphius	8m		
Susan A.	2f		

77-78			
Perry,Thomas	25m	VA	farm
Cintha	21f	WV	
William M.	4m		
Anna E.	3f		
Joshua M.	2m		

78-79			
Morris,Benjamin	38m	Va	farm
Malon S.	15m	WV	
Benjamin	11m		
Julia A.	9f		
Lucretia	7f		
Lucy	5f		

79-80			
Rousey,John J.	22m	VA	farm
Sarah	18f	WV	
Heath,Sallie	42f		
Smith,Margaret	26f		
Smith,Elvery	11m		

80-81			
Perry,John J.	22m	VA	farm
Jenetta	20f	WV	

81-82				
	Gill,George	27m	Eng	farm
	Mary A.	51f		
	Charles J.	23m		lab
p603a	John F.	21m	WV	lab
	Henry A.	16m		
	Thomas J.	13m		

82-83			
Heath,Joshua	28m	WV	farm
Jane	25f		
Robert	9/12m		

83-84			
Bias,James	54m	WV	farm
Mary	47f		
Millington	19m		lab

64

83-84 Bias(con't)			
Blackburn	17m	lab	
Marion	15m	lab	
Letha	13f	sch	
Galiton	9m	sch	
James W.	6m		
Mary W.	3f		

84-85			
Roffe,James H.	54m	WV	farm
Mary	54f		
William	12m		
Holt,Sarah	50f		

85-85			
Pettit,John	23m	VA	farm
Sarah C.	28f		
William	5m	WV	
Charles	3m		
John	10/12m		

86-87			
Walters,William	53m	VA	farm
Catherine	46f		
James L.	26m	lab	
Rebecca A.	18f		
Rachel A.	15f		
Francis	15m	lab	
Dora G.	12f		
Ulysses G.	5m	WV	

87-88			
Gill,Joseph	34m	Eng	farm
Fannie	37f	WV	
Emily	10f		
Elisha	8m		
Mary A.	6f		
Laura	3f		
Cora	1f		

p 604

88-89			
McComas,David	37m	WV	farm
Sarah	27f		
Emily	11f		
Walter	8m		
Albert	6m		
James J.	3m		
Shelton,Martha	3f		

89-90			
Bias,James M.	23m	WV	farm
Rebecca A.	23f		
William	2m		
America	9/12f		

90-91			
Midkiff,Solomon	65m	VA	farm
America	38f	WV	
Henry C.	15m		sch
Lewis E.	12m		sch
Roland W.	8m		
Julia M.	4f		
John T.	11/12m(2/12)?		

91-92			
Porter,Jerurhel	63m	VA	farm
Sarah J.	33f	WV	
Adaline	32f		
Jacob G.	30m		lab
James H.	28m		lab
Nancy A.	21f		
Louisa C.	18f		
Julia A.	14f		
John J.	12m		

92-93			
Rose,Robert	55m	OH	farm
Elizabeth	56f	WV	
George	27m		teach
Hugh	26m		farm
Nancy	21f		teach
Robert	19m		lab
John H.	19m		Lab
Walter	17m		lab
Hugh	14m		lab

93-94			
Harris,Reuben	54f	KY	
Elizabeth	51f		
William J.	21m	WV	
Arminda	17f		
p604a John F.	14m		

94-95			
Miller,Jessey	50f	WV	kph
Fredrick	25m		lab
Luncinda	20f		
Jacob	20m		
Henry	14m		
James W.	8m		

95-96			
Kirk,Jemima	45f	WV	kph
Emerine	20f		
Sallie	18f		
William	17m		lab
James	15m		lab
Fannie	13f		

8

5

```
96-97
  Gue,James          31m WV farm
    Mary             31f
    James            12m
    Julia A.          6f
    Ulysses           4m
    Nancy             2f
    Linsey            1m

97-98
  Gue,Nancy          57f VA kph
    Taney            23m WV lab
    Lucy             21f
    Mary             18f
    Permilla         15f

98-99
  Doland,John        65m VA farm
    Judy             60f
    Frances          30f WV
    John D.          10m
    Sarah             8f

99-100
  Booth,Ballard      35m WV farm
    Eliza            30f
    John S.           3m

100-101
  Lucas,Vinson       55m VA   farm
    Rebecca          40f WV
    Parke            26m      lab
    Edward           18m      lab
    David            16m      lab
    Rebecca          15f
    Irvin             9m
p605
101-102
  Venath,Irvin       26m WV farm
    Delpha           22f
    Amanda            5f
    George F.         1m

102-103
  Adkins,Randle      30m WV farm
    Laddie           31f
    Spicer            8f
    James M.          4m
    Noah              1m
  Bartrem,Rebecca    69f

103-104
  Adkins,Champ       33m WV farm
    Polley           24f
    Viney             9f
    Victoria          7f
    Dicy              4f
    Viola             2f

104-105
  Adkins,Robert G.   24m WV farm
    Mary             29f
    Lettie            2f
    Martha          5/12f
  Lucas,John         19m      lab

105-106
  Childers,Bettie    59f WV farm
    Daniel           23m      teach
    Benjamin         17m      lab
    Adaline          14f

106-107
  Childers,Filman S. 21m WV farm
    Cintha           18f
    Walter          8/12m

107-108
  Bias,Thomas A.     28m WV farm
    Hester A.        32f
    Clifton           4m
    Benjamin          2m
    Millard           1m

108-109
  Childers,Shim      28m WV farm
    Carolina         22f
    Joseph            1m

109-110
  Cremeans,Hiram     56m OH farm
    Catherine        56f VA
    Mintie           26f WV
    Mary             21f
p605a
----111
  Eplin,Sherid       23m WV farm
    Catherine        24f

110-112
  Cremeans,Wesley    22m WV farm
    Mahaley          21f
    Haley             3m
    Mary A.           2f
```

111-113				
Adkins,John	63m	WV	farm	
Bettie	53f			
Martha	30f			
Oma F.	24f			
Jeramiah	20m		lab	
William V.	17m		lab	
Jones	14m		lab	

112-114				
Cremeans,Lewis	37m	WV	farm	
Susanna	28f			
Arminta	10f			
Perlina H.	6f			
Delpha	4f			
Stalina	1f			

113-115				
Lucas,William	25m	WV	farm	
Palina	20f			
Helina	8/12f			

114-116				
Cremeans,William	24m	WV	farm	
Palina	20f			
Andrew	2m			

115-117				
Clay,James	23m	KY	farm	
Cintha A.	32f	WV		
Berton	4/12m			

116-118				
Adkins,Elijah	42m	WV	farm	
Margaret	25f			
Chestina	5f			
Stirling	3m			
Sarah	2f			
Hezekiah	8/12m			

117-119				
Dunnahoo,William	27m	KY	farm	
Lucinda	25f	VA		
Alexander	4m	WV		
Joel	2m			

118-120				
Adkins,Everman	43m		farm	
Anjaline	36f			
p606 McHerston	16m		lab	
Thomas J.	13m			
Adaline	10f			
Amacetta	7f			
Intia A.	5f			
James H.	2m			
Albright,Elias	30m		lab	

119-121				
Adkins,Albert	23m	WV	farm	
America	18f			

120-122				
Adkins,Jesse	59m	WV	farm	
Elizabeth	43f			
Everett	18m		lab	
Pleasant	13m	KY	lab	
Hezekiah	3f	WV		
Dicy	7/12f			
Eplin,Mary	17m			
Eplin,Fredrick	13m			

121-123				
Adkins,Enoch	24m	WV	farm	
Margret	19f			
Tenasee	1f			

122-124				
Adkins,Sylvester	57m	WV		
Elizabeth	48f	VA		
John D.	20m	WV		
Susun	22f			
Nancy	16f			
Anderson	15m			
Champion	12m			
Francis M.	7/12m			
Jefferson	2m			

123-125				
Johnson,William	29m	WV	farm	
Mahaley	25f			
Almeda	5f			
Armilda	3f			
Marietta	2f			
Jefferson	3/12m			

124-126				
Johnson,Isom	22m	WV	farm	
Zerilda	20f			

125-127				
Adkins,Green L.	45m	WV	farm	
Annie	43f			
Martin	19m		lab	
p606a Kandith	18f			
Sarah	17f			
Jarrett	12m		lab	
Amildie	10f			
Rebecca	8f			
Lee	4m			
Wesley	2m			

126-128			
Johnson,Merritt	58m	WV	farm
Rody	50f		
Marion	23m		farm
Spicy	23f		
Lucas,Marion	10m		

127-129			
Adkins,Randolph	59m	Va	farm
Elizabeth	48f		
Ephram	23m		lab
Parker	17m		lab
William	8m		

128-130			
Adkins,James A.	39m	WV	farm
Sarah	38f		
Jessey	16m		lab
Jackson	13m		lab
Mary T.	12f		
Randolph	10m		
James M.	5m		
Mathew	3m		

129-130			
Porter,Samuel	45m	Wv	farm
Sarah	38f		
Letha	21f		
John	18m		
Milley	15f		
Malinda	13f		
Frank	5m		
Elizabeth	3f		
Polley	1f		

130-132			
Adkins,Enoch	25m	WV	farm
Zerilda	25f		
Alice	2f		
Bettie	9/12f		

131-133			
Eplin,Bazel	28m	WV	farm
Eliza A.	28f		
p307 Polley	4f		
William	3m		

132-134			
Eplin,Rundolph	36m	WV	farm
Polley	30f		
Amacetta	17f		
Elizabeth	15f		
Merritt	13m		
Angaline	12f		

132-143 Eplin (con't)			
Marshall	9m		
Nancy A.	5f		
Melvina	3f		

133-135			
Johnson,John	66m	WV	farm
Elizabeth	54f		
Evaline	33f		
Joseph	18m		
Elizabeth	14f		
Lucinda	13f		
Irvin	13m		

134-136			
Adkins,Winchester	20m	WV	farm
Delphia	18f		

135-137			
Adkins,Winchester	45m	WV	farm
Pollie	44f		
Mahaley	15f		

136-138			
Elkins,Harvey	34m	WV	farm
Nancy	27f		
Francis M.	4m	KY	
Andrew J.	1m	WV	

137-139			
Eplin,William	47m	WV	farm
Susanna	53f	VA	

138-140			
Adkins,Shered W.	33m	WV	farm
Mary J.	31f		
Rebecca	9f		
Cintha A.	7f		
Lee	6m		
Polley A.	4f		
Cloey	1f		

139-141			
Adkins,John C.	36m	WV	farm
Ruth P.	23f	WV	

140-142			
Morrison,Frances	58f	NC	kph
Telitha	19f	WV	sch

p307a

141-43			
Morrison,Henry	23m	WV	farm
Mary	25f		

68

142-144
Childers,Benjamin   36m WV farm
   Greenville   42m   farm
   Nancy   42f   kph
   Elizabeth   17f   sch
   Mary M.   14f   sch
   Jeneva   11f
   Royal A.   9m
   Melina   33f   kph
   Andrew   J.   10m
   Florence   7f
   Sarah E.   4f

143-145
Childers,Abreham M.44m WV farm
   Elizabeth   40f
   Mary J.   21f
   Almeda V.   18f
   Alexander   15m   lab
   Louisa   13f
   Albert   9m
   Elizabeth   6f

144-146
Childers,Royal   64m VA farm
   Nancy   66f
   Royal B.   26m WV farm
   Sarah J.   31f

145-147
Roberts,Rebecca   35f VA kph
   Mary E.   34f VA kph

146-148
Childers,William   43m WV farm
   Mary F.   19f
   Joseph   17m   lab
   Colonel   15m   lab
   Nancy M.   13f
   Albert   12m
   Greenville   10m
   Wheeler,William   75m   lab
   Wheeler,Margaret 42f

147-149
Tooley,Tandy   54m VA farm
   Cintha A.   46f WV
   Harrison,George W.14m   lab p608a
   Harrison,David   11m   lab
p608
   Bias,Joseph B.   19m
   Bias,Thomas   21m   lab
   Bias,William   18m   lab
   Morrison,Virnilla 42f

148-150
Swan,John K.   58m WV farm
   Nancy   55f
   Elizabeth   37f
   Enoch A.   27m   teach
   William J.   24m   farm
   Rezin   23m   lab
   McHerston   20m   lab
   Jasper   15m   lab

149-151
Hall,Henry W.   34m VA farm
   Ann   35f WV
   Thomas   3m
   Mary E.   1f

150-152
Bramlett,William   45m VA farm
   Armelda   40f WV
   Josephine   15f
   Eugenia   13f
   Linnie M.   7f

151-153
Childers,Melville M.45m WV farm
   Ann C.   41f
   John T.   19m   lab
   Spencer   18m
   Amanda   16f   sch
   James   14m
   Jacob G.   9m
   Childers,Nancy   70f VA
   Sheratz,Canaro   25m   farm
   Sheratz,Nancy   28f WV
   Harless,Pollie   33f   dom

152-154
Brown,Jefferson   34m WV farm
   Anjalina   34f
   Isabell   16f   sch
   Polina   12f   sch
   Lemuel   11m
   Beverly   8m
   Ann   5f

153-155
Nicely,James   50m VA farm
   Elizabeth   40f WV
   Sarah   23f
   Henry   20m   lab
   Albert   19m   lab
   Emily   17f
   William   15m   lab
   Louisa   13f

```
153-155 Nicely (con't)                 160-162 Huffman (con't)
      Adaline           11f                  Brown,Anna M.         1f  WV
      Andrew             9m                   Eplin,Marion        17m  VA  lab
      Joshua             7m
      George             5m            161-163
      Hughey             3m                   Porter,Alexander    59m  WV  farm
      Thomas          1/12m                         Harriet       56f
                                                     Patrick H.   17m       lab
153-156                                              Susan A.      9f
   Nicely,James H.     22m  WV  farm
      Margaret         20f            162-164
      Waldin,Thomas     6m  VA              Porter,John          26m  WV  farm
                                                  Catherine       22f
155-157                                           Mary A.          2f
   Bias,Daniel B.      24m  WV  farm             America V.     8/12f
      Malissey J.      26f  KY
      Mary M.           2f  WV        163-165
      Levie O.          1f                  Bayless,Thomas H.    35m  WV  farm
                                                  Mary S.         25f
156-158                                           Thomas           3m
   Bias,Daniel         62m  VA  farm             William A.     4/12m
      Jenetta          62f
      Cordoria         17f  WV        164-166
      George           14m                  Swan,John R.         25m  WV  farm
                                                  Mollie          26f
157-159                                           Georgia       3/12f
   Savage,George       58m  KY  farm
      Manerva          46f  WV        165-167
      Judy             15f                  Swan,Leven C.        55m  WV  farm
      George           14m                       Susan A.        48f
                                                  Shelby J.       27m       lab
158-160                                           Joseph W.       22m       lab
   Martin,John B.      56m  PA  farm             Cintha A.       18f
      Emily            35f  VA                    James H.        16m       lab
      Butler            3m  WV                    Manville        12m       lab
      Grace             2f
                                        166-168
159-161                                    Porter,James S.      49m  WV  farm
   Cremeans,James      35m  WV  farm             John            9m
      Elizabeth        35f                        Eliza           5f
      Daniel D.        13m                        Sarah           4f
      James W.         11m                        Robert       7/12m
      William L.        7m                   Toney,John          19m
      Henry S.          4m                   Becket,Thomas       13m  OH
      Burton            2m
      Sarah S.       7/12f               167-169
p609                                       Porter,John          33m  WV  farm
160-162                                          Margaret       32f  KY
   Huffman,Thomas      53m  VA  farm             William        11m  WV  lab
      Rosanna          39f  OH      p609a        Martha          9f
      Rachel           15f  VA  sch             Eliza            7f
      William          11m                       Elijah          5m
   Hutchinson,Washington   21  VA  lab           John            2m
   Brown,Margaret      19f                        Robert       3/12m
```

70

168-170					175-177			
Smith,David F.	38m	WV	farm		Bias,Roland	76m	VA	farm
Amanda	29f				Martha	51f		
Walter L.	8m				Catherine	10f	WV	
Olive F.	6f				Markins,Elizabeth	18f		
Georgie	4f				Markins,John	25m	OH	lab
Grant	1m							
					176-178			
169-171					Bias,Hughie	32m	WV	farm
Morrison,John E.	50m	WV	farm		Sarah	28f		
Mary E.	39f				Dolphin	11m		
James	19m		lab		William	8m		
Catherine	17f				Elizabeth	14m		sch
William	14m				Richard	5m		
Mary E.	21f				Sarah	2f		
John E.	5m							
Smith,Henry	11m	M			177-179			
					Keyser,Ephram	44m	WV	farm
170-172					Eliza	42f		
Rogers,Fenton	32m	WV	farm		Hughy	21m		lab
Amanda	35f	VA			Thomas	20m		lab
Bascom	9m	WV			William	18m		lab
Cintha R.	8f				Ephram	13m		lab
Wilburn B.	5m				George	10m		
					Vila A.	10f		
171-173					Gallitin	8m		
Morrison,Nancy B.	48f	WV	kph		Dora	5f		
Martha A.	28f				John	2m		
Nancy	24f							
John T.	22m				178-180			
Calvary	15m				Nipps,Jacob	48m	WV	farm
Napoleon B.	12m				Juriah	68f		
172-174					179-181			
Roberts,Richard J.	32m	WV	farm		Keysor,David	50m	WV	farm
Ellie	23f				Vetera F.	46f		
Lincoln	5m				William	23m		tmer
Arther B.	3m				Eliza F.	19f		
					Elizabeth	21f		
173-175					Patrick H.	19m		lab
King,Mary	34f	WV	kph		John	17m		lab
William	15m		lab		David	15m		lab
Martha J.	13f				Albert	12m		
George	8m		p610a		Oscar	10m		
					Annie	8f		
174-176					Charles	6m		
Diel,John	48m	WV	farm		Fannie	2f		
Tabitha	28f							
p610 Emily	8f				180-182			
Alexander	5m				Smith,Ambros	40m	WV	farm
Catherine	3f				Telitha	40f		
Diel,Nancy	83f	VA			Anna A.	17f		sch
Porter,Elisha	21m	WV	lab		Sarah E.	15f		sch
Porter,Mary	21f		dom		Randolph	13m		sch

71

180-182 Smith (con't)
          Mary G.   9f
          Vetria   8f
          Sigman   6m

181-183
          Barnett,Charles   21m WV farm
          Louisa   20f
          Vila W.   2f

182-184
          Montgomery,Alexander 60m Ire far
          Joanna   42f WV

183-185
          Davidson,William   46m WV farm
          Martha   50f
          Charles A.   19m   lab
          Sarah D.   17f
          Samuel H.   16m
          William C.   13m
          John A.   11m

184-186
          Meadowrs,Balester   71m VA farm
          Mirem   63f
          Salena   34f
          Mandona   19f
          Nannie   21f
          Dunn,Arthur   6m WV
          Dunn,Lutiecha   1f

185-187
          Love,Peter E.   35m WV farm
          Ann A.   36f
          Charles   16m
          John   14m
          Conwelsa   11m
          James   8m
          Thomas   6m
          Leonades   4m
          Allen   1m
page 611
186-188
          Gibson,William   36m WV farm
          Malissey   35f
          Franklin   14m
          Isabel   12f
          Randolph   10m
          William   8m
          George   6m
          John   4m
          Ann   2f
          Lizzie   6/12f

187-189
          Henrick.Lewis   39m Hes farm
          Ann   34f WV
          Joseph   12m
          Catherin   6f
          Sylvester   2m

188-190
          Simmons,Conwelsa   45m WV farm
          Elizabeth   45f
          Smith,Lucy   16f

189-191
          Seamonds,Sampson   26m WV farm
          Agnis G.   19f
          Ruffner,Elizabeth   21f

----192
          Shumaker,Charles   31m WV lab
          Sarah M.   30f
          James   10m
          Robert   5m
          Elizabeth   3f
          Conwelsa   1m

190-193
          Doland,George   39m VA river
          Letha   47m WV
          Jonna E.   15f
          Martha L.   13f

191-194
          Meadowrs,John O.   34m WV farm
          Rebecca F.   16f WV
page

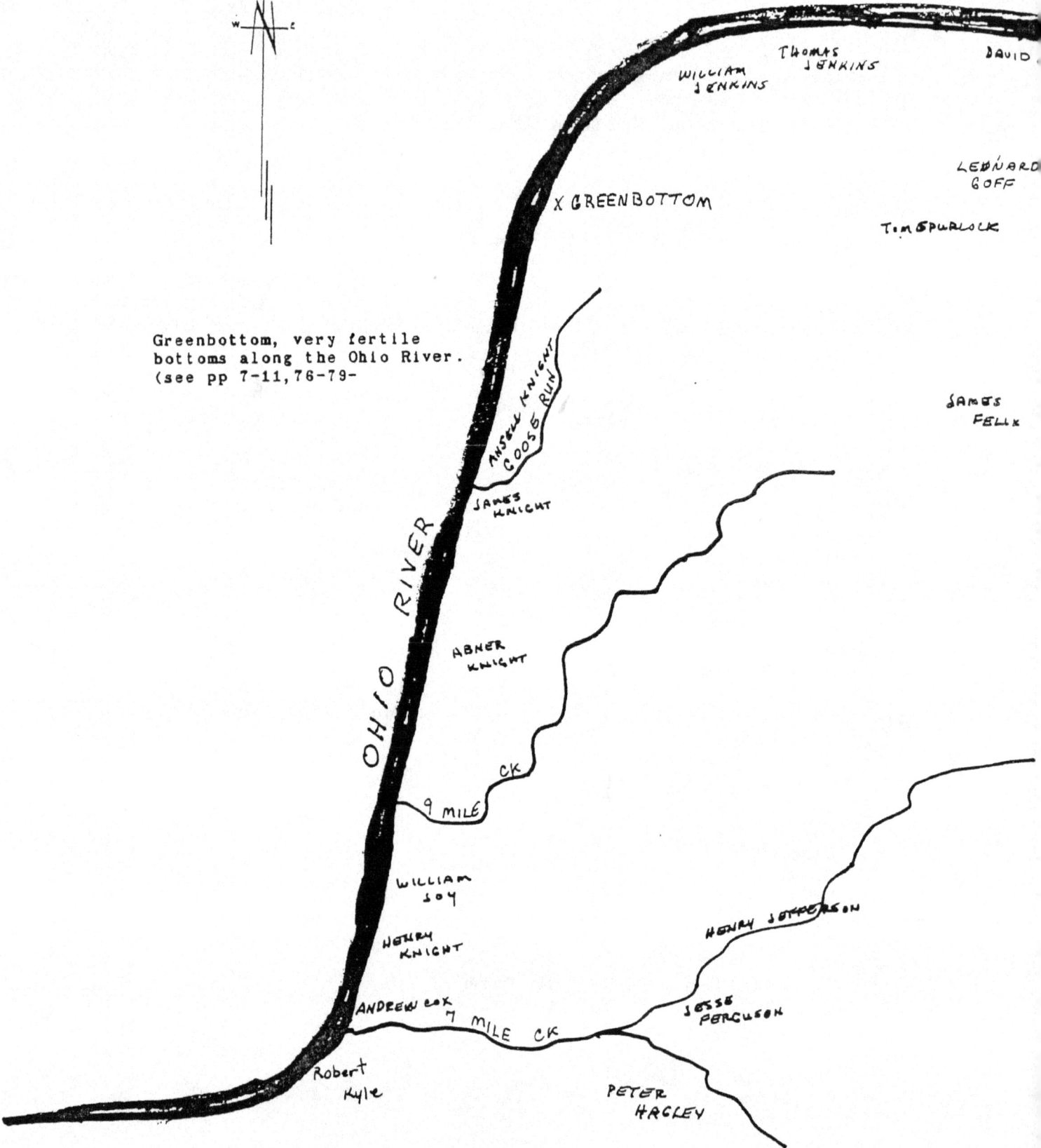

Greenbottom, very fertile
bottoms along the Ohio River.
(see pp 7-11, 76-79-

71 F

OHIO RIVER

GOFF

EH HANNON

SPURLOCK CK

R GWINN

JENNING GWINN

TOM SPURLOCK

TAL WALLACE

Union/Barkers Ridge a wide ridge
between the Ohio River and Teays
Valley.(see pp 74-83)

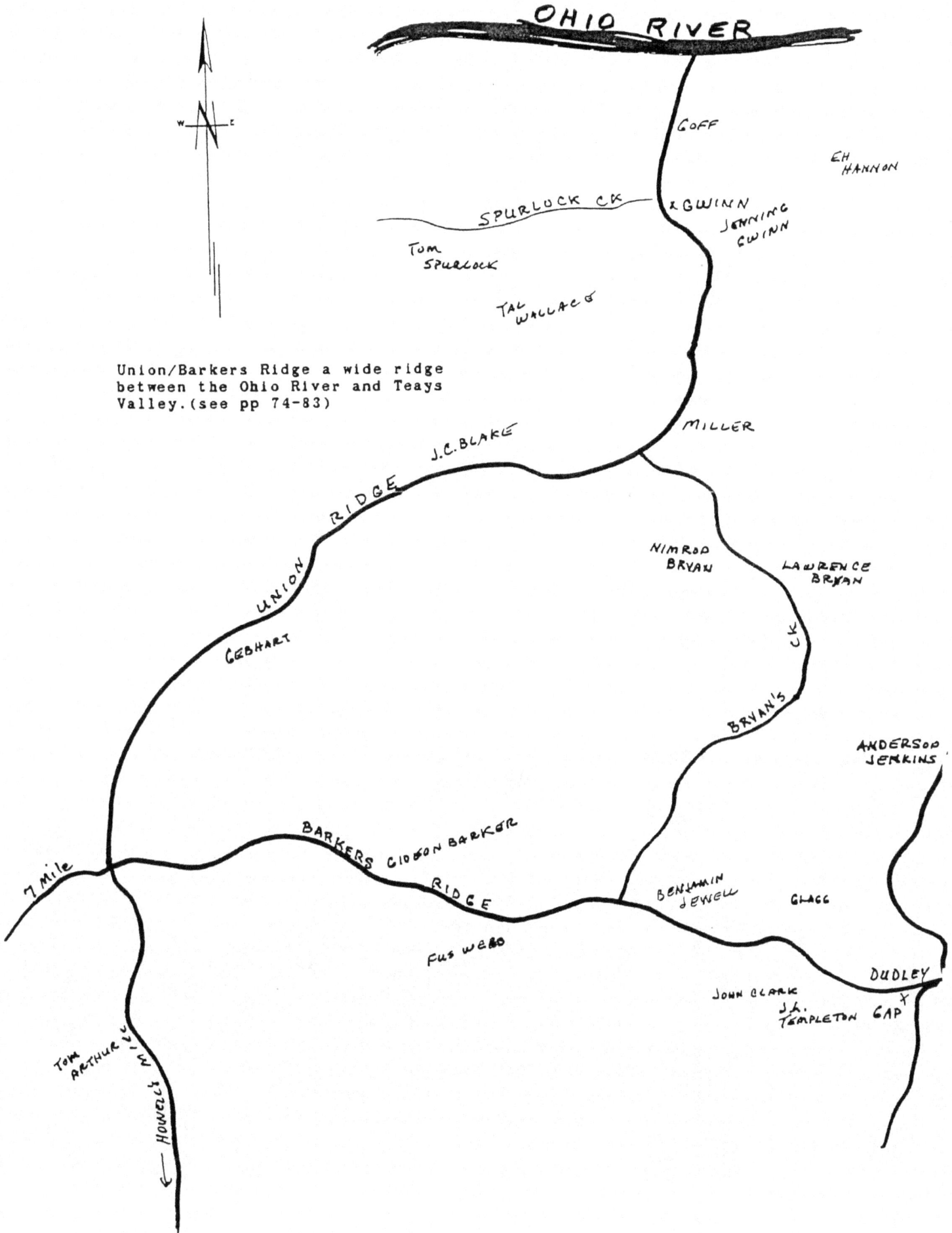

MILLER

J.C.BLAKE

UNION RIDGE

NIMROD BRYAN

LAWRENCE BRYAN

GEBHART

CK

BRYAN'S

ANDERSON JENKINS

BARKERS GIDEON BARKER

7 Mile

RIDGE

BENJAMIN JEWELL

GLASS

FUS WEBB

DUDLEY

JOHN CLARK

J.L. TEMPLETON GAP

TOM ARTHUR

← Howell's Mill

72

page 613 Union Township-Thorndike PO

1-1
Douglass,William	41m	VA	carp
Mahaley	39f	WV	
Mary E.	13f		
Cora V.	2f		
Mattie L.	8/12f		

2-2
Reynolds,Hardon	42m	VA	farm
Twintna	32f	WV	
Mary	15f		
Nipps,George	10m		

3-3
Wray,Henry	45m	WV	farm
Nancy	46f		
George	15m		lab
Wilson	13m		lab
Wray,Rody	79f	VA	

4-4
Chapman,Taswell	28m	WV	lab
Abigail	25f		
Georgia	2f		
Ida	5/12f		

5-5
Spencer,James	70m	VA	farm
Anna E.	46f		
Mary	17f	WV	

6-6
Rose,Cintha	38f	WV	kph
Malinda	15f		
Mary R.	13f		
Sarah C.	11f		
Virginia	4/12f		

7-7
Collins,Nathan	39m	WV	farm
Mary J.	37f	VA	
Smith,Granville	21m		lab
Smith,Ellen	16f	WV	
Smith,Collins	13m		lab

8-8
Jordan,John P.	36m	OH	farm
Cintha	27f	WV	
Jeremiah	17m		lab
John W.	14m		lab
Joseph	9m		
Lafayette	7m		
Margaret	5f		

8-8 Jordan (con't)
| Edward | 2m | | |
| Ida | 4/12f | | |

p 613a

9-9
Dennison,John	55m	Eng	farm
John	23m		lab
George	18m	WV	lab
Mary	20f		
James A.	15m		
Jenett	11f		

10-10
Adams,William	60m	VA	farm
Susan	39m	WV	
Francis	21m		lab
Knight,Eliza	16f		
Knight,Abigal	13f		
Jordan,Jeremiah	23m		lab

11-11
Davis,Samuel H.	46m	VA	farm
America	43f	WV	
Joseph S.	20m		lab
Nancy	19f		
Allen B.	16m		lab
Lisha	12m		
Jackson J.	10m		
Jefferson	7m		
Thomas W.	3m		

12-12
Arther, Isaac	60m	WV	farm
Julia	36f		
Likergus	13m		
Mary J.	11f		
Rosetta	9f		
Alice	8f		
Ammasetta	3f		
Sallie	1f		

13-13
Arther,James	56m	WV	farm
Elizabeth	55f	VA	
Lewis F.	22m	WV	lab
James C.	20m		
Eliza J.	15f		

14-14
Arther,John M.	51m	WV	farm
Sarah A.	48f		
William	26m		lab
John V.	22m		lab

14-14 Arther (con't)				
Mary M.	19f			
Anna E.	16f			
p114 Isaac	13m			
Albert J.	10m			
Sallie	6f			
15-15				
Davis,Elizabeth	52f	WV	kph	
Charles	24m		lab	
Jesse	22m		lab	
Sarah	19f			
Mary J.	15f			
16-16				
Buxfield,Richard	44m	Eng	farm	
Mary	38f	WV		
Joseph	18m		lab	
James	17m		lab	
Thomas	5m			
17-17				
Blake,Jeremiah	80m	WV	farm	
Margaret	70f			
Valentine	28m		farm	
Clarressey	27f			
Emily J.	6f			
John P.	5m			
18-18				
Gibson,Leroy	55m	VA	farm	
Jane	50f	WV		
19-19				
Jefferson,Henry	91m	VA	farm	
Bettie	84f			
America	35f	WV		
Elizabeth	10f			
20-20				
Ferguson,James	53m	WV	farm	
Martha	64f	VA		
Jesse	24m	WV	lab	
Martha	21f			
Henry	17m		lab	
Jackson	15m		lab	
Mahaley	13f			
21-21				
Perry,Richard	72m	WV	farm	
Annie	70f			
Henry	30m		lab	
Harrison	27m		lab	
Addie	25f			
Lucinda	10f			

22-22				
Ferguson,Jesse	55m	WV	farm	
Hannah	60f			
p614a Joseph	15m		lab	
Catherine	9f			
23-23				
Newman,Alexander	69m	NC	farm	
Elizabeth	68f	WV		
Emily	37f			
James	7m			
24-24				
Pulley,William	35m	NC	lab	
Julia	38f	WV		
Rebecca	17f			
Mary	5f			
David	7m			
William	15m			
25-25				
Clark,Daniel	63m	VA	farm	
Harriet	49f	WV		
Grimes,Roberta	16f		sch	
Grimes,George F.	14m		sch	
Grimes,Robert A.	12m			
Grimes,Thomas J.	9m			
Grimes,Abreham	7m			
26-26				
Johnston,Lewis	56m	WV	farm	
Jane	54f			
Squire	18m	OH		
Edward P.	14m	WV		
Andrew	10m			
Ferguson,Walter	2m			
27-27				
Johnston,William	22m	WV	farm	
Sarah	21f	OH		
Eliza J.	1f	WV		
28-28				
Perry,Richard	86m	NC	farm	
Annie	70f	MD		
Hagley,Ariadna	38f	WV		
Hagley,Harrison	24m		lab	
Hagley,Henry	25m		lab	
Hagley,Lucinda	11f			
29-29				
Deal,Lewis	50m	Pru	farm	
Rosey D.	49f	Han		
Lewis	19m	PA	lab	

74

```
29-29 Deal (con't)              p615a
      Albert          17m PA lab   34-34
      Robert          10m WV          Toney,Joel      40m WV farm
      Liddie           8f               Edith         33f
p615 Bettie            6f               Lucinda       16f
      Frank            4m               Elena E.      14f
                                        Nancy         12f
30-30                                   Elizabeth     10m
   Baley,George       57m WV farm        John          7m
      Sarah           28f OH            William        5m
      George          16m    lab        Thomas L.      2m
      Elizabeth       13f               Joel A.      2/12m
      John            11m
      Catherine        9f WV        35-35
      Susan            6f              Lapole,John     30m PA lab
      Addie            5f                 Rebecca      20f
      James            3m
      Sylvester        1m          36-36
                                       Bryan,Lewis     30m WV lab
31-31                                     Sarah G.     20f OH
   Perry,William      39m WV farm
      Eliza J.        34f          37-37
      John H.         17m    lab      Gapehart,John    60m Rad farm
      Susa            14f                Elizabeth     57f
      Lucy            12f                John          20m       lab
      Albert          10m                Kate          17f WV
      Nancy            8f                Mary          15f
      Rachel           6f                William       10m
      Virginia         4f
      William          2m          38-38
   Perry,John         65m NC lab       Schlagal,John   52m Bav farm
   Perry,Lucy         64f VA             Mary          50f
                                         John           8m WV
32-32                                    Mary          21f Bav
   Miller,Carolina    50f Sax kph        Henry          2m WV
      Leanina         28f Sax
      Rose A.         14f WV        39-39
      Isabel          10f             Colwell,Robert   31m VA farm
      Arrova           9f                Elizabeth     19f OH
      Charles        3/12m               Fleming     10/12m WV
      Carolina        17f
                                   40-40
33-32(33)                             Henry,Gutliff    52m Sax farm
   Spurlock,Thomas    60m WV farm       Emily          45f
      Catherine       35f PA            Thradore       22m       lab
      William M.      16m WV farm       Gusta          17f
      Lonora S.       14f
      Lora A.         13f          41-41
      Ira J.          10m             Smick,Phillip    51m PA hotel
      Lillie B.        8f               Sarah          51f OH hotel
      John E.          6m               Semantha       20f
      Andrew           4m               Mary           16f
                                        James B.       14m
                                        Albert         10m
```

75

```
41-41 Smick (con't)                          48-48
   Williams,George    42m WV clk             Jefferson,John W.    46m WV farm
                                                Anjaline          33f
42-42                                           Albert            13m
   Rouse,Richard      36m KY farm  p616a        Willie            11m
p616 Eliza            27f                        Harriet           9f
     Charles           5m                        Alga              7f
     Drucilla          3f                        Effie             5f
     Frances           1f                        Cora              3f
   Rouse,Samuel       80m NJ farm               Ammasetta       10/12f
   Rouse,Spencer      27m KY
                                             49-49
43-43                                           Hagley,Peter      50m WV farm
   Taylor,Isaac       50m OH eng                Mary E.           43f
     Rody             34f WV                     Pollie A.         22f
     Mary             15f                        Hannah            19f
     George           14m                        Elizabeth         18f
     Henry             4m                        Sarah M.          15f
     Melcina           2f                        Mahaley S.        12f
   Jefferson,Franklin 11m                        Martha S.          6f
   Jefferson,William   8m                        George H.          2m
   Jefferson,Virginia  6f                      Hagely,Peter       22m

44-44                                        50-50
   Knight,William     33m WV farm              Mobley,William     23m OH farm
     Harriet          26f                        Margaret          22f
     Rosa B.           5f                        Rachel            1f WV
     Verena J.         4f
     Sarah S.          3f                     51-51
     Henry L.       5/12m                       Hagely,Joseph     57m WV farm
                                                 Louisa           41f
45-45                                            Pollie           22f
   File,Able S.       51m OH farm                Joseph           21m      lab
     Nancy            25f                        Hannah F.        20f
     George            5m                        George P.        18m      lab
     Hester            3f WV                     Louisa J.        16f
     Joseph            1m                        James            15m
                                                 Malachiah        12m
46-46                                            Mary E.          10f
   Woodard,William    46m WV farm
     Frances          23f WI                  52-52
     Martha            3f WV                     Lesage,Francis    34m NY farm
     William           2m                        Mary M.          28f VA
                                                 Mary F.          12f WV
47-47                                            Zelia J.          9f
   Neuman,William     36m WV farm                Lvesa S.          7f
     Lucinda          26f                        Julius C.         4m
     Mary              9f                        Francis J.        1m
     Mariah            7f OH
     Albert G.         6m                     53-53
     Viola             4f WV                     Paulees,Ernest    45m Fra paint
     Carolina          2f                        Henrietta        45f
                                                 Henry            20m      limer
                                                 Lvesa            18f
```

p617				
54-54				
Cornell,Martin	46m	NY	lab	
Levisa	50f			
55-55				
Knight,John	37m	WV	farm	
Margaret	35f			
John H.	10m			
Martha	7f			
Virginia	4f			
Laura E.	1f			
56-56				
Knight,Abner	35m	WV	farm	
Parthena	31f			
Henry M.	6m			
Phillip S.	4m			
Lafyette	2m			
James	1m			
57-57				
Johnston,Wesley	52m	VA	farm	
Sina	47f	WV		
Bettie A.	22f		dom	
Anjalina	19f		dom	
America	18f			
Sarah	16f			
James M.	13m			
Sirena	11f			
Emily F.	8f			
58-58				
Jefferson,Thomas	58m	VA	farm	
Parthena	58f	WV		
Malinda	23f			
Abner L.	19m		lab	
Nancy L.	15f			
Mary E.	11f			
Burns,Allen J.	22m		lab	
59-59				
Ansell,Michael	54m	WV	farm	
Elizabeth	42f			
Jack,Eliza	10f	OH		
Weeks,Franklin	9m			
Baker,Susan	21f	WV		
Baker,Elizabeth	3f			
Baker,Michael	1m			
60-60				
Howard,Allen	67m	WV	carp	
Cristina	63f			
Louisa	27f			

p617a				
60-60 Howard (con't)				
Hannah	24f	OH		
Hugh A.	19m		lab	
Oliver,Ann	15f			
Oliver,Rachel	13f			
Oliver,Nancy	11f			
Howard,Marion	6m	WV		
61-61				
Floyd,John	25m	WV	coop	
Frances	23f	OH		
William A.	3m	WV		
Allen	2m			
Finley	2/12m			
62-62				
Lesage,Julius	59m	Fra	farm	
Mary M.	65f			
63-63				
Knight,George	56m	NC	farm	
Mary	56f	VA		
George	23m	WV	lab	
Alsindra	16m			
Eliza F.	14f			
Wilson,Charles	9m			
Wilson,William	1m			
64-64				
Winters,Lemuel	27m	WV	farm	
Mary	22f			
William F.	7m	OH		
Henry J.	4m	WV		
Alice R.	1f			
Winters,Esther	66f	NY		
65-65				
Knight,Abner P.	34m	WV	farm	
Caroline	34f			
William	10m			
Walter	8m			
Newman,Harvey	21m		lab	
66-66				
Blake,Pennell	70m	WV	farm	
Nancy	45f			
Sarah C.	16f			
Auslun	14m			
Preston	12m			
John T.	10m			
Lafyette	8m			
Robert L.	6m			

67-67				
Winters,George	29m	WV	farm	
p618 Mary E.	30f			
George	8m			
Henry V.	6m			
Laura E.	4f			
Charles	11/12m			
68-68				
Peters,John L.	28m	VA	lab	
Rachel	24f	OH		
Franklin	5m			
John T.	3m			
69-69				
Mobley,James	58m	MD	lab	
Rachel	59f			
James	27m	OH	lab	
Margret	26f			
Thomas J.	25m		lab	
Isaac	21m		lab	
Mason	16m		lab	
Scarberry,William	7m			
70-70				
Berry,Philo.B.	37m	OH	farm	
Mary J.	38f			
Letecia	17f	WV		
Carlie L.	15f			
Mary J.	13f			
Sarah	11f			
Eliza	9f			
Samuel	6m			
Alice	4f			
Louisa A.	1f			
71-71				
Curnell,James	38m	OH	lab	
Bettie	38f			
John	12m			
Mary	14f			
James	10m			
Catherine	8f			
Sheriden	4m			
72-72				
Ansell,Malchiah	38m	WV	farm	
Abreham	33m		farm	
Ann C.	43f			
Sarah	45f			
Hagley,Tabitha	14f			
73-73				
Morton,John	27m	WV	farm	
p618a Caroline	26f	OH		
Helena	1f			
74-74				
Houchin,Francis	40m	VA	farm	
Rebecca	39f	WV		
Henry	15m		lab	
William	13m			
Mary A.	11f			
Sarah E.	8f			
Clarressey	7f			
Adalade	5f			
Charles E.	3m			
75-75				
Blake,William H.	29m	WV	farm	
Mary F.	22f			
Robert M.	4m			
Marilla	6/12f			
Linkfield,Alice	14f			
76-76				
Arther,Thomas	32m	WV	farm	
Julia A.	23f			
Mary A.	11f			
Benjamin	8m			
Thomas	2m			
Elizabeth	4f			
77-77				
Spurlock,Harvey	52m	WV	farm	
Elizabeth	55f			
James H.	26m		lab	
Levery W.	23m		lab	
David	22m		lab	
Charles J.	20m		lab	
Jesse	17m		lab	
Daniel A.	14m		lab	
Campbell,Seena	25f			
78-78				
French,William	31m	OH	blks	
Martha	27f	WV		
Alice	9f			
Ellie	6f			
Lemuel	4m			
Laura	5/12f			
79-79				
Spurlock,Thomas D.	21m	WV	farm	
Mary E.	18f	OH		
Spurlock,Jesse	50m	WV	farm	

p619
79-79 Spurlock (con't)
    Spurlock,Margaret 40f WV

80-80
    Spurlock,Simeon   26m WV farm
        Margret   24f OH
        Anetta M.   4f WV
    Knop,Sarah   17f

81-81
Bowen,Sylvester   33m WV farm
    Susan   30f
    Monroe   11m
    Susan   6f
    Mary   3f
    Emma   6/12f

82-82
    Spurlock,Stephen   44m WV farm
        Jane A.   44f
        William   22m   lab
        Sarah A.   18f
        Abner   16m   lab
        Nancy E.   10f
        Susan   5f
        Linkfield,Riley   20m

83-83
    Weekly,Elias   23m WV farm
        Sarah   18f OH

84---
84-85
    Knight,Anselum   39m WV farm
        Matilda   40f
        Leelie   22f
        Abner   19m
        Missouri E.   18f
        Sarah E.   12f
        William   10m
        Eliza E.   8f
        Jefferson   5m
        Julia   2f
        John   6/12m

86-85
    Bowen,Zayes   26m WV lab
        Anna C.   20f
        William   5m
        Ammasetta   2f

87-86
    Knight,Lenard   25m WV farm
        Martha A.   19f
        Mary J.   4/12f

p619a
88-87
    Jenkins,William   41m WV farm
        Julia M.   39f MO
        Jenetta A.   15f WV
        William J.   14m
        Julia M.   7f
        Susan   7f

89-88
    Cremeans,Richard   25m WV lab
        Mary   22f OH
        Henry   6m

90-89
    Jenkins,Thomas J.   41m WV farm
        Susan   32f
        Julia   12f   sch
        Laura P.   11f
        Dudley   9m
        Addie   4f
    Mathena,Mary   26f VA dom

91-90
    Hews,Decalb   23m OH lab
        Jane A.   23f WV
        William   3m

92-91
    Bowen,Ezekiel   47m WV lab
        Ann   44f
        William   28m   lab
        Missouri   17f
        Charles   14m
        Albert   13m
        Ezekiel J.   11m
        Mary S.   9f
        Alice V.   5f

93-92
    Merrimen,Thomas   36m PA farm
        Frances   27f OH
        Hester   9f KY
        Nellie   5f OH
        Mathew   1m WV

---93
    Herren,Austin   30f OH lab
        Abbie   29f
        Harvey   3m WV

```
94-94                                   101-101
  Well,Jesse        30f OH farm           Weekly,James      49m WV farm
    Elizabeth       30f MD                  Phebe           50f
    Angela           9f OH      p620a       Joseph          16m    lab
    Emadelia         7f                     Amanda          14f
    George           8m                     Henry           11m
    Lenard        8/12m                     Alcinda          6f
p620
95-95
  Christy,Thomas    34m OH lab
    Jemima          32f                   102-102
    Jerome          16m WV lab             Moore,William    35m VA farm
    James           11m                      Edith C.       26f
    Jefferson        8m                      Julia A.        9f WV
                                             Sarah           7f
                                             Roda J.         4f
96-96                                        John            1m
  Boulin,James B.   66m VA farm             Emmerson,Elisa   1f
    Margret         51f                     Moore,Anna      56f VA
    Rebecca         50f
    Rose,Anderson   35m B WV lab
    Lacy,Mary       35f B   dom          103-103
    Lacy,George     15m B   lab            McKindy,Azel     35m VA lab
    Lacy,Cristina   12f B                    Mary           33f
    Lacy,John P.     3m M                     George L.      15m
                                             Elmore S.      13m
97-97                                        Lurania        10f
  Chapman,George    30m OH lab               Benjamin        9m
    Eliza           25f                      Ida J.          8f
    William          6m                      Cora B.         4f
    Frances          4f                      Olive P.        2f
    Laura J.         1f WV                    Baze        3/12m

98-98                                   104-104
  Lane,Charles      33m WV lab            Johnson,Joseph    77m NJ farm
    Mary J.         28f                     Rachel          46f WV
    Varena          10f                      Joseph         16m
    Albert           4m                      Mary           18f
                                             David          14m
                                             Malissey       12f
99-99                                        Martha          5f
  Michael,William   49m WV farm             Melvena          4f
    Olive           47f                     Burres,Daniel   34m    lab
    John            27m OH lab
    David           25m    lab
    Daniel          23m    lab          105-105
    Sarah           22f                    Trippeet,Jesse G. 33m WV farm
    Elizabeth       19f                      Jane           32f
    Malissey J.     17f                      Caleb           2m
    Wilson          15m                      William         1m
    Ulysses          7m                     Campbell,Wesley  42m WV coop
  Michael,Elizabeth 25f
  Michael,Mary M.    1f                  106-106
100-100                                    Holley,Samuel    32m OH lab
  Lacy,David        73m BA brkm             Sarah           27f
    Eustatia        64f                      Mary H.         6f
```

```
107-107                                114-114 Chase (con't)
  Reed,William      29m WV farm           Clarinda          2f
p621 Margret       25f                    William F.    6/12m WV
     John H.        6m               p621a
     Sarah C.       4f               115-115
     Charles        3m                 Rariden,John       50m WV lab
                                         Ammazella        45f
108-108                                   Henry            19m
  Blake,Jeremiah   22m WV farm            Melvina          15f
     Dolph         14m                    Sarah            11f
     Elizabeth     12f
     Louisa A.     11f               116-116
  Blake,Ivana J.   52f VA              Wallace,Tolaver    65m VA farm
                                         Malinda          48f OH
109-109                                   Emily            13f WV
  Harris,James     29m WV farm            Laura             9f
     Telitha       28f                  McComas,John       24m    lab
     Martha      5/12f                  McComas,Elisha     16f

110-110                              117-117
  Blake,Morris     52m WV farm         Knapp,Henry        39m NY stmn
     Teletha       49f                    Elizabeth        32f PA
     Sarah M.      20f                    Lymon            12m OH    --
     John M.       17m       lab          Samuel           12m      --
     Lecetta       14f                    David            12m      --
     Daniel M.     12m                    William           3m
     Nancy         10f                    Catherine         5f
     Rosa           8f                    Ira               1m WV
     Mattie         5f
                                     118-118
111-111                                Riggs,Albert       25m WV farm
  Lapool,John      84m PA blks           Virginia         25f
     Zerilda       40f OH                 Vida              2f
     Pedilla A.     5f                 Riggs,Thomas J.    22m      lab
     Margret        1f WV              Riggs,Celila A.    62f

112-112                              119-119
  Canard,William H. 33m WV lab         McComas,William    24m OH lab
     Elsea         33f VA                 Ellen            21f
     Thomas         2m                    William          16m      lab
     Cora Bell    3/12f
                                     120-120
113-113                                Lenard,Reuben E.   36m PA farm
  Hagley,Joseph    26m WV lab             Margret          34f
     Eliza         22f                    Anna B.          15f      sch
     Mahaley        1f                    John F.          13m      sch
  Ferguson,Elizabeth 20f                  William           7m
                                          Emma              5f
114-114                                   Frank M.          1m WV
  Chase,Abel J.    37m OH farm
     Sarah J.      30f MD            121-121
     Sienda         8f OH              Sheff,Andrew       69m VA farm
     McCellen       6m                   Catherine        32f WV
     Sheriden       4m                 Wilks,Mary         27f
```

81

```
122-122
  Wilson,Lemuel        30m WV farm          129-129
    Susan              26f                    Templeton,Jesse A.  44m VA farm
    Alice E.            4f           p622a      William           21m      lab
p622 Leonades           2m                       Julia            19f
    Sheff,Lerrie        8f                        John L.          18m      lab
                                                  Charles          14m      lab
123-123                                           Francis J.       12m      lab
  Ball,Lafayette       38m WV farm                Thomas           10m
    Mary               27f                         Mary J.          7f
    Joseph             11m                          Claressey E.     4f
    Willie E.           9m                          Bennett V.   10/12m
    Martha E.           7f                     Houchen,Rebecca      34f
    Jennie              6f
    Fannie              5f                    130-130
    Emily               3f                      Smith,Joseph       43m WV lab
                                                  Mary             30f
124-124                                           William J.       17m      lab
  Davis,Adison         28m WV farm                Mary F.          15f
    Elizabeth          20f                         Sarah M.         13f
    John M.         10/12m                         James R.         10m
                                                  Joseph S.          7m
125-125                                           John W.            5m
  Yates,John T.        40m WV farm                Julia A.           2f
    John W.            10m
    William             8m                    131-131
    Jacob               6m                      Howard,William     59m VA farm
    Rebecca            42f                         Ann              45f WV
    Lucretia           21f
    Ezra W.            20m      lab            132-132
    Julia              14f MO                    Legg,Willis        44m WV farm
    James              10m WV                      Rebecca          39f
    Adaline             5f                          Elias           20m
                                                  Adison           14m
126-126                                           Thomas           10m
  Barker,John          30m VA lab                 Charles W.       10m
    Sarah C.           25f WV                      Mary E.           7f
    Jeneva              2f                          James A.          4m
    Julia               2f                          Martha L.         3f
    Nimrod          10/12m
                                               133-133
127-127                                          Cremens,Winget     65m WV lab
  McComas,John         48m WV farm                Pollie           60f VA
    Lucinda            46f VA                       Menitha         29f WV dom
    William            16m WV lab                   Delila          27f      dom
    Job                14m      lab                 Walter           5m
    Thomas J.          10m
    George C.           8m                    134-134
    Andrea              2m                       Legg,John H.       21m WV lab
                                                  Sallie A.         23f
128-128                                           Daniel         9/12m
  Houchin,William      38m WV lab
    Mary J.            20f
    Claressey           1f
```

135-135
```
Cremeans.Amanda      56f WV kph
   Montaville        15m
```
p623
136-136
```
Cremens,Nathan       55m WV farm
   Elizabeth         57f VA
   Mary              25f WV
   Sarah C.          19f
Smith,Jesse          25m
Holley,Lorenzo       10m
Holley,Martha         7f
Holley,Sarah C.       2f
```

137-137
```
Ceremens,John W.     21m WV farm
   Nancy             21f
```

138-138
```
Jenkins,Anderson     94m KY farm
   Menitha           48f WV
   John J.           19m    lab
   William           15m
   Colonel           12m
```

139-139
```
McClasky,Nancy       52f WV kph
   Robert            23m    lab
   Hamilton          22m    lab
   John H.           20m    lab
   James W.          17m    lab
   Sarah T.          14f
```

140-140
```
McClasky,Floyd       23m WV farm
   Mareom            22f NY
Smith,Elizabeth      60f
```

141-141
```
Smith,Gohram         24m NY farm
   Mary              22f
   William            1m WV
```

142-142
```
McClasky,Emily       58f WV kph
   Nancy J.          22f
   Alexander         17m    lab
   Thomas            12m
```

143-143
```
McWharter,James      44m WV farm
   Calferna          37f
   Mahaley F.        16f    sch
   Marietta          13f    sch
```

143-143 McWarther (con't)
```
   Elizabeth         10f
   Edna P.            7f
   Consentine         4m
   James H.           1m
Shoemaker,Joseph      9m
```

144-144
```
Medows,William       53m WV farm
   Sarah             56f VA
   Hezekiah          18m WV lab
   Sylvester         15m    lab
Suter,James P.       25m    phy
```

145-145
```
Medows,Ranson        24m WV farm
   Margaret          19f
   William            4m
```

146-146
```
Bryon,Nimrod         47m WV farm
   Matilda           22f
   Gabriel           17m    lab
   Thomas            16m    lab
   Mary A.           12f
   Julia A.          11f
   Semantha           9f
   Robert E.          7m
```

147-147
```
Clagg,Julius         37m WV farm
   Rebecca           28f
   John W.           12m
   Mary F.           11f
   James              9m
   Nancy              8f
   Matilda            7f
   Thomas             5m
   Bennett V.      9/12m
Smith,Eliza          50f
Smith,James          13m
```

148-148
```
White,James H.       40m VA farm
   Lucy              50f WV
   Sarah J.          20f
   Catherine         16f
   John H.           13m
   Nimrod            10m
   William            7m
```

149-149
```
Medows,James J.      36f WV
   Drucilla          36f VA
```

83

149-149 Medows (con't)

Sarah E.	14f	WV	sch
Mary A.	11f		
Laurinda J.	9f		
Henry J.	6m		

p624

150-150

Amoss,Joshua	47m	OH	farm
Mary	41f	WV	
William	21m		coop
Sarah C.	13f		
Mary F.	11f		
Luvena E.	8f		
Claressey M.	5f		
Agnisetta	2f		
Cremens,Sarah	94f	VA	

151-151

Templeton,Ransom	27m	WV	farm
Mary A.	21f		
Minisota	7/12f		
Holley,Joanna	17f		dom
Holley,Gorden	9/12m		

152-152

Templeton,Harvey	48m	WV	farm
Mary	46f		
John L.	29m		lab
Isaac	24m		lab
Esom T.	22m		lab
William	21m		lab
Mary A.	17f		
Lucinda	15f		
Adison H.	13m		
Charles H.	11m		
Elizabeth	8f		

153-153

Fox,James	22m	KY	farm
Smith,Matilda	40f		
Fox,William	19m	OH	lab
Smith,Mary	12f	WV	
Smith,Leander	10m		
Smith,Missouri	7f		
Smith,Frances	3f		

154-154

Bryon,Lawrence	50m	WV	farm
Mary E.	45f	VA	
Clarissey C.	19f	WV	
John H.	18m		lab
Parthenia	16f		
Adaline F.	14f		
Nimrod F.	12m		

154-154 Bryon (con't)

Verena	8f	

p624a

155-155

Bryon,William	24m	WV	farm
Julia	22f	OH	
Albert G.	2m	WV	

156-156

Smith,Frank	45m	Sax	farm
Amie	46f		
Albert G.	2m	WV	

157-157

Hamberger,Joseph	55m	Pru	farm
Henrietta	48f		
Cosaline	16f	PA	sch
Mary	13f	WV	sch
Lucy	11f		
Annie	9f		

158-158

Stowater,Frank	53m	Pru	farm
Cristina	48f	Sax	

159-159

Beaker,Henry	50m	Bav	farm
Joanna	62f	Pru	
Anthony	35m	Bav	farm

160-160

Felix,Julius	31m	Swi	survy
Susan	29f	OH	
Isabel	9f	WV	
Felix,Julia	57f	Swi	
Golden,Gustaves	46m		lab
Felix,James	65m		survy

161-161

Felix,Arnold	27m	Swi	paint
Penila	20f	WV	
Werner	2m		
James F.	1m		

162-162

Telgner,Emile	37m	Pru	farm
Agnis	33f	Aus	
Julia A.	12f	WV	
Teressey	10f		
Merkl,George	72m	Aus	farm

163-163

Beils,Edward	39m	Aus	farm
Catherine	38f		

```
163-163 Biels (con't)
      Matilda              17f NY
      Henry                16m WV lab
      Frank                14m    lab
      Joseph               13m
      Emily                11m WI
      Julia                 9f
p625 Mary                   6f
      Augusta           10/12m WV

164-164
  Biels,Anthony            32m Aus farm
    Barbery                27f
    Almira                 11f WI
    Georgia                 7f
    Anna A.                 5f
    William                 4m WV
    Isabel                  2f
    John                 9/12m
  Cinstater,Catherine 60f Aus

165-165
  Turner,Lenard            50m WV farm
    Sarah E.               35f VA
    America                12f WV
    Andrew                 10m
    Joseph                  9m
    Mary                    7f
    Lucy                    5f
```

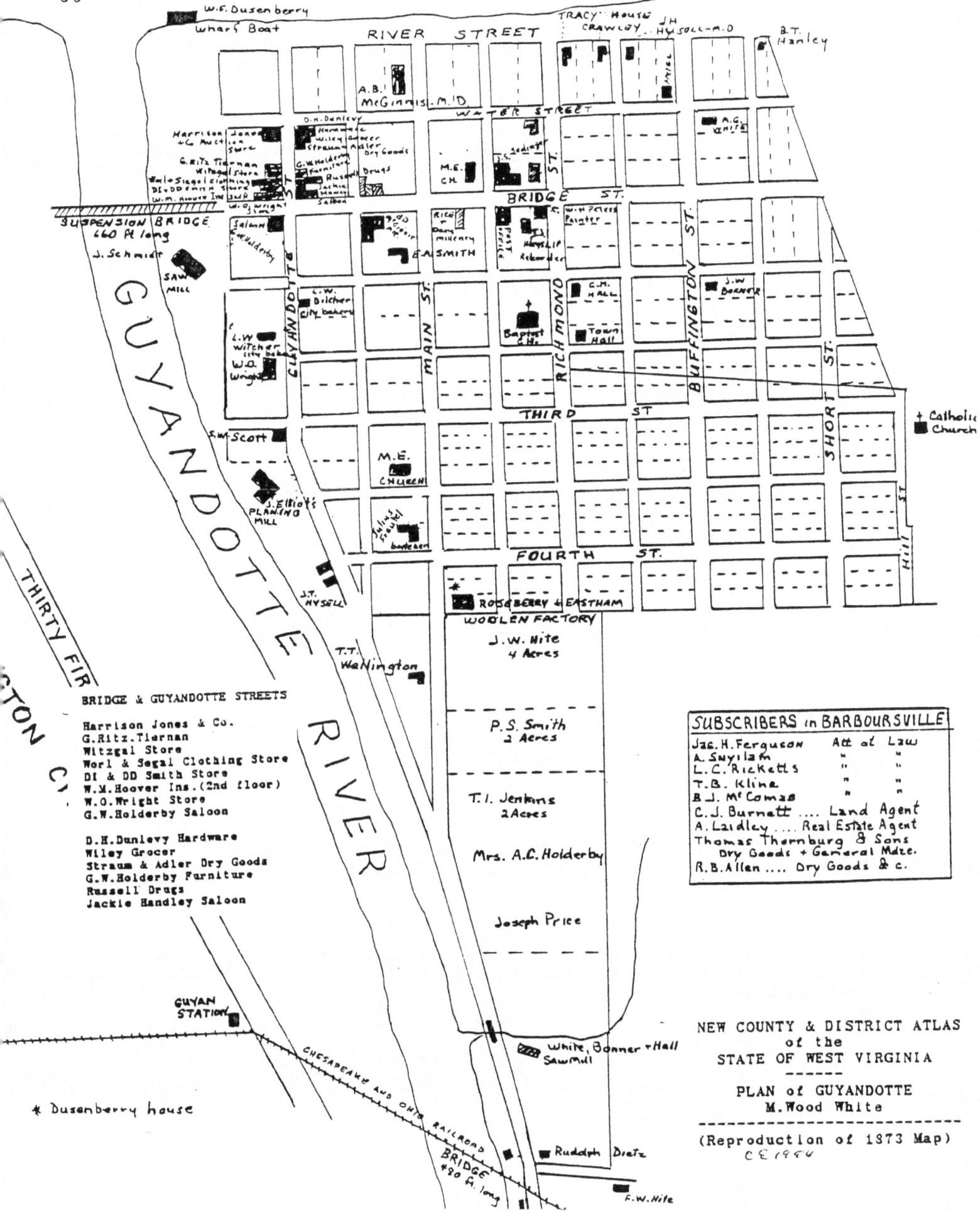

85

OHIO RIVER

W.F. Dusenberry
Wharf Boat

RIVER STREET

TRACY HOUSE
CRAWLEY   JH HYSOLL-M.D

B.T. Hanley

A.B. McGinnis. M.D

WATER STREET

A.G. WHITE

Harrison Jones & Co. Auction
D.H. Dunlevy
Hardware
Wiley Grocer
Straum Adler
Dry Goods

G.Ritz Tiernan
Witzgal Store
Worl & Siegel clothing
DI & DD Smith Store
W.M. Hoover Ins. 2nd fl
W.O. Wright Store

G.W Holderby
Furniture
Russell Drugs
Jackie Handley
Saloon

M.E. CH.

Saloon
W. Holderby

T.S. Seddler

BRIDGE ST.

SUSPENSION BRIDGE
660 Ft long

J. Schmidt

SAW MILL

W.O. Wright Jas

Salm
E.W.Holderby

W.O. Wright Barber

Rice
Dressmillinery

Post office

W.H Peters
Painter

HaysLIP
Releewaker

E.A. SMITH

L.W. Dilcher
City bakery

C.H. HALL

J.W BONNER

L.W. Witcher
city bank

Baptist
C. Hs.

Town Hall

W.O. Wright

S.W. Scott

M.E. CHURCH

THIRD ST

Catholic Church

J. Elliot's
PLANING MILL

Julius
Freudel
barber

FOURTH ST.

Rosaberry & Eastham
WOOLEN FACTORY

J.T. HYSELL

T.T. Wellington

J.W. Hite
4 Acres

P.S. Smith
2 Acres

T.I. Jenkins
2 Acres

Mrs. A.C. Holderby

Joseph Price

RICHMOND ST.

BUFFINGTON ST.

SHORT ST.

Hill ST.

MAIN ST.

GUYANDOTTE ST.

GUYANDOTTE RIVER

THIRTY FIRST

...TON C.

BRIDGE & GUYANDOTTE STREETS

Harrison Jones & Co.
G.Ritz.Tiernan
Witzgal Store
Worl & Segal Clothing Store
DI & DD Smith Store
W.M.Hoover Ins.(2nd floor)
W.O.Wright Store
G.W.Holderby Saloon

D.H.Dunlevy Hardware
Wiley Grocer
Straum & Adler Dry Goods
G.W.Holderby Furniture
Russell Drugs
Jackie Handley Saloon

SUBSCRIBERS in BARBOURSVILLE

Jas.H.Ferguson	Att at Law
A.Smylam	" "
L.C.Ricketts	" "
T.B.Kline	" "
B.J.McComas	" "
C.J.Burnett	Land Agent
A.Laidley	Real Estate Agent
Thomas Thornburg & Sons	Dry Goods + General Mdze.
R.B.Allen	Dry Goods &c.

GUYAN STATION

CHESAPEAKE AND OHIO RAILROAD

* Dusenberry house

White, Bonner + Hall
Sawmill

BRIDGE 480 ft long

Rudolph Dietz

F.W. Hite

NEW COUNTY & DISTRICT ATLAS
of the
STATE OF WEST VIRGINIA

PLAN of GUYANDOTTE
M.Wood White

(Reproduction of 1873 Map)
C E 1954

CABELL COUNTY PRESS.

Devoted to Literature, Agriculture, Morality, General Intelligence and Industrial Improvements; Local News &c.

VOL. I.   CABELL COURT-HOUSE, WEST VIRGINIA, MONDAY, AUGUST 23, 1869.   NO. 6

The Cabell County Press.

Terms of Subscription:
One copy one year $2.00 | One copy 6 months $1.00
INVARIABLY IN ADVANCE.

Rates of Advertising:

One square, 1 insertion _____ $1.00
Each additional insertion _____ 50
One square 3 months _____ 5 00
One square 6 months _____ 7 00
One square 12 months _____ 10 00

A reasonable deduction on all yearly advertisements occupying one fourth of a column or more.

All yearly advertisements collected quarterly in advance.

Transient advertisements must be paid for in advance.

Announcing candidates for county offices $3 00; for State and Federal Offices $10 00; payment required in advance.

Communications solicited, but every article must be accompanied with the name of the writer. No notice taken of anonymous letters.

Rejected communications are not returned.

All legal advertisements must be paid for before the Proof of Publication can be obtained. Plaintiffs are required by law to pay the cost of Orders of Publication before the Proof of Publication is issued.

For Special Notices fifteen cents per line will be charged.

PROFESSIONAL.

T. L. MOSS.   C. D. MOSS.

DRS. V. R. & C. D. MOSS,

Physicians and Surgeons,

BARBOURSVILLE, W. VA.

PROMPT to attend calls both from town and country. Especial attention paid to the treatment of all chronic diseases, Scrofula, Consumption &c. Can always be found at their office when not professionally engaged.

LARAN T. MOORE,   T. B. KLINE.

MOORE & KLINE,

ATTORNEYS AT LAW.

WILL practice in Cabell, Wayne and adjoining counties. Prompt attention given to the collection of claims.
Address, Laran T. Moore, Catlettsburg Ky.
T. B. Kline, Cabell Court House. W. Va.

C. P. T. Moore.   Lucien C. Ricketts.

MOORE & RICKETTS,

ATTORNEYS AT LAW.

CABELL COURT HOUSE. WEST VA.

WILL practice in the counties of Wayne, Cabell and Lincoln. Especial attention given to the collection of claims.
Address
C. P. T. Moore, Point Pleasant. W. Va. or
Lucien C. Ricketts. Cabell C. H. W. Va.

B. D. McGINNIS,

ATTORNEY AT LAW.

GUYANDOTTE, W. VA.

WILL practice in Cabell and adjoining counties and the United States District Court of West Virginia. Prompt attention given to the collection of claims.

TOMLINSON & KLINE,

ATTORNEYS AT LAW

WILL attend to all business entrusted to them in Lincoln and Logan counties.
Address
Wm. H. Tomlinson, Pt. Pleasant. W. Va. or
T. B. Kline, Cabell C. H. W. Va.

ABRAHAM SUYDAM.

ATTORNEY AT LAW.

STATE OF WEST VIRGINIA.

AT Rules held in the Clerk's office of the circuit court of Cabell county on the first Monday in October, 1869.
V. W. Masher.
vs.
M. Berger and Ladwic Schmidt, partners doing business under the firm name of M. Berger & Co.—In Assumpsit.

The object of this suit is to recover of the defendants the sum of $157.70 due by account together with the interest thereon and to attach and sell the estate of the defendant M. Berger for the payment of the same. The order of attachment awarded in this case having been returned by the Sheriff showing that he has levied the same upon

---

B. D. McGINNIS,

ATTORNEY AT LAW.

GUYANDOTTE, W. VA.

WILL practice in Cabell and adjoining counties and the United States District Court of West Virginia. Prompt attention given to the collection of claims.

TOMLINSON & KLINE,

ATTORNEYS AT LAW

WILL attend to all business entrusted to them in Lincoln and Logan counties.
Address
Wm. H. Tomlinson, Pt. Pleasant. W. Va. or
T. B. Kline, Cabell C. H. W. Va.

ABRAHAM SUYDAM.

ATTORNEY AT LAW,

CABELL COURT HOUSE. W. VA.

WILL practice in the counties composing the Twelfth Judicial Circuit.

J. S. P. CARROLL,

ATTORNEY AT LAW.

WAYNE COURT-HOUSE. W. VA.

WILL practice in the counties of Wayne, Cabell, Lincoln, Boone & Logan. Especial attention given to the collection of claims.

The Cabell County Press

A WEEKLY RECORD OF

General and Local News,

PUBLISHED EVERY MONDAY

Cabell Court House W. Va.

The publisher of this paper would respectfully announce to the citizens of this and adjoining counties that he has commenced the publication of the Press under new and favorable circumstances, and is happy to inform his readers that he is now able to furnish them as good a newspaper as is printed in this section of the State. The intention of the Publisher is to give them the Very Latest News, Both Foreign and Domestic and to furnish in each issue a suitable amount of GOOD READING MATTER, from the best authors, while giving information relative to all important events taking place in this section of the country.

The columns of the Press will also be open at all times to the discussion of interesting questions of the day.

The Market Prices will be carefully noted.

Minutes of National, State and Local meetings given in detail.

☞ The Press is the Official newspaper of the 12th Judicial Circuit, comprising the counties of Cabell, Wayne, Logan, Lincoln and Boone, and as such will contain all Decrees of Court, Land Sales, &c.

Terms of Subscription:

One copy one year $2.00
One copy six months 1.00
Five copies one year 9.00
Ten copies one year 18.00

The publisher of the Press is also prepared to do

All Kinds of Job Work,

In the Best Style, at the Lowest Prices, and on Short Notice.

Fancy and Ornamental Printing a Speciality.

Large and Small Bills, Business and Visiting Cards, Pamphlets, Circulars, Posters, Law Blanks, Legal Forms, Bonds, Deeds, Promissory Notes, &c. &c.

Business men in all part of the State should increase their trade by advertising in the Press. It has a large circulation in this and adjoining counties, and is rapidly increasing, in all parts of the State and County. For reaching the people of this section of the country, by advertisements the Press is the very best medium. Any information concerning this section of country will be cheerfully given upon application either in person or by letter.

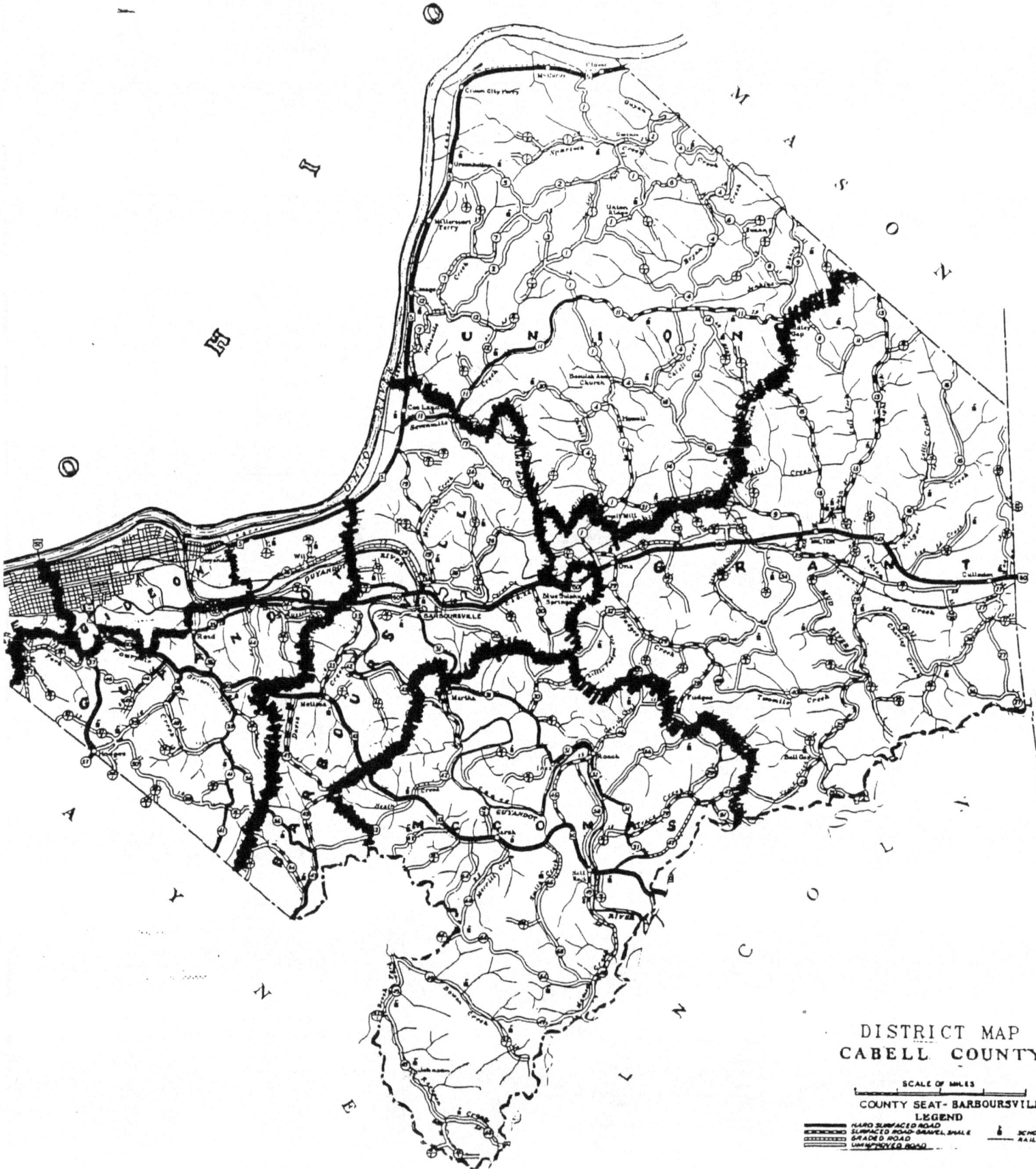

DISTRICT MAP
CABELL COUNTY

SCALE OF MILES

COUNTY SEAT- BARBOURSVILLE
LEGEND

DISTRICTS IN CABELL COUNTY

The present district system was created in West Virginia by a Township Commission in 1852 and revised in 1863. The Original Districts were: District 1 - Lower Guyan
                    District 2 - Barboursville
                    District 3 - Mud River and Ohio
                    District 4 - Valley and Upper Mud District
                    District 5 - Upper Guyan

In 1863, the new state of West Virginia renamed these districts, but kept the same division lines because "We are unabel at this time to have the line of the said townships surveyed for the reason that a large portion of the county is in the possession of the Rebels".(Cabell Commissioners)

District 1: Guyandotte - begining on the Ohio River at the mouth of 4 Pole at the Wayne County line hence up the river to the mouth of Files Branch(Pyles) hence across the ridge to the Guyandotte River to Widow Shelton's and toward the Wayne county line along the dividing ridge between 4 Pole and Davis Creek. (After Huntington was incorporated this district was sudivided adding Gideon and Kyle)

District 2: Barboursville - Begining on the Ohio River at the mouth of Files Branch with Guyandotte line hence up the river to James Knight's ferry across ridge to 9 Mile at Lemuel Cornell house hence along road to Richard Perry house, hence along road to James Cushing house then in a straight line to the Mud River Ford above Harshbarger's Mill hence to the Turnpike the south along the dividing ridge around the head waters of Fudge Creek and Little Cabell Creek and down the next ridge to the mouth of Little Cabell hence in a straight line to the Wayne County line at the old Carson place hence along county line to Guyandotte.

District 3: Union - Begining at the Ohio River with the Barbousville line hence to the line to the Turnpike the to Putnam County line hence north to Mason County line and to river.

District 4: Carroll (Grant) - Beginging at the Turnpike at junction of Union and Barboursville lines hence along Turnpike to Putnam County line south to the Boone County line the west to the Logan County line hence to the top of the dividing ridge between Mud River and Guyandotte River hence North along ridge to Barboursville line and then the begining. (Carroll included part of Lincoln County when that section was removed the District took the name Grant.)

District 5: McComas - Begining at the southwest corner of the Barboursville line at the Wayne County line hence to the Logan County line hence to Carroll District hence along said line to the Barboursville line and the begining. (Also contained part of Lincoln County)

*Aams,Elijah 33
Aams,Eliza 33
Aams,Farman 33
Aams,Jane 33
Aams,Mark L. 33
Aams,Martha A. 33
Aams,Mary J., 33
Adams,Agnis 22
Adams,Allen L. 22
*Adams,Amos 51
Adams,Anna L. 51
Adams,Asden 36
Adams,Bettie (x) 13
Adams,Charles S. 11
Adams,Elizabeth 36
Adams,Emily J. 51
Adams,Emma 36
Adams,Emma E. 11
Adams,Fannie 36
Adams,Francis 72
Adams,George (x) 11
Adams,James F. 11
*Adams,Jeremiah 36
Adams,John (x) 39
Adams,John H. 22
*Adams,Joshua A. 22
Adams,Mary F. 22
Adams,Minnie 11
Adams,Nancy (x) 11
Adams,Nancy J. 14
Adams,Samuel 36
Adams,Sarah 22
Adams,Sarah 51
Adams,Sarah A.(x) 39
Adams,Sarah L. 14
Adams,Sarah M. 14
Adams,Sophia 14
Adams,Susan 72
Adams,Thomas 36
Adams,Thomas 51
*Adams,William 14
Adams,William 22
*Adams,William 72
Adkins,Adaline 66
*Adkins,Albert 66
Adkins,Alice 67
Adkins,Amacetta 66
Adkins,America 66
Adkins,Amildie 66
Adkins,Anderson 66
Adkins,Anjaline 66
Adkins,Ann E. 12
Adkins,Anna 12
Adkins,Annie 66

Adkins,Bettie 66
Adkins,Bettie 67
*Adkins,Champ 65
Adkins,Champion 66
Adkins,Chestina 66
Adkins,Cintha A. 67
Adkins,Cloey 67
Adkins,Cordelia 12
Adkins,Delphia 67
Adkins,Dicy 65
Adkins,Dicy 66
*Adkins,Edward 12
*Adkins,Elijah 66
Adkins,Elizabeth 66
Adkins,Elizabeth 67
Adkins,Emily J. 12
*Adkins,Enoch 66
*Adkins,Enoch 67
Adkins,Ephram 67
Adkins,Everett 66
*Adkins,Everman 66
Adkins,Frances 38
Adkins,Frances 5
Adkins,Francis M. 66
Adkins,George 38
*Adkins,Green L. 66
Adkins,Hezekiah 66
Adkins,Hezekiah 66
Adkins,Intia A. 66
Adkins,Jackson 67
Adkins,James (x) 63
Adkins,James 5
*Adkins,James A. 67
Adkins,James H. 66
Adkins,James M. 65
Adkins,James M. 67
Adkins,Jarrett 66
Adkins,Jefferson 66
Adkins,Jeremiah 66
*Adkins,Jesse 66
Adkins,Jessey 67
Adkins,John 4
*Adkins,John 66
*Adkins,John C. 67
Adkins,John D. 66
*Adkins,John S. 4
Adkins,Jones 66
Adkins,Kandith 66
Adkins,Laddie 65
Adkins,Lee 66
Adkins,Lee 67
Adkins,Lettie 65
Adkins,Mahaley 67
Adkins,Margret 66

Adkins,Margret 66
Adkins,Martha 5
Adkins,Martha 65
Adkins,Martha 66
Adkins,Martin 66
Adkins,Mary 4
Adkins,Mary 65
Adkins,Mary E. 12
Adkins,Mary J. 67
Adkins,Mary T. 67
Adkins,Mathew 67
Adkins,McHester 66
Adkins,Nancy 4
Adkins,Nancy 66
Adkins,Noah 65
Adkins,Olaver 4
Adkins,Oma F. 66
Adkins,Parker 67
Adkins,Peter 38
Adkins,Pleasant 66
Adkins,Polley (x) 62
Adkins,Polley 65
Adkins,Polley A. 67
Adkins,Pollie 67
*Adkins,Randle 65
*Adkins,Randolph 67
Adkins,Rebecca 66
Adkins,Rebecca 67
*Adkins,Riley 5
*Adkins,Robert G. 65
Adkins,Ruth P. 67
*Adkins,Sarah 38
Adkins,Sarah 66
Adkins,Sarah 67
*Adkins,Shered W. 67
Adkins,Sidney 12
Adkins,Spicer 65
Adkins,Sterling 66
Adkins,Susan 12
Adkins,Susun 66
*Adkins,Sylvester 12
*Adkins,Sylvester 66
Adkins,Tenasee 66
Adkins,Thomas J. 66
Adkins,Victoria 65
Adkins,Viney 65
Adkins,Viola 65
Adkins,Wesley 66
Adkins,West (x) 62
Adkins,William 12
Adkins,William 38
Adkins,William 67
Adkins,William V. 66
*Adkins,Winchester 67

Adkins,Zerilda 67
Albers,John (x) 42
Albers,John (x) 53
Albert,Benjamin(x)22
Albright,Elias (x)66
Aljoe,Ammacetta 58
Aljoe,Augusta V. 58
Aljoe,Bevely 58
Aljoe,Mary E. 58
Aljoe,Rachael 58
Aljoe,Wiliam W. 58
*Aljoe,William 58
Allen,Dexter 37
Allen,Eliza 37
Allen,Elizabeth 37
Allen,Ellen 37
Allen,Frances l. 12
Allen,Ida 37
*Allen,James 37
Allen,Jennie B. 12
Allen,John 37
*Allen,John W. 37
Allen,Martha 37
Allen,Minnie 37
Allen,Nancy 37
*Allen,Reynolds 37
*Allen,Robert 37
*Allen,Robert B. 12
Allen,Samuel 37
Allen,Sarah 37
Allen,Virginia 37
Allen,Willie 37
Amoss,Agnisetta 83
Amoss,Claressey M. 83
*Amoss,Joshua 83
Amoss,Luvena E. 83
Amoss,Mary 83
Amoss,Mary F. 83
Amoss,Sarah C. 83
Amoss,William 83
*Anderson,Baxter 16
Anderson,Camey 16
Anderson,Clarence(x)12
Anderson,David (x) 21
Anderson,Fannie (x) 12
Anderson,Harriet 16
Anderson,James(x)23
Anderson,John D.(x)21
Anderson,Julia (x) 21
Anderson,Melcina (x)21
Anderson,Perlina(x)23
Anderson,Peter (x) 21
Anderson,William (x)12
Angle,Calvin 55

Angle,Elvira 55
*Angle,Peter 55
Angle,Stephen 55
Ansell,Abreham 77
Ansell,Ann C. 77
Ansell,Elizabeth 76
*Ansell,Malchiah 77
*Ansell,Michael 76
Ansell,Sarah 77
Arther,Albert J. 73
Arther,Alice 72
Arther,Ammasetta 72
Arther,Ann 40
Arther,Anna E. 73
Arther,Benjamin 77
Arther,Bradford 47
Arther,Catherine 47
Artur,Clara B.42
Arthur,Eliza 40
Arther,Eliza J. 72
Arthur,Elizabeth 40
Arthur,Elizabeth 47
Arther,Elizabeth 72
Arther,Elizabeth 77
Arthur,Ella 40
Arthur,Emily 41
Arthur,Emma 54
Arthur,George W.54
Arthur,Georgie 47
Arther,Isaac 72
*Arther,Isaac 73
*Arther,James 72
Arther,James C. 72
Arthur,Jenna 41
Arhtur,John L. 42
*Arther,John M. 72
Arther,John V. 72
Arthur,Josephine 40
Arther,Julia 72
Arther,Julia A. 77
*Arthur,Lewis 40
Arther,Lewis F. 72
Arthur,Lewis V.54
Arthur,Lucetta 47
Arthur,Lucy 40
Arthur,Lucy F. 42
Arthur,Marion 54
Arthur,Martha 47
Arther,Mary A. 77
Arthur,Mary E. 54
Arther,Mary J. 72
Arther,Mary M. 73
Arthur,Morris S.54

*Arthur,Pennel 54
Arther,Rosetta 72
Arther,Sallie 72
Arther,Sallie 73
*Arthur,Sanders 40
Arther,Sarah A. 72
Arthur,Thomas 40
Arthur,Thomas 54
Arther,Thomas 77
Arthur,Thomas H.54
Arthur,Virginia 54
*Arthur,William 41
Arthur,William (x)42
*Arthur,william 47
Arther,William 72
*Ash,Daniel 7
Ash,Hudly B.7
Ash,Levory 7
Ash,Margaret 7
Ash,Marshall 7
Ash,Mary M. 7
Ash,Peter D.7
Ash,Sarah C. 7
Ash,Stephen C.
Ashworth,Elizabeth 27
Ashworth,Harriet 27
Ashworth,Jane 27
Ashworth,Martha 27
Ashworth,Taylor 27
*Ashworth,William 27
Babcock,William (x) 61
Bailey,Andrew (x) 19
Bailey,Harvey (x) 15
Baley,Addie 74
Baley,Catherine 74
Baley,Elizabeth 74
*Baley,George 74
Baley,James 74
Baley,John 74
Baley,Sarah 74
Baley,Sylvester 74
Baker,Elizabeth
Baker,Henry P. (x) 48
Baker,John (x) 16
*Baker,John C. 43
Baker,Leanora 43
Baker,Michael
Baker,Mary O. (x) 48
Baker,Susan
Ball,Albert 24
Ball,Allice 21
Ball,Bell 21
Ball,Bennett 29
Ball,Calvary 21

Ball,Conwelsa 21	Bates,Lucy E. 32	Beckett,Hannah 63
Ball,Edna 29	Bates,Manoah 32	Becket,Henry 29
Ball,Emily 81	Bates,Martha 32	Becket,Isiah O. 28
Ball,Fannie 81	Bates,Martha 39	Becket,James 29
Ball,George 21	Bates,Mary E. 32	Beckett,James R. 63
*Ball,Henry 29	*Bates,Nancy 32	Becket,John H. 28
Ball,Hezekiah 29	Bates,Olive E. 32	Becket,John L. 29
*Ball,Isaac 21	Bates,Peter 39	Becket,Julia A. 29
Ball,Jennie 24	Bates,Susan 32	*Beckett,Lewis C.63
Ball,Jennie 81	Bates,Susan A. 32	Becket,Louisa 28
*Ball,Jeremiah 24	Bates,Thomas 32	Becket,Lucinda 29
Ball,John C. 29	Bates,Willis R. 32	Becket,Martha A. 28
Ball,Joseph 81	Baumgardner,Alonzo 16	Becket,Mary 28
*Ball,Lafayette 81	Baumgardner,Charles A. 16	Becket,Mary S. 28
Ball,Louisa 24	Baumgardner,Cora V. 16	Beckett,Mary S. 63
Ball,Luella 29	Baumgardener,Enery 17	Becket,Moses 28
Ball,Martha E. 81	Baumgardener,Frank 17	Becket,Oliver 29
Ball,Mary 25	Baumgardner,Fredrick 17	Becket,Rebecca 28
Ball,Mary 81	Baumgardiner,Grant 5	Becket,Rebecca M. 28
Ball,Mediva 29	*Baumgardiner,James 5	Becket,Samuel 29
Ball,Parilla 29	Baumgardiner,John 5	Beckett,Susan 63
Ball,Susan 21	*Baumgardener,John 17	Becket,Susan J. 28
Ball,Telitha 29	*Baumgardner,John B. 16	Becket,Susanna 29
Ball,Virginia (x) 28	Baumgardner,Louisa 16	Beckett,Thomas (x)69
Ball,Willie 21	Baumgardener,Malinda 17	Becket,William C. 28
Ball,Willie E.81	Baumgardiner,Margaret 5	Beckett,William L.13
Barbour,Elisha 33	Baumgardener,Margaret 17	Beckley,Charles 21
Barbour,Henry E. 33	Baumgardener,Motire 17	Beckley,Henrietta 21
*Barbour,Henry 33	Baumgardiner,Phillip 5	Beckley,Rodrick 21
Barbour,Jacob D. 33	Baumgardiner,Sarah 6	*Beckley,William 21
Barbour,Martha 33	Baumgardiner,Valentine 5	Beils,Almira 84
Barbour,Samuel 33	Baumgardiner,Welcom 5	Beils,Anna A.84
Barbour,Sarah J. 33	*Baumgardiner,William 6	*Beils,Anthony 84
Barbour,Susan 33	Baumgardner,William L. 16	Beils,Augusta 84
Barger,Elizabeth (x)50	Baumgardener,Worth 17	Beils,Barbery 84
Barger,Wiliam (x) 50	Bayless,Mary S. 69	Beils,Catherine 83
Barker,Jeneva 81	Bayless,Thomas 69	*Beils,Edward 83
*Barker,John 81	*Bayless,Thomas H. 69	Beils,Emily 84
Barker,Julia 81	Bayless,William A. 69	Beils,Frank 84
Barker,Nimrod 81	Beaker,Anthony 83	Beils,Georgia 84
Barker,Sarah C. 81	*Beaker,Henry 83	Beils,Henry 84
*Barnett,Charles 71	Beaker,Joanna 83	Beils,Isabel 84
Barnett,John F. (x) 11	Becket,Adaline 28	Beils,John 84
Barnett,Louisa 71	*Becket,Andrew L. 29	Beils,Joseph 84
Barnett,Martha F.(x)11	Becket,Arvilla 28	Beils,Julia 84
Barnett,Vila W. 71	Becket,Charles 28	Beils,Mary 84
Bartrem,Rebecca (x) 65	Beckett,Charles M. 63	Beils,Matilda 84
*Bates,Andrew 32	Becket,Charles W. 29	Beils,William 84
Bates,Eliza 39	Becket,Cora 28	Bell,Marion(x)26
Bates,Farelander 32	Becket,Emesly 28	Bellemy,Georgie E. 17
Bates,Georgie 39	Becket,Emily S. 29	*Bellemy,Henry C. 17
Bates,John 39	Becket,Fannie 28	Bellemy,Mary 17
Bates,Julia 39	Beckett,Francis M. 63	Bellemy,Sarah T. 17
*Bates,Lee 39	Becket,George 28	Benam,John A. (x)20

Bench,Carolina 25
Bench,Eliza J. 25
Bench,Elizabeth 25
*Bench,James 25
Bench,James R. 25
Bench,John 25
Bench,Margaret 25
Bench,Mary 25
Bench,Sallie 25
Bench,Sarah 25
*Bench,William 25
Benchfield,Harriet 36
Benchfield,Henry 36
Benchfield,James C. 36
*Benchfield,John 36
Benchfield,Levisa 36
Benchfield,Manerva 36
Benchfield,Margaret 36
Benchfield,Martha 36
Benchfield,Samuel 36
Benchfield,Susana 36
Benchfield,Wader H. 36
Benchfield,William 36
Bensen,Hester A. 4
Bensen,Hugh B. 4
*Bensen,John L. 4
Bensen,Laura W. 4
Bensen,William 4
Berry,Alice 77
Berry,Carlie L. 77
Berry,Eliza 77
Berry,Letecia 77
Berry,Louisa A. 77
Berry,Mary J. 77
*Berry,Philo B. 77
Berry,Samuel 77
Berry,Sarah 77
Beuhring,Francis E. 36
*Beuhring,Fredrick 36
Beuhring,Henry H. 36
Beuhring,Lee D. 36
Beuhring,Mary L. 36
Beuhring,Nora B. 36
Beuhring,Virginia E. 36
Bias,Almedd (x) 53
Bias,America 64
Bias,Andersen 6
Bias,Andrew 55
Bias,Benjamin 65
*Bias,Beny 6
Bias,Blackburn 64
Bias,Catherine 70
Bias,Clifton 65
Bias,Cordoria 69

*Bias,Daniel 69
*Bias,Daniel B. 69
Bias,David A. 22
Bias,Dolphin 70
Bias,Elisha 62
Bias,Elizabeth 55
Bias,Elizabeth 70
Bias,Emaline 6
Bias,Galiton 64
Bias,George 69
Bias,George H. 55
Bias,George W. 57
Bias,Hester A. 65
Bias,Hester Ann 6
*Bias,Hughie 70
Bias,Jacob B. 62
Bias,James (x) 6
*Bias,James 63
Bias,James A. 22
*Bias,James F. 57
Bias,James L. 55
*Bias,James M. 64
Bias,James W. 64
Bias,Jenetta 69
Bias,John 6
Bias,Joseph B.(x) 68
Bias,Leandir 6
Bias,Letha 64
Bias,Levie O. 69
Bias,Lewis 6
Bias,Linzy (x) 53
Bias,Lucinda 55
Bias,Lucy A. 62
Bias,Malissey J. 69
Bias,Marion 64
Bias,Martha 62
Bias,Martha (x) 53
Bias,Martha 70
Bias,Martha F. 55
Bias,Martha R. 22
Bias,Mary 6
Bias,Mary 63
Bias,Mary A. 62
Bias,Mary M. 55
Bias,Mary M. 69
Bias,Mary W. 64
Bias,Millard 65
Bias,Millington 63
Bias,nancy 6
Bias,Pricilla 62
Bias,Rebecca A. 64
Bias,Richard 70
Bias,Riley M. 22
*Bias,Roland 62

*Bias,Roland 70
Bias,Roland S. 62
Bias,Sarah 6
Bias,Sarah 70
Bias,Sarah A. 57
Bias,Sereptha 62
Bias,Thomas (x) 68
*Bias,Thomas A. 65
Bias,Wilbert 55
Bias,William (x) 68
*Bias,William 22
*Bias,William 55
Bias,William 57
Bias,William 64
Bibb,Clara 9
Bibb,George 9
Bibb,Hattie 9
Bibb,Hellen 9
Bibb,James 9
Bibb,John 9
Bibb,Joseph 9
Bibb,Margaret 9
*Bibb,Robert 9
Bibb,Victoria 9
Bibb,Virginia 9
Bird,Hannah (x) 58
Bishop,Elizabeth 5
Bishop,James S. 5
*Bishop,John 5
Bishop,Martha 5
Black,Allice 20
Black,Ametha 20
*Black,Camel 20
Black,Cintha 20
Black,Elizabeth 20
Black,Ezra 20
Black,Ida 20
Black,Isabel 20
Black,Jane 20
Black,John 20
Black,Lovie 20
Black,McCellen 20
Black,Theodore 20
Black,Virginia 20
*Black,William 20
Blackwood,Charles W. 21
Blackwood,James H. 21
Blackwood,Joel H. 21
*Blackwood,Joseph 21
Blackwood,Mary (x)18
Blackwood,Robert E. 21
Blag,Eli A. 19
Blag,Ella B. 19
Blag,Hannah 19

Blag, John 19
*Blag, Joseph 19
Blag, Laley 19
Blag, Loley 19
Blag, Mary A. 19
Blake, Anna 52
Blake, Auslin 76
Blake, Ceraus 53
Blake, Clarressey 73
Blake, Daniel M. 80
Blake, Dolph 80
Blake, Edna (x) 13
Blake, Elizabeth 80
Blake, Emily J. 73
Blake, Emma 52
Blake, Henry (x) 51
*Blake, Isaac 52
Blake, Ivana J. 80
*Blake, Jeremiah 73
*Blake, Jeremiah 80
Blake, John M. 80
Blake, John P. 73
Blake, John T. 76
Blake, Lafyette 76
Blake, Lecetta 80
Blake, Louisa (x) 51
Blake, Louisa 80
Blake, Maggie 53
Blake, Margaret 73
Blake, Marilla 77
Blake, Mary 52
Blake, Mary F. 77
Blake, Mattie 80
*Blake, Morris 80
Blake, Nancy 76
Blake, Nancy 80
Blake, Pennell 76
Blake, Preston 76
Blake, Robert L. 76
Blake, Robert M. 77
Blake, Rosa 80
Blake, Rose (x) 51
*Blake, Sarah 11
Blake, Sarah C. 76
Blake, Sarah M. 80
Blake, Teletha 80
Blake, Valentine 73
Blake, Virginia 53
Blake, William H. 77
Blankenship, Almeda 55
*Blankenship, Aranna 5
Blankenship, Charles A. 55
Blankenship, Charles E. 32
Blankenship, Charlott 43

*Blankenship, E.D. 43
Blankenship, Gerald 43
Blankenship, Gerturde 55
*Blankenship, Henry 32
Blankenship, James (x)3
Blankenship, Jefferson (x)2
Blankenship, John (x) 2
Blankenship, Louisa L. 43
Blankenship, Margaret 32
*Blankenship, Marlin 55
Blankenship, Mary F. 32
Blankenship, Mary V. 43
Blankenship, Rosalie 32
Blankenship, Samuel D.(x)55
Blankenship, Sarah 43
Bledsew, Allice 60
*Bledsew, Charles L. 62
Bledsew, Emily F. 62
Bledsew, Francis 60
Bledsew, Grant 60
Bledsew, Hannah 60
*Bledsew, James A. 62
Bledsew, John 60
Bledsew, Malissey 60
Bledsew, Rachel 62
Bledsew, Waldon 60
*Bledsew, William 60
Blume, Albert 16
Blume, Evaline 16
*Blume, Evan W. 16
Blume, George 16
Blume, Henry C. 16
Blume, Ida A. 16
Blume, Luke 16
Blume, William 16
Boggs, Eliza 50
Boggs, James H. 50
Boggs, John A. 50
*Boggs, John G. 50
Boggs, Josephine 50
Boggs, Kate 50
Boggs, Lorenzo 50
Boggs, Sarah 50
Boggs, Ulysses W. 50
Boice, Anna F. 9
*Boice, James 9
Boice, Mary L. 9
Boice, Matilda 9
Boland, Thomas (x) 2
Bonner, Amelia 43
Bonner, Isaac N. 43
*Bonner, John W. 43
Booten, Elizabeth(x)36
*Booth, Ballard 65

Booth, Eliza 65
Booth, Emily J. 5
Booth, John S. 65
Booth, Mary 5
*Booth, William 5
*Boulin, James B. 79
Boulin, Margaret 79
Boulin, Rebecca 79
Bowden, Baxter(x)38
*Bowden, Cintha 40
Bowden, Columbus 40
Bowden, Elizabeth 40
Bowden, Evaline J. 40
*Bowden, James 40
Bowden, John E. 40
Bowden, Mary E.(x)38
Bowden, Stewart 40
Bowden, Susan(x)38
Bowen, Albert 78
Bowen, Alice V. 78
Bowen, Ammasetta 78
Bowen, Ann 78
Bowen, Anna C. 78
Bowen, Charles 78
*Bowen, Dyke 7
Bowen, Edward 7
Bowen, Emma 78
Bowen, Ezekiel 78
Bowen, Ezekiel J. 78
Bowen, Flora A. 20
Bowen, Georgie J. 20
Bowen, Garland 7
Bowen, Grovener 20
Bowen, Henry L. 20
Bowen, Hensen H. 7
Bowen, Isadira 7
Bowen, Mary 78
Bowen, Mary E. 20
Bowen, Mary S. 78
Bowen, Missouri 78
Bowen, Monroe 78
Bowen, Morris 7
Bowen, Sarah A. 7
*Bowen, Strother 20
Bowen, Susan 20
Bowen, Susan 78
*Bowen, Sylvester 78
Bowen, Wayne P. 7
Bowen, William 78
*Bowen, Zayes 78
Boyer, Philip (x) 40
Bramlett, Armelda 68
Bramlett, Eugenia 68
Bramlett, Josephine 68

Bramlett, Linnie M. 68
*Bramlett, William 68
*Brammer, Clark K. 48
Brammer, George L. 48
Brammer, Sarah P. 48
Brammer, Sarah V. 48
Brammer, Willie V. 48
*Branam, Catherine 24
Branam, Elizabeth 24
Branam, George 24
Branam, John 24
Branam, Mary 24
Branam, Michael 24
Branam, Peter 24
Branam, William 24
Bread, James (x)20
Bright, Emma D. 13
*Bright, Rodick D. 13
Brooks, Fredrick (x) 15
Brown, Adaline 31
Brown, Amasetta 31
Brown, Ammasetta 31
Brown, Anjalina 68
Brown, Ann 68
*Brown, Anna M. (x) 69
Brown, Beverly 68
Brown, Cintha 18
Brown, Edgar S. 18
Brown, Eliza (x) 17
Brown, Isabell 68
*Brown, James 31
Brown, Jane 31
*Brown, Jefferson 68
Brown, Josephine 31
Brown, Kitty 31
Brown, Labon L. 31
Brown, Lemuel 68
Brown, Lenvita 18
Brown, Levina A. 18
Brown, Margaret (x) 69
Brown, Mary O. (x) 16
Brown, Morris G. 18
Brown, Permilla 31
Brown, Polina 68
Brown, Sarah M. 18
*Brown, Thomas 18
Brown, William W. 31
Brown, William (x) 16
Brown, William (x) 17
Brown, William (x) 48
Bruce, John 5
Bruce, Rebecca 5
Bruce, Riley 5
Bryon, Adaline F. 83

Bryon, Albert G. 83
Bryan, Chapman, 21
Bryon, Clarissey C.83
Bryan, Elizabeth 13
Bryan, Francis 21
Bryon, Gabriel 82
Bryon, John H. 83
Bryon, Julia 83
Bryon, Julia A. 82
*Bryon, Lawrence 83
*Bryan, Lewis 74
*Bryan, Lucy 21
Bryon, Mary A. 82
Bryon, Mary E. 83
Bryon, Matilda 82
*Bryon, Nimrod 82
Bryon, Nimrod F. 83
Bryon, Parthenia 83
Bryon, Robert E. 82
Bryan, Sarah G. 74
Bryon, Semantha 82
Bryon, Thomas 82
Bryon, Verena 83
*Bryan, Whitfield 13
*Bryon, William 83
Bryant, Andrew 40
*Bryant, Dennis 40
Bryant, Isabella 2
Bryant, James 2
Bryant, John R. 40
Bryant, Lebert 40
Bryant, Lucy F. 40
*Bryant, Marion 2
Bryant, Martha E. (x) 56
Bryant, Mary A. 40
Bryant, Thomas 49
Bryant, Virginia 40
Bryant, William (x) 56
*Buffington, Peter C. 52
Buffington, Garland 52
Buffington, Sarah 52
*Buck, Anthony 10
Buck, Bridget 10
Buck, James 10
Buck, John 10
Buck, Mollie 10
Buck, Thomas 10
Bukey, Eveline 48
Bukey, Preston M. 48
Bukey, Rebecca 48
*Bukey, Rudolph 48
Burdett, Elizabeth 18
Burdett, Frank L. 18
*Burdett, James R. 18

Burdett, Mary E. 18
Burdett, Jeneva C. 18
Burdett, William 18
*Burks, Beverly B. 51
Burks, Georgie(x)36
Burkley, Charles (x)7
Burkley, Eliza (x)7
Burks, Charlers H. 56
Burks, Eliza L. 52
Burks, Elizabeth 35
Burks, Elizabeth 51
Burks, Elizabeth 56
Burks, George 51
Burks, Helen M. 52
*Burks, Jesse 35
Burks, John 35
*Burks, Lewis H. 52
Burks, Martha 51
Burks, Martha E. 51
Burks, Mary 35
Burks, Minnie L. 51
Burks, Sarah 35
Burks, Thomas (x)49
*Burks, William 35
Burns, Allen J. (x) 76
Burrel, Ashberry (x)51
Burres, Daniel (x) 79
Burton, Allice 20
Burton, America 20
Burton, Andrew 20
Burton, John 20
Burton, Mary 20
Burton, Morris 20
Burton, Victoria 20
*Burton, William 20
Butcher, Ann F. 43
Butcher, Charles 45
Butcher, Clemtine 45
Butcher, Edward 45
*Butcher, Getmont 45
*Butcher, James 11
Butcher, Jennie B. 45
Butcher, Margery 11
Butcher, Mattie E. 45
Butcher, Morton 45
Butcher, Rachael 11
Butcher, Reuben 11
Butcher, Sarah M. 43
Butcher, Temima 45
Butcher, Wiliam 45
Butcher, William H. 11
*Butcher, Worden 43
Buxfield, Joseph 73
Buxfield, Mary 73

*Buxfield,Richard 73
Buxfield,Thomas 73
Cain,Ann 59
Cain,Bryan 59
Cain,Henry C.59
*Cain,Martin 59
Cain,Mary 59
Cain,Michael 59
Cain,Peter 59
Cain,Thomas 59
Cain,Walter 59
Cain,William T.59
Camard,Frank 25
*Camard,George 25
Camard,Mary 25
Campbell,Clayton 44
Campbell,Harriet 19
*Campbell,Henry C.44
Campbell,Henry J. 44
Campbell,Leinta 44
Campbell,Seena (x)77
Campbell,Wesley(x)79
*Campbell,William 19
Canard,Cora Bell 80
Canard,Elsea 80
Canard,Ephram (x)26
*Canard,Howard 27
Canard,Joseph 27
Canard,Mary M. 27
Canard,Nancy 27
Canard,Sarah A. 27
Canard,Thomas 80
*Canard,William H.80
Cannon,Matilda (x)63
Cardwell,Henry 36
*Cardwell,Manoah 36
Cardwell,Melvil 36
Cardwell,Sarah 36
Cardwell,Semantha 36
cardwell,Susan 36
Cardwell,William 36
Carpenter,Fannie 22
Carpenter,Frances 22
*Carpenter,John 22
Carpenter,Mahaley 22
Carpenter,Matilda S. 22
Carpenter,Savina(x)28
Carroll,Augustis 43
Carroll,Charles 43
Carroll,Ellen 43
Carroll,Kate V.43
Carroll,Margaret 43
Carroll,Mary 43
*Carroll,Thomas 43

Carson,Albey(x)9
Carson,Allice(x)9
Carson,Arkansas(x)9
Carson,Caroline (x)9
Carson,George(x)9
Carson,James 37
*Carson,John 37
Carson,Mary 37
Carson,Stephen(x)9
Carter,Algalena 60
Carter,Benjamin 34
Carter,Eliza (x)53
Carter,Eliza 31
Carter,George H.34
*Carter,James 31
Carter,Jennie 31
*Carter,Lemuel 34
Carter,Louisa 34
Carter,Matilda F.34
*Carter,Salem 60
Carter,Thomas 60
Carter,Thornton 31
Carver,Elmira 49
*Carver,James A. 49
Carver,James J.49
*Cassell,John W.36
Cassell,Lura B.36
Cassell,Margret 36
Cassell,Mary 36
Chapman,Abigal 72
Chapman,Albert 25
Chapman,Albert 4
Chapman,Charles 23
Chapman,Charles 24
Chapman,Charles 25
Chapman,Edna S.30
Chapman,Elen 29
*Chapman,Eli 23
Chapman,Elijah 29
Chapman,Eliza 79
Chapman,Eliza 8
Chapman,Elizabeth 29
Chapman,Ellen 23
Chapman,Everman 23
Chapman,Ezra 23
Chapman,Fannie 4
Chapman,Frances 79
Chapman,George 79
Chapman,Georgia 72
Chapman,Green 25
Chapman,Henrietta 24
Chapman,Henry 23
*Chapman,Henry 24

Chapman,Henry G. 29
chapman,Ida 72
Chapman,Ira 23
Chapman,Isa 24
Chapman,James 8
Chapman,Jenetta 23
Chapman,Jennie 23
*Chapman,Jerman 23
Chapman,John 23
Chapman,John G. 29
Chapman,John S. 25
Chapman,Julia 24
Chapman,Laura J. 79
Chapman,Linnie 24
Chapman,Luana 23
Chapman,Lucy 25
Chapman,Lucy M.8
Chapman,Luella 23
Chapman,Mary 4
Chapman,Mary A. 25
Chapman,Matilda 30
Chapman,Milda 23
Chapman,Missouri 4
Chapman,Oliva 29
Chapman,Randolph 23
Chapman,Sarah H. 29
*Chapman,Taswell 72
Chapman,Thersey 25
Chapman,Thomas 24
Chapman,Thomas 8
Chapman,Verina 29
*Chapman,William 25
*Chapman,William 29
Chapman,William 24
Chapman,William 79
Chapman,William 8
*Chapman,Willie 4
*Chase,Abel J. 80
chase,Clarinda 80
Chase,McCellen 80
Chase,Sarah J. 80
Chase,Sheriden 80
Chase,Sienda 80
Chase,William F.80
Chatterton,Amanda 34
Chatterton,Edna 34
*Chatterton,George 34
Chatterton,Mary 34
Chatterton,Richard 34
Chatterton,Roxey 34
Childers,Abreham M.68
Childers,Ada 57
Childers,Adaline 65
Childers,Alexander 68

Childers,Almeda V.68
Childers,Amanda 68
Childers,Andrew 68
Childers,Ann 4
childers,Ann C. 68
Childers,Anna B. 5
Childers,Benjamin 5
Childers,Benjamin 65
*Childers,Benjamin 68
*Childers,Bettie 65
Childers,Carolina 65
Childers,Cathrine 5
Childers,Charles F.5
Childers,Cintha 65
Childers,Colonel 68
Childers,Daniel 65
Childers,Elizabeth 68
Childers,Elizabeth 68
*Childers,Filman 65
Childers,Florence 68
*Childers,George W.6
Childers,Greenville 68
Childers,Jacob G. 68
Childers,James 68
Childers,James M. 5
Childers,Jeneva 68
Childers,John A.6
Childers,John M. 5
Childers,John T. 68
Childers,Joseph 65
Childers,Joseph 68
*Childers,Louisa 57
Childers,Louisa 68
Childers,Mary 6
Childers,Mary F. 68
Childers,Mary J. 68
Childers,Mary M. 68
Childers,Melina 68
Childers,Melville M.68*
Childers,Nancy 68
Childers,Nancy 68
Childers,Nancy M.68
Childers,Nancy(x)68
Childers,Newton 5
Childers,Oliver 57
Childers,Patrick H. 5
Childers,Phillips M. 5
*Childers,Royal 68
Childers,Royal A. 68
Childers,Royal B. 68
Childers,Rufus J. 5
Childers,Samuel 5
-*Childers,Samuel 5
Childers,Sarah A.6

Childers,Sarah E. 5
Childers,Sarah E. 68
Childers,Sarah J.68
*Childers,Shim 65
Childers,Spencer 68
Childers,Victoria 6
Childers,Virginia 6
Childers,Walter 65
*Childers,William 4
*Childers,William 6
*Childers,William 68
Chinn,John W.(x)51
Christian,James 49
Christian,Mary 49
*Christian,William 49
Christy,Agnes 19
Christy,James 79
Christy,Jane 19
Christy,Jefferson 79
Christy,Jemima 79
Christy,Jerome 79
Christy,John 19
Christy,John M.19
christy,Martha 19
*Christy,Thomas 79
*Christy,William 19
Church,Archibald(x)15
*Cinstater,Catherine 84
Clagg,Bennett V.82
Clagg,James 82
Clagg,John W. 82
*Clagg,Julius 82
Clagg,Mary F. 82
Clagg,Matilda 82
Clagg,Nancy 82
Clagg,Rebecca 82
Clagg,Thomas 82
*Clark,Abel H.50
Clark,Alexander 44
Clark,Alma 50
Clark,Angelia(x)3
Clark,Catherine 7
*Clark,Charles 9
*Clark,Daniel 73
Clark,Edward 50
Clark,Elizabeth(x)19
Clark,Elizabeth 44
Clark,Emaline 50
Clark,Emily 44
Clark,Frank 45
Clark,Franklin C.(x)19
Clark,Fredrick 44
Clark,Hanner 50
Clark,Harriet 73

*Clark,Harvey 50
Clark,James L. 50
clark,John A. 50
Clark,John B. 42
Clark,John R.50
Clark,Julia A. 44
Clark,Lorenzo 44
Clark,Martha 42
Clark,Martha 44
Clark,Mary E.44
Clark,Mary M.7
Clark,Minnie 44
Clark,Mirtie 50
Clark,Nancy 9
Clark,Nancy(x)29
Clark,Robert 44
*Clark,Roland 45
Clark,Sarah 50
*Clark,Silas M.44
Clark,Susie 45
*Clark,Taylor 7
Clark,Thomas 42
Clark,Thomas 44
*Clark,William 42
Clark,William 50
*Clark,William L.44
*Claughton,Richard 42
Claughton,Susan 42
Clay,Berton 66
Clay,Cintha A. 66
*Clay,James 66
Clements,Malinda(x)58
Clemonds,Henry (x)49
Coalman,Loucilla(x)20
Coalman,Margaret(x)20
Coalman,Mary E.(x)20
Coalman,William(x)20
Cochran,Abey J.43
Cochran,Amelia C.43
*Cochran,Andrew 16
Cochran,Ella D.16
Cochran,Ida A.43
*Cochran,Jacob 43
Cochran,Mary 16
Cochran,Thomas 16
Cochran,Vallentine 16
Cockings,Anna M.12
Cockings,Carrie L. 12
Cockings,Joseph 12
Cockings,Mariah 12
*Cockings,Thomas 12
Coe,John 52
Coe,Lewis R. 52
Coe,Margaret 52

Coe, Mary 52
*Coe, Sheldon S. 52
Coffman, Alfred 41
Coffman, Athen 41
Coffman, Elizabeth 41
Coffman, James 41
Coffman, Lucy 41
*Coffman, Noah 41
*Collins, Aaron 6
Collins, Enoch 6
Collins, John (x) 19
Collins, Mary J. 72
Collins, Millie J.(x)53
Collins, Nathan 72
Collins, Susan 6
*Collins, William 6
Collins, Zilpha 6
Colwell, Elizabeth 74
Colwell, Fleming 74
*Colwell, Robert 74
Comer, America 28
Comer, Elizabeth 28
Comer, Susanna 28
*Comer, William 28
Condon, Catherine 15
Condon, John 15
*Condon, Michael 15
*Conner, Adison 22
*Conner, Andrew 28
Conner, Charles 28
*Conner, Conwelsa 28
Conner, Eliza 28
Conner, Emeretta 22
Conner, Everman 26
Conner, Harriet 26
*Conner, James 26
Conner, James 28
Conner, John (x)19
Conner, John 28
Conner, John M. 22
*Conner, John M. 26
Conner, Joseph 22
*Conner, Joseph 26
Conner, Lewis (x)26
Conner, Luvina 26
Conner, Martha 26
Conner, Mary 28
Conner, Milley 28
Conner, Randolph 26
Conner, Sarah E. 28
Conner, Virginia 28
*Conner, William 28
*Cook, Abner 3
*Cook, Abner 48

Cook, Catherine 3
Cook, Clarinda 41
Cook, Eliza A. 3
Cook, Elizabeth 40
Cook, Emily J. 41
Cook, Florena 49
Cook, General 41
Cook, George A. 3
Cook, Henry (x)39
Cook, Henry L. 3
Cook, James (x)2
*Cook, James 41
Cook, John 40
Cook, Julius(x)59
Cook, Louisa 47
Cook, Martha 47
Cook, Martha A. 3
Cook, Mary 3
Cook, Mary F. 49
Cook, Nancy 48
*Cook, Peter 40
Cook, Sarah 40
*Cook, Thomas 47
Curnell, Bettie 77
Curnell, Catherine 77
*Curnell, James 77
Curnell, John 77
Cornell, Levisa 76
*Cornell, Martin 76
Curnell, Mary 77
Curnell, Sheriden 77
Cox, Adelia 7
Cox, Albert E. 7
Cox, Alvin H. 18
Cox, Edward 7
Cox, Eugene L. 7
Cox, Frank L. 18
Cox, Georgie 18
Cox, Harris, M. 7
*Cox, James O. 18
Cox, Jennie C. 18
*Cox, John A. 7
*Cox, Joseph 7
Cox, Margaret 18
Cox, Mariah 7
Cox, Saka 7
Cox, Sarah 7
Cox, William L. 7
*Creel, George A. 16
Creel, Lizzie 16
Creig, Anna A. 17
Creig, John H. 17
Creig, Lorena F. 17
Creig, Martha E. 17

Creig, Mary I. 17
Creig, Mary J. 17
Creig, Sarah 17
Creig, Thomas A. 17
*Creig, William 17
Creig, William R. 17
*Cremeans, Amanda 82
Cremeans, Andrew 66
Cremeans, Arminta 66
Cremeans, Burton 69
Cremeans, Catherie 65
Cremeans, Daniel D. 69
Cremens, Delila 81
Cremeans, Delpha 66
Cremeans, Elizabeth 69
Cremens, Elizabeth 82
Cremeans, Haley 65
Crimens, Henova 9
Cremeans, Henry 78
Cremeans, Henry S. 69
*Cremeans, Hiram 65
Cremeans, James (x)6
*Cremeans, James 69
Cremeans, James W. 69
*Crimens, John 9
*Cremens, John W. 82
*Cremeans, Lewis 66
Cremeans, Mahaley 65
Cremeans, Mary 65
Cremeans, Mary 78
Cremens, Mary 82
Crimens, Mary A. 9
Cremeans, Mary A. 65
Cremens, Menitha 81
Cremeans, Mintie 65
Cremeans, Montaville 82
Cremens, Nancy 82
Cremeans, Nathan 82*
Cremeans, Palina 66
Crimens, Patrick 9
Cremeans, Perlina H. 66
Cremens, Pollie 81
*Cremeans, Richard 78
*Cremens, Sarah 83
Cremeans, Sarah A.(x)6
Cremens, Sarah C. 82
Cremeans, Sarah S. 69
Cremeans, Stalina 66
Cremeans, Susan (x)6
Cremeans, Susanna 66
Cremens, Walter 81
*Cremeans, Wesley 65
*Cremeans, William 66
Cremeans, William L. 69

Cremens, Winget 81
Crooks, Ann E. 14
Crooks, Everman(x)33
*Crooks, John C 14
Crooks, John W. 14
Crooks, Lucy E. 14
Crooks, Lucy H.31
Crooks, Mary W. 14
Crooks, Mitchell(x)31
*Crooks, Morran 31
Crooks, Robert E. 14
Crooks, Virginia H.14
Crooks, William 31
Crooks, William H.14
Crowder, David 21
*Crowder, Henry 21
Crowder, John J.21
Crowder, Mirum 21
Crowder, Sarah A.21
Crowder, Sarah M.21
Crump, Elizabeth 56
Crump, Ella 56
Crump, George 56
*Crump, George W.41
*Crump, Isaac 56
Crump, Martha 56
Crump, Mary 56
Crump, Nancy 56
Crump, Nannie 56
Crump, Nettie 41
Crump, Susan 41
Cunningham, Amanda(x)19
Cunningham, Harry C. 19
*Cunningham, John M.19
Cunningham, Johnathan 19
Cunningham, Lucy H. 19
Cunningham, Mary 19
Cunningham, Mary J. 19
Curnell see Cornell
Currey, Bennett 22
Currey, Ida M.22
Currey, James F. 22
Currey, John C. 22
Currey, Martha 22
*Currey, William 22
Dalmer, James (x)16
Daulton, James W.(x)62
Davidson, Charles A.71
Davidson, John A. 71
Davidson, Martha 71
Davidson, Samuel H. 71
Davidson, Sarah D. 71
*Davidson, William 71
Davidson, William C.71

Davis, Abreham 4
Davis, Adaline 4
*Davis, Adison 81
Davis, Alfred 4
Davis, Allen B.72
*Davis, Alven 4
Davis, America 72
Davis, Bradford(x)54
Davis, Charles 73
Davis, Cintha 4
Davis, Cora 29
Davis, Cortis(x)31
Davis, Drucilla 31
Davis, Edna(x)4
*Davis, Elizabeth 73
Davis, Elizabeth 81
Davis, Flora 31
Davis, Florence 55
Davis, Francis 4
Davis, Gallaton(x)56
Davis, Georgie 55
*Davis, Greenville 55
*Davis, Harrison 31
Davis, Henderson 31
Davis, Henry L.29
Davis, Ida 55
Davis, Isabel 55
Davis, Jackson, J.72
Davis, Jane 29
Davis, Jefferson 4
Davis, Jefferson 72
*Davis, Jesse 29
Davis, Jesse 73
Davis, Jesse M.29
Davis, John M.81
Davis, Joseph S. 72
Davis, Lilla 55
Davis, Lisha 72
Davis, Louisa 31
Davis, Lucinda 29
Davis, Lunetta 22
Davis, Manera 29
Davis, Margaret(x)2
Davis, Mary 31
Davis, Mary 55
Davis, Mary E. 22
Davis, Mary J.73
DAvis, Mary(x)31
Davis, Milton J. 4
Davis, Missouria 31
Davis, Nancy 72
Davis, Otis 4
Davis, Paul 31

Davis, Permilla(x)14
Davis, Randolph 4
Davis, Samuel H.72
Davis, Sarah 73
Davis, Susan 22
*Davis, Thomas 22
*Davis, Thomas J.29
Davis, Thomas W.72
Davis, Ulysses 31
*Davis, Valentine 4
Davis, Victor 55
Davis, Walter 4
Davis, William 29
Davis, William 55
Davis, William B.4
Davis, William W. 31
Deal, Albert 74
Diel, Alexander 70
Diel, Almeda 60
Diel, Benjamin 60
Deal, Bettie 74
Deal, Cad C.22
Diel, Catherine 70
Deal, Elenyey 22
*Diel, Elisha 60
Diel, Emily 70
Deal, Frank 74
*Deal, Henry H.22
*Diel, John 70
Deal, Lewis 73
*Deal, Lewis 73
Deal, Liddie 74
Diel, Mary F. 60
Diel, Nancy(x)70
Deal, Robert 74
Deal, Rosey D.73
Deal, Ruth 22
Diel, Tabitha 70
Dean, Arabella 16
*Dean, Patsey 15
Delantern, Elizabeth(x)58
Dennison, James A. 72
Dennison, Jenett 72
*Dennison, John 72
Dennisson, Mary 72
Derton, Albert A. 6
Derton, Ann 15
Derton, Elizabeth(x)17
Derton, Elmore F.15
Derton, George 15
*Derton, Harrison 15
Derton, Henrietta 6
*Derton, Henry 6
Derton, Henry J.17

Derton,Isabel 15
*Derton,John 16
Derton,John T.16
Derton,Joseph 15
Derton,Louisa 16
Derton,Louisa A.16
*Derton,Maggie 15
Derton,Mary 15
Derton,Mary A.15
Derton,Mary E. 6
Derton,Sarah F.6
*Derton,William 15
Derton,William Z.16
Devore,Fannie(x)25
Devore,Susan(x)25
Diamond,Emma 50
Diamond,Isabel 50
Diamond,Isabella 50
Diamond,James 50
*Diamond,Obadiah 50
Diamond,Susan 50
Diamond,William T.50
*Dick,Andrew 16
Dick,Anna E.(x)58
Dicks,Ballard 59
Dicks,Benjamin 59
Dicks,Casander 59
Dicks,Catherine 59
Dicks,David H. 59
Dicks,Henry J.59
Dick,Henry L.(x)58
Dick,Ida A.16
*Dicks,Joseph 59
Dick,Lena E.16
Dicks,Margaret 59
Dick,Mary V.16
Dick,Morris F.(x)58
Diel see Deal
Dietz,Benjamin 50
Dietz,Charles H.51
Dietz,Charlott 45
Dietz,George 45
*Dietz,Hugo 45
Dietz,Nonnan 51
*Dietz,Otto 51
Dietz,Rosanna 51
Dietz,Willie G.50
Dillon,Adalade 2
*Dillon,Benjamin 2
Dillon,Catherine 2
Dillon,Charles 2
Dillon,Claudius 2
Dillion,Elizabeth 32

*Dillon,John L.2
Dillon,John M.2
Dillon,John R.2
Dillion,Julia 32
Dillon,Julius 2
Dillon,Mary A. 2
Dillon,Nannie 2
Dillon,Orenda J.2
*Dillon,Reece P.2
Dillon,Ruth A. 2
Dillon,Sarah E. 2
Dillon,Stephen D.2
Dillon,Susan 2
Dillon,Thomas J.2
Dillon,William J. 2
*Dillion,William 32
Dodds,Charles V.11
Dodds,Harriet V.11
*Dodds,John 11
Dodds,Margaret 11
Dodds,Rebecca J.11
Dodson,Albert G.32
Dodson,Amanda 32
Dodson,Edgar 32
Dodson,Henry 32
Dodson,Ida 32
Dodson,Jese B.32
Dodson,Lucetta 32
Dodson,Nancy (x)32
Doland,Bridget 19
Doland,Frances 65
*Doland,George 71
*Doland,John 65
Doland,John D.65
Doland,Jonna E.71
Doland,Letha 71
Doland,Martha L.71
Doland,Mary 19
Doland,Sarah 65
*Doland,Thomas 19
Dolanmd,Judy 65
Dorman,----(x)15
Douglas,Mary E.72
Douglass,Cora V. 72
Douglass,Mahaley 72
Douglass,Mattie L. 72
*Douglass,William 72
Douthit,Charlott 42
Douthit,Clara 42
Douthit,Edward 42
Douthit,Elizabeth 42
Douthit,Frank W.43
Douthit,Gracy 42
Douthit,Jane A.43

*Douthit,John L.42
Douthit,Richard 42
*Douthit,William 42
*Douthit,William H.43
Droun,David 31
Droun,Elby 31
Droun,Hellen 31
Droun,John P.31
Droun,Leat 31
Droun,Newton 31
*Droun,Rufus 31
Droun,Sarah 31
Duding,Alfred 27
Duding,Casandia 27
*Duding,John 27
Duding,Madlem 27
Dudley,Elizabeth 5
Dudley,John 5
*Dudley,John 5
Dudley,Julia A. 5
Dudley,Mahaly 5
Dudley,Margaret 5
Dudley,Pollie 5
Dundass,Betty 8
Dundass,Charles 8
Dundass,Croney 30
Dundass,Eliza 8
*Dundass,James 8
*Dundass,John 10
Dundass,Lucy(x)15
Dundass,Martha 30
Dundass,Mary 10
Dundass,Mary J.8
Dundass,Sallie 8
*Dundass,Thomas 30
Dundass,Virginia 30
Dunkle,Catherine 3
Dunkle,Daniel(x)56
Dunkle,Eliza(x)56
*Dunkle,Henry C.3
Dunkle,James A.3
Dunkle,John A.3
Dunkle,Minnie 3
Dunkle,William H.3
Dunn,Arthur(x)71
Dunn,Lutiecha(x)71
Dunnahoo,Alexander 66
Dunnahoo,Joel 66
Dunnahoo,Lucinda 66
*Dunnahoo,William 66
Dunsford,Mary J.27
*Dunsford,William 27
Dusenberry,Anna F.47
Dusenberry,Caleb C.45

*Dusenberry,Charles O.47
Dusenberry,Cintha 45
Dusenberry,Edwin M.57
Dusenberry,Flora F.58
Dusenberry,Francis L.48
Dusenberry,George 48
Dusenberry,James B.48
Dusenberry,Jessie 45
*Dusenberry,Justin T.48
Dusenberry,Louisa 48
Dusenberry,Louisa 48
Dusenberry,Mary A.57
Dusenberry,Mary E.48
Dusenberry,Nancy(x)47
Dusenberry,Nellie B.47
*Dusenberry,Robert 57
Dusenberry,Robert W.58
*Dusenberry,Samuel 58
Dusenberry,Sarah G. 58
Dusenberry,Sarah K.45
Dusenberry,Theodore W.48
*Dusenberry,William 45
Dusenberry,William C.47
Dyer,Ann L. 13
Dyer,James E. 13
*Dyer,James R. 13
Dyer,John W.13
Dyer,Margaret M.13
Dyer,Morgan H.13
Dyer,Rebecca 13
Dyer,Rowena 13
Edens,Benjamin 3
Edens,Benjamin F. 59
*Edens,Edward 3
Edens,Emma J. 59
Edens,Harriet A. 59
*Edens,James A. 59
Edens,Jenevra 59
Edens,Lucy A. 3
Edens,Martha J.3
Edens,Mary E. 3
Edens,Mary I.3
Edens,Mary V.59
Edens,Melvin E. 59
Edens,Samuel H.3
Edens,Sarah B.59
Edens,Sarah F.3
Edens,William 59
Edens,Willie E. 59
*Edwards,Sarah 36
Eggers,Adaline 26
Eggers,Elizabeth 13
Eggers,Fleming 26
Eggers,John(x)13

*Eggers,Joseph 13
Eggers,Mary 26
*Eggers,Nancy 26
Eggers,Samuel 26
Eggers,Wilbert (x)13
Eggers,William(x)13
Elkins,Andrew J.67
Elkins,Celey 36
Elkins,Charles H. 36
*Elkins,Dudley 36
Elkins,Francis M.67
*Elkins,Harvey 67
Elkins,James M.36
Elkins,Mary E. 36
Elkins,Nancy 67
Elkins,Sarah E.36
Ellis,Addison 39
*Ellis,Addison 41
Ellis,Albert 41
Ellis,Ellen 39
Ellis,Gilbert 41
Ellis,Lewis 39
*Ellis,Preston 39
Ellis,Sarah A.41
Ellis,Siles 39
Elmore,Bennett 5
Elmore,Edward 58
Elmore,Edwin 5
Elmore,Jeanna 5
Elmore,Jefferson 5
Elmore,Pascal 5
Elmore,Roddie 5
Elmore,Sarah 5
*Elmore,William 5
Emmerson,Elisa(x)79
Eplin,Amacetta 67
Eplin,Angaline 67
*Eplin,Bazel 67
Eplin,Catherine 65
Eplin,Eliza A. 67
Eplin,Elizabeth 67
Eplin,Fredrick(x)66
Eplin,Marion(x)69
Eplin,Marshall 67
Eplin,Mary(x)66
Eplin,Melvina 67
Eplin,Merritt 67
Eplin,Nancy A. 67
Eplin,Polley 67
*Eplin,Rundolph 67
*Eplin,Sherid 65
Eplin,Susanna 67
*Eplin,William 67
Epps,Harrison(x)58

Epps,Sophia(x)58
Erls,Cela 37
Erls,Charles H.37
Erls,Columbia 37
Erls,David 37
Erls,George 37
Erls,Lucien E.37
Erls,William R.37
Esherman,Edward(x)24
Esherman,Ida(x)24
Estep,Corbin 33
Estep,Elizabeth 33
Estep,George 33
*Estep,John 33
Estep,Harrison 33
Estep,Mary 33
Estep,Nancy 33
Estep,Susan A.33
Estus,Elizabeth(x)24x
Estus,James(x)24
Estus,John(x)24
Estus,Mary E.(x)24
Everett,Clayton 48
Everett,Elizabeth 25
Everett,Elizabeth 48
Everett,Emily 51
Everett,Emma 51
Everett,Emma C. 48
Everett,Flecther 51
Everett,George 390
Everett,George F.(x)53
Everett,George S. 48
Everett,Hannah 44
*Everett,James 25
*Everett,John 44
Everett,John H.51
*Everett,John S. 51
Everett,Kate 39
Everett,Kate M.(x)53
Everett,Labon T.48
Everett,Lucy F. 39
Everett,Mary T.48
Everett,Mary(x)53
Everett,Peter 39
Everett,Peter 51
Everett,Peter R.(x)53
Everett,Rebecca J.(x)53
Everett,Sallie(x)75
*Everett,Samuel 39
Everett,Sarah 51
*Everett,Talton 48
Everett,Temperana 39
Eves,Eliza 34
Eves,Eliza E.34

Eves,Elizabeth 34
Eves,James F.34
*Eves,John 34
Eves,Mary A. 34
Eves,Mary E. 34
Eves,Sarah 34
Eves,Sulvira 34
Eves,Thomas 34
Eves,Thomas A. 34
*Eves,Thomas M.34
Farley,Anges 10
Farley,Ann 10
Farley,Edwin 10
*Farley,Elijah 10
Farley,Franklin 10
Farley,Fredrick 10
Farley,John 10
Farley,Sarah 10
Farley,Thomas 10
Farley,William 10
Farrell,Elizabeth 12
*Farrell,Francis M.12
Farrell,Isaac 12
Farrell,Lawrence 12
Farrell,Mary S. 12
Farrell,William 12
Farrist,Anna E.40
Farrist,Dorenda 40
Farrist,Elijah 40
Farrist,Francis 40
*Farrist,James 40
Farrist,Jugley 40
Farrist,Julia R.40
Farrist,Lewis 40
Farrist,Lucy A.40
Farrist,Lurena 40
*Felix,Arnold 83
Felix,Isabel 83
Felix,James F.83
Felix,James(x)83
Felix,Julia(x)83
*Felix,Julius 83
Felix,Penila 83
Felix,Susan 83
Felix,Werner 83
Ferguson,Areanna 47
Ferguson,Ardel 47
Ferguson,Catherine 73
Ferguson,Charles 41
Ferguson,Elias 41
Ferguson,Elizabeth 16
Ferguson,Elizabeth(x)80
Ferguson,George 41
Ferguson,Hannah 73

Ferguson,Henry 73
Ferguson,Jackson 73
*Ferguson,James 73
*Ferguson,James H.16
Ferguson,Jesse 73
*Ferguson,Jesse 73
*Ferguson,John 41
Ferguson,John A. 41
Ferguson,Joseph 73
Ferguson,Julia 41
Ferguson,Julius(x)40
Ferguson,Leanora(x)40
Ferguson,Lenard 6
Ferguson,Levera(x)40
Ferguson,Lucien C.41
Ferguson,Lucy 41
Ferguson,Mahaley 73
Ferguson,Martha 73
Ferguson,Mary A.47
Ferguson,Polley 6
Ferguson,Rebecca(x)40
Ferguson,Samuel 41
*Ferguson,Sarah 47
Ferguson,Sarah S.47
Ferguson,Walter(x)73
*Ferguson,William 6
Ferguson,William 41
Ferguson,William(x)40
Fetters,Ada S.11
Fetters,Carrie F.11
Fetters,Eli R.11
Fetters,Flora F.11
*Fetters,Henry 11
Fetters,Louisa 11
Fetters,Nettie D.11
Fetters,Willie B.11
*File,Able S.75
File,George 75
File,Hester 75
File,Joseph 75
File,Nancy 75
Flinn,Thomas(x)16
*Flowers,Alford C.46
Flowers,Alonzo 46
Flowers,Amasetta 34
Flowers,Daniel C.34
Flowers,Edgar 46
Flowers,Emily 46
Flowers,Esra 46
Flowers,Fildred 34
Flowers,Frances 34
*Flowers,Fredrick 34
*Flowers,George 34
Flowers,Gerard 34

Flowers,Henry L.34
Flowers,Hermina 34
Flowers,James F.46
Flowers,James L.34
Flowers,John A.34
Flowers,John R.34*
Flowers,Julia 34
Flowers,Lorenzo 34
Flowers,Martha 34
Flowers,Nancy 46
Flowers,Oscar 46
Flowers,Sadler R.34
Flowers,Sarah 46
*Flowers,Thadeus 46
Floyd,Allen 76
Floyd,Allice (x)55
Floyd,Editha 7
Floyd,Elizabeth 7
Floyd,Finley 7
Floyd,Finley 76
Floyd,Frances 76
*Floyd,James 7
*Floyd,John 76
Floyd,Margaret 7
Floyd,Rossey 7
Floyd,William A.76
Ford,Nancy(x)3
Foster,Arno(x)27
Foster,Ellen(x)27
Foster,John(x)44
Foster,Lizzie(x)44
Foster,Walden(x)44
Fowler,Frances 41
Fowler,Gray 41
*Fowler,Harrison 41
*Fox,James 83
Fox,William(x)83
Frampton,Albert (x)54
Frampton,David (x)54
Frampton,James(x)54
France,Adaline 8
*France,Benjamin 4
France,George 8
France,Harvey 8
*France,Henry 8
France,Henry L. 4
*France,Isaac 8
France,Isabel 8
France,James 4
France,James G.8
France,Lidea 4
France,Matilda 8
France,Nancy 8
France,Nancy A. 8

France,Patience 8
France,Pheby J.8
France,Roxey 4
France,Thomas 8
France,Viley 4
France,William 4
Francisco,Anetta A. 57
Francisco,Elisha 57
Francisco,Elizabeth 57
Francisco,Emily J. 57
Francisco,Floyd 57
*Francisco,Jacob 57
Francisco,Mary 57
Francisco,Nancy 57
Frasier,Alfred(x)26
Frasier,Effie(x)26
Frasier,Mary J.(x)26
French,Alice 77
French,Ellie 77
French,Henry(x)38
French,John(x)38
French,Laura 77
French,Lemuel 77
French,Martha 77
*French,William 77
Frey,William(x)19
Fruitell,Alexander 46
Fruitell,Christian 46
Fruitell,Henry A.46
*Fruitell,Julius 46
Fruitell,Mary C.46
Fruitell,Sophia M.46
Fruitell,William 46
*Frye,Fleming 61
Frye,Francis 61
Frye,Randolph 61
Fulks,James J.6*
Fulks,Luhatta 6
Fulks,Mary A. 6
Fuller,Elizabeth(x)49
Fuller,Ida M.49
*Fuller,John W.49
Fuller,Lillie B.49
Fuller,Rosalie 49
Fuller,Sarah A. 49
Fuller,Sarah A.49
Fuller,Sarah F. (x)55
Fuller,William 49
Fulwiler,Ella 12
*Fulwiler,George 12
Fulwiler,John 12
Fulwiler,Kate 12
Fulwiler,Mary 12
Fulwiler,Matilda 12

Fulwiler,William 12
Galliher,Drucilla 56
Gallaher,Edward(x)36
Galliher,Edward 56
Galliher,Elizabeth 56
*Galliher,John 56
Galliher,Lora 56
Gallaher,Sarah(x)53
Galliher,Sarah 56
Gapehart,Elizabeth 74
Gapehart,John 74
*Gapehart,John 74
Gapehart,Kate 74
Gapehart,Mary 74
Gapehart,William 74
Gardiner,Elizabeth(x)45
*Gasner,George 46
Gasner,Henry 46
Gasner,Mary 46
Gasner,Stella 46
Gasner,Victoria 46
Gates,Alvira 49
Gates,Edward S.49
Gates,Ella A.49
Gates,Hatta A.49
Gates,John M.49
Gates,Laura 49
Gates,William 49
*Gates,William W.49
Gaven,Michael(x)19
Gaven,William(x)19
*Ghear,Acy 5
Ghear,Acy M.5
Ghear,Liddie J.5
Ghear,nancy 5
Gibb,William(x)14
Gibbons,Paul(x)19
Gibson,Albert J.62
Gibson,Ann 71
Gibson,Elizabeth 62
Gibson,Franklin 71
Gibson,George 71
Gibson,Isabel 71
Gibson,James 62
Gibson,Jane 73
*Gibson,Job 62
Gibson,John 71
Gibson,John L.(x)35
Gibson,Joseph 62
*Gibson,Leroy 73
Gibson,Lizzie 71
Gibson,Lucetta 62
Gibson,Malissey 62
Gibson,Malissey 71

Gibson,Mary(x)63
Gibson,Randolph 71
Gibson,Robert L.62
*Gibson,William 71
Gill,Charles J.63
Gill,Cora 64
Gill,Elisha 64
Gill,Emily 64
Gill,Fannie 64
*Gill,George 63
Gill,Henry A. 63
Gill,John F.63
*Gill,Joseph 64
Gill,Laura 64
Gill,Mary A. 64
Gill,Mary A.63
Gill,Thomas J.63
Gillen Sarah 21
*Gillen,John 21
Gillen,Milten 21
Golden,Gustaves(x)83
Graf,Caroline(x)43
*Granway,John 9
Granway,Mary A. 9
Granway,Sarah A. 9
Grass,George(x)18
Grayham,Aratitum 34
Grayham,Georgie 35
Grayham,Ivda 35
*Grayham,Jefferson 35
*Grayham,Marion 34
Grayham,Mary 35
Grayham,Mary E. 34
Grayham,William J.35
*Grayham,Jonas 35
Griffin,Cora A.(x)49
Griffin,Elizabeth(x)49
Griffin,James W.(x)49
Grimes,Abreham(x)73
Grimes,George F.(x)73
Grimes,Roberta(x)73
Grimes,Thomas J.(x)73
*Gross,George W.44
Gross,Grant 44
Gross,Martha 44
Gross,Theadore 44
Gross,William 44
*Gue,James 65
Gue,Julia A. 65
Gue,Linsey 65
Gue,Lucy 65
Gue,Mary 65
Gue,Nancy 65
Gue,Permilla

Gue,Tandy 65
Gue,Ulysses 65
*Guinn,Andrew 24
*Gwinn,Andrew 24
Guinn,Charles 24
Gwinn,Charles 25
Gwinn,Conwelsa 25
Gwinn,Elizabeth 25
*Gwinn,George 25
Guinn,Harriet 24
Guinn,James 24
Gwinn,Jefferson 24
Gwinn,Margaret 25
Gwinn,Marietta 25
Gwinn,Mary 25
Gwinn,Robert E. 25
Gwinn,Sampson 25
Gwinn,Thomas 25
Gwinn,Rachel 24
Guinn,William 24
Hackworth,Annie 25
Hackworth,Eliza(x)39
*Hackworth,George 25
Hackworth,George(x)39
Hackworth,Georgie 25
Hackworth,Hetti 25
Hackworth,Martha(x)39
Hackworth,Pleasent(x)39
Hackworth,Randolph 25
Hackworth,Robert 25
Hackworth,Thomas 25
Hagan,Emogene 51
Hagan,Hugh A.51
Hagan,James W.51
Hagan,Mary J.51
Hagan,Nannie S.51
Hagan,Stella 51
*Hagan,William H.51
Hagely,Ariadna(x)73
Hagely,Elizabeth 75
Hagely,George H.75
Hagely,George P.75
Hagely,Hannah 75
Hagely,Hannah F.75
Hagely,Harrison(x)73
Hagely,Henry(x)73
Hagely,James 75
*Hagely,Joseph 75
Hagely,Louisa 75
Hagely,Louisa J.75
Hagely,Lucinda(x)73
Hagely,Mahaley S.75
Hagely,Malachiah 75
Hagely,Martha S.75

Hagely,Mary E. 75
Hagely,Mary E.75
*Hagely,Peter 75
Hagely,Peter(x)75
Hagely,Pollie 75
Hagely,Pollie A.75
Hagely,Sarah M.75
Hagley,Eliza 80
*Hagley,Joseph 80
Hagley,Mahaley 80
Hagley,Tabitha 77
Hale,Mary J.3
Hale,Nancy J.3
Hale,Robert H.3
*Hale,Samuel 3
Hall,Amanda 57
*Hall,Andrew H.40
*Hall,Andrew J.49
Hall,Ann 68
*Hall,Charles 17
Hall,Christofer 38
Hall,Eliza A.49
Hall,Elizabeth 40
Hall,Filora 49
Hall,Harriet M.17
Hall,Henry 40
*Hall,Henry W.68
Hall,Luticia 40
Hall,Martha J.49
Hall,Martha 40
Hall,Mary E.68
*Hall,Nancy 38
Hall,Samuel 40
Hall,Thomas 68
*Hall,William 57
Hall,William T.17
Halls,James J.49
Hamberger,Annie 83
Hamberger,Cosaline 83
Hamberger,Henrietta 83
*Hamberger,Joseph 83
Hamberger,Lucy 83
Hamberger,Mary 83
Hamlin,Sallie(x)13
Hanley,Ann 19
Hanly,Augusta 47
*Hanly,Benjamin 47
*Hanley,Charles 18
Hanley,Charles 18
*Hanley,Cornelius 19
Hanly,Eliza 26
Hanley,Elizabeth 18
Hanley,Ellen 19
Hanley,Frank W. 18

*Hanly,Harrison 26
Hanly,Jackson 26
Hanly,Jefferson 26
Hanly,John W. 26
Hanley,Leondas 18
Hanley,Marion L. 18
Hanly,Martha 26
Hanly,Nancy 26
Hanley,Ona 18
Hanly,Samuel 18
Hanly,Sarah 26
Hanly,Sarah E.26
Hanly,Susie 47
*Harless,Pollie 68
Harmon,Amey F.26
Harmon,Indson 26
Harmon,Leondas 26
*Harmon,Thomas 26
Harmon,Victoria 26
Harmon,Virginia 26
Harris,Arminda 64
Harris,Elizabeth 64
Harris,James 80
Harris,John F.64
Harris,Martha 80
Harris,Netta (x)35
*Harris,Reuben 64
Harris,Telitha 80
Harris,William J.64
Harrison,Arianna 38
Harrison,Catherine 35
Harrison,Charles O.52
Harrison,David(x)68
Harrison,Elizabeth 61
Harrison,Ella 52
Harrison,Ellen 14
Harrison,Eugenia 52
Harrison,Flora A. 52
Harrison,Francis 38
Harrison,George W.(x)68
*Harrison,Greenville 14
*Harrison,Henry 38
Harrison,Henry B.61
Harrison,Henry H.37
Harrison,John A.(x)8
Harrison,Luciene 52
Harrison,Lucy A.37
Harrison,Lucy A.38
Harrison,Luvenia(x)8
Harrison,Margaret(x)20
Harrison,Mary 14
Harrison,Mary V.38
Harrison,Mary V.52
Harrison,Matilda 61

Harrison,Orren B.52	Hatfield,Editha (x)60	Heath,Edward 32
*Harrison,Otis 52	Hatfield,Effie A.12	*Heath,George A.32
Harrison,Phenton 37	Hatfield,Eliza A. 60	Heath,Jane 63
Harrison,Robert 37	Hatfield,Eliza J.61	*Heath,Joshua 63
Harrison,Ruth L.52	Hatfield,Emily C.61	Heath,Lucetta 32
Harrison,Sarah Q.(x)8	Hatfield,Francis 60	Heath,Mary A. 32
Harrison,Sarah V.(x)8	*Hatfield,George 60	Heath,Robert 63
Harrison,Selina R.35	Hatfield,Hannah 58	Heath,Sallie(x)63
Harrison,Sina 35	*Hatfield,Henry 61	Heath,Tom Kline 32
Harrison,Thomas 14	Hatfield,Henry J. 60	Henckly,Bell 35
*Harrison,Thomas 61	*Hatfield,Henry M. 60	*Henckly,Jacob 35
Harrison,Thomas E.61	Hatfield,Isaac 61	Henckly,John L.35
*Harrison,William 35	Hatfield,James A. 60	Henckly,Lois 35
*Harrison,William 37	Hatfield,James G. 58	Hendrick,Ann 71
Harrison,William(x)8	*Hatfield,John L,12	Hendrick,Cathrin 71
Harshbarger,Charles 25	Hatfield,John M. 60	Hendrick,Jospeh 71
*Harshbarger,David 9	Hatfield,Josaphine 60	*Hendrick,Lewis 71
Harshbarger,Dora M.9	Hatfield,Joseph M. 58	Hendrick,Sylvester 71
Harshbarger,Drucilla 23	Hatfield,Joseph N. 60	Henry,Emily 74
Harshbarger,Edna 23	Hatfield,Lucinda 58	Henry,Gusta 74
Harshbarger,Edna A. 9	Hatfield,Lucinda H. 60	*Henry,Gutliff 74
*Harshbarger,Elizabeth 25	Hatfield,Maggie A. 13	Henry,Thradore 74
Harshbarger,Elizabeth 8	Hatfield,Malind 12	Hensley,Allice 3
Harshbarger,Ellen 8	Hatfield,Margaret 60	Hensley,Amanda 59
Harshbarger,George 25	Hatfield,Martha J. 60	Hensley,Andrew J. 59*
Harshbarger,George 9	Hatfield,Millard 13	Hensley,Ann 4
Harshbarger,Gracy 23	*Hatfield,Moses 58	Hensley,Ann(x)38
*Harshbarger,Henry 23	Hatfield,Nancy A.61	*Hensley,Bird 3
Harshbarger,Henry 9	Hatfield,Peninah 58	*Hensley,Bird 56
Harshbarger,Ida 9	Hatfield,Rufus A. 60	Hensley,catherine 3
Harshbarger,Ira J. 9	Hatfield,Thomas 60	Hensley,Charles L.3
*Harshbarger,John 8	Hatrly,Isabel(x)40	Hensley,Columbus 3
Harshbarger,Josephine 9	Hatton,Edmond 35	Hensley,David 56
Harshbarger,Mary 9	Hatton,Elizabeth 35	Hensley,Elizabeth 56
Harshbarger,Mary F.9	Hatton,Lincoln 35	*Hensley,Ephram 59
Harshbarger,Samuel 9	Hatton,Mary A.35	Hensley,Eugenia(x)49
Harshbarger,William 25	Hatton,Perlows 35	Hensley,Fannie 3
Harvey,America 50	Hatton,Sanford 35	Hensley,George B.3
*Harvey,Calvary 50	*Hatton,Solomon 35	Hensley,George W.3
Harvey,Elizabeth 50	Hatton,William 35	Hensley,Hellana M. 56
Harvey,Florence 50	Hayslip,Cary B.45	Hensley,Ida May 4
Harvey,Henry L.50	Hayslip,Charles H.46	*Hensley,James 4
Harvey,John W.50	Hayslip,George 43	*Hensley,James A.4
Harvey,Mary E.50	*Hayslip,James L.43	*Hensley,John 56
Harvey,Octava 50	Hayslip,Margery 45	Hensley,John F. 59
Harvey,William 50	Hayslip,Minnie 43	*Hensley,John L.3
Hatfield,Adam S. 60	Hayslip,Nancy 1.46	Hensley,John W. 56
Hatfield,Albert 58	Hayslip,Okey K.46	Hensley,Julius 4
Hatfield,Allice(x)8	Hayslip,Richard B.45	Hensley,Lucy 3
Hatfield,America L. 60	Hayslip,Rubie K.46	Hensley,Malinda 56
*Hatfield,Andrew 60	*Hayslip,Samuel D.46	Hensley,Marengo 3
Hatfield,Catherine 61	Hayslip,Thomas J.45	Hensley,Mary A. 3
Hatfield,Charles F. 60	*Hayslip,Thomas J.45	Hensley,Mary E. 59
Hatfield,David J,61	Hayslip,Victoria 43	Hensley,Mary F. 4

Hensley,Minnie H. 56
Hensley,Nancy 3
Hensley,Olive 59
Hensley,Rufus(x)49
*Hensley,Samuel 3
Hensley,Sarah 3
Hensley,Sarah C. 59
Hensley,Thona 3
Hensley,William 59
Hensley,William G. 56
Hensley,Willie 3
Hensley,Willie A. 4
Herd,America 33
Herd,Carrie 10
Herd,Ella 10
*Herd,Isriel 33
Herd,Melia 10
Herd,Sarah 10
Hord,Sarah 52
*Herd,William 10
Hord,William W.52*
Herd,Willie 10
Herndon,Charles S.18
Herndon,James F. 18
*Herndon,James L.18
Herndon,Mary A. 18
Herndon,Mortica V.18
Herndon,Susan E.18
Herold,Nancy J.4
*Herold,William 4
Herren,Abbie 78
*Herren,Austin 78
Herren,Harvey 78
*Herrenkohl,Albert 6
Herrenkohl,Charles 6
Herrenkohl,Envil 6
Herrenkohl,Hellena 6
Herrenkohl,Louisa 6
Herrenkohl,Milinka 6
Hews see Hughs
Higgins,Patrick(x)19
Hill,Mary J.19
Hill,Susan S. 63
*Hill,William S.63
Hiltbruner,Anna 48
Hiltbruner,Hiram 48
Hiltbruner,Isiah 48
*Hiltbruner,Jacob 48
Hiltbruner,Maggie R.48
Hiltbruner,Martha V.48
Hiltbruner,Mary 48
Hiltbruner,Stephen C.48
Hiltbruner,William P.48
*Hinchman,Adam 59

Hinchman,Eliza J.61
Hinchman,Elizabeth(x)61
Hinchman,George W.61
Hinchman,John W.61
Hinchman,Joseph A. 59
*Hinchman,Lewis 61
Hinchman,Margaret 61
Hinchman,Martha A. 59
*Hinchman,Wesley 61
Hite,Charles 48
*Hite,Edward 48
Hite,Eliza 44
Hite,Elizabeth 44
*Hite,Frances 48
Hite,Gerturde 48
Hite,Henry C.48
Hite,Izza(x)52
Hite,John 44
*Hite,John B.44
Hite,Malinda 44
Hite,Maretta 44
Hite,Mary 44
Hite,Mary 48
Hite,Sarah(x)52
*Hite,William 44
Hite,William 48
Hoback,Franklin 2
Hoback,Hannah 2
Hoback,Ida 2
*Hoback,Lorenzo 2
Hoback,Martha 2
Hoback,Mary S.2
Hodges,Allice A.34
Hodge,Charles A.11
Hodges,Edgar L.22
Hodges,John 22
*Hodges,John 34
Hodges,Lewis 22
*Hodge,Margaret 11
Hodges,Mary E. 22
Hodges,Mary J.22
Hodges,Peter 22
*Hodges,Stephen 22
Hodges,William 22
Hoffman see Huffman
Hoffman,Catherine 52
Hoffman,Thomas 52
*Hoffman,William 52
Hoges,Ellen 18
Hoges,Leah 18
Hoges,Preston 18
Hoges,Sarah 18
Holderby,Addie 46
Holderby,Edward(x)53

*Holderby,George W.46
Holderby,James A.(x)52
Holderby,Jessie R.46
Holderby,Susie 46
Holderby,William(x)52
Holdroyd,Anna M. 47
Holdroyd,Elizabeth 8
Holdroyd,George 47
Holdroyd,Maggie 47
*Holdroyd,Peter 47
Holdroyd,Robert 47
*Holdroyd,Sarah 8
Holdroyd,Susan E. 47
Hollenback,Ellen(x)36
Holley,Gorden(x)83
Holley,Joanna(x)83x
Holley,Lorenzo(x)82
Holley,Martha(x)82
Holley,Mary H.79
*Holley,Samuel 79
Holley,Sarah 79
Holley,Sarah C.82
Holmes,James L.(x)54
Holmes,John W.(x)54
Holmes,Lucinda(x)54
Holt,Elizabeth(x)55
Holt,Elizabeth(x)62
Holt,Eunice (x)55
Holt,Flora(x)23
Holt,Henrietta (x)55
Holt,Sarah(x)64
Holt,Sarah L.(x)55
*Hoops,Isiah 47
Hoops,Mary 47
Hord see Herd
Houchin,Adelade 77
Houchin,Charles E.77
Houchin,Claressey 81
Houchin,Clarressey 77
*Houchin,Francis 77
Houchin,Henry 77
Houchin,Mary A. 77
Houchin,Mary J.81
Houchin,Rebecca 77
Houchen,Rebecca(x)81
Houchin,Sarah E.77
Houchin,William 77
*Houchin,William 81
*Howard,Allen 76
Howard,Ann 81
*Howerd,Aaron 8
Howard,Cristina 76
Howerd,David 8
Howerd,Ellen 8

Howard,Hannah 76
Howerd,Hugh 8
Howard,Hugh A. 76
Howerd,Louisa 8
Howard,Louisa 76
Howerd,Lucy A.8
Howerd,Lydia 8
Howard,Marion(x)76
Howerd,Margaret 8
*Howard,William 81
Howell,Alice 18
*Howell,Armstead 18
Howell,Fannie 18
Howell,John 18
Howell,Josephine 58
*Howell,Sallie 58
Howell,Sarah 58
Howkins,Ann 24
Howkins,Martin 24
Howkins,Mary 24
Howkins,Thomas 23
Howkins,Thomas 24
Howkins,William 24
Huffman see Hoffman
*Huffman,Andrew 38
Huffman,Matilda 38
Huffman,Meteoni 38
Huffman,Rachel 69
Huffman,Rosanna 69
*Huffman,Thomas 69
Huffman,William 69
Hughs,Beverly 2
*Hews,Decalb 78
Hughs,Electir 2
Hughs,Isadora 38
Hughs,James 38
Hews,Jane A.78
Hughs,Julia A.38
*Hughs,Lorenzo D.2
Hughs,Margaret V.2
Hughs,Mary 2
Hughs,Mary E.2
Hughs,Ora S.38
*Hughs,Ralph 2
Hughs,Richard 38*
Hews,William 78
*(Hull),James O.53-Wall
Hunter,Charles(x)37
Hunter,Eliza(x)37
Hunter,Emma(x)37
Hunter,Jessie(x)37
Hunter,John(x)37
Hunter,Julia A.(x)37
Hunter,Mary(x)37

Hunter,Nancy L.(x)37
Hutchinson,Washington(x)69
Huxham,Charles H.38
Huxham,Elizabeth 38
Huxham,Florence 38
Huxham,Harry 38
*Huxham,Henry 38
Huxham,Sarah 38
Huxham,Victoria 38
Hyder,Federal 47
*Hyder,Henry 47
Hyder,Virginia 47
Hysell,Elizabeth 42
Hysell,Fitz H.46
*Hysell,James H.46
*Hysell,Joseph L.42
Hysell,Mary L.46
Hysell,Nannie 42
Insco,Amasetta 32
Insco,Eliza J. 38
Insco,Ellen(x)52
Insco,George 38
Insco,James(x)52
*Insco,Joseph 32
Insco,Martha 38
Insco,Mollie(x)52
Insco,Olive C.38
Insco,Sarah 32
*Insco,William 38
Irby,Berry 34
Irby,Charles 34
Irby,Edward 34
Irby,George (x)34
Irby,John(x)33
Irby,Julia 34
*Irby,Lacheriah 34
Irby,Marg.A.34
Irby,Mary E.34
Irby,Nancy E.34
Irby,Robert A.34
*Irby,Samuel T.34
Irby,Sarah 34
Irby,Sarah A.34
*Irvin,Amanda 22
Irvin,David 21
Irvin,Delia 21
Irvin,Edward 21
Irwin,Eliza 61
Irvin,Elizabeth 21
Irwin,Hannah 21
Irwin,James A.61
Irvin,John H.22
Irwin,Martha A.61

Irwin,Mary A.61
Irvin,Mary E.21
Irwin,Mary E.61
*Irvin,Mathew 21
Irvin,Nancy 21
Irvin,Nancy J.22
Irvin,Napeleon 21
Irwin,Sarah A.61
Irwin,Sarah J.61
Irwin,Semintha 61
Irvin,Virginia 22
*Irwin,William 61
Jack,Eliza(x)76
Janney,Anna L.27
Janney,Elizabeth 27
*Janney,John 27
Janney,Manerva 27
Janney,Mary L.27
Janney,Michael 27
Janney,Viley A.27
*Jarrell,Ambrose 33
Jarrell,Mary E.33
Jarrett,Martha(x)20
Jefferson,Abner L.76
Jefferson,Albert 75
Jefferson,Alga 75
Jefferson,America 73
Jefferson,America E.7
Jefferson,Ammasetta 75
Jefferson,Anjaline 75
Jefferson,Bettie 73
Jefferson,Charles 7
Jefferson,Cora 75
Jefferson,Effie 75
Jefferson,Elizabeth 73
Jefferson,Franklin(x)75
Jefferson,Harriet 75
*Jefferson,Henry 7
*Jefferson,Henry 73
Jefferson,John W.7
*Jefferson,John W.75
Jefferson,Louisa 28
Jefferson,Louisa E.7
Jefferson,Lucetta 7
Jefferson,Malinda 7
Jefferson,Malinda 76
Jefferson,Marenda 7
Jefferson,Mary A.7
Jefferson,Mary E. 76
Jefferson,Nancy L.76
Jefferson,Parthena 76
Jefferson,Samuel 7
*Jefferson,Thomas 76
Jefferson,Virginia(x)75

Jefferson,William 7
Jefferson,William(x)75
Jefferson,Willie 75
Jenkins,Addie 78
*Jenkins,Anderson 82
Jenkins,Colonel 82
Jenkins,Dudley 78
Jenkins,Ida E. 5
Jenkins,Jackson 5
Jenkins,John J.82
Jenkins,Julia 78
Jenkins,Laura P.78
Jenkins,Mary J.5
Jenkins,Medina B.5
Jenkins,Menitha 82
*Jenkins,Phillip E.5
Jenkins,Susan 78
*Jenkins,William 78
Jenkins,William 82
Jennings,Mary(x)29
Jerry,Anna M.(x)15
*Jewel,Daniel 48
Jewel,Emma 48
Jewel,Mary E. 48
Joel,James(x)16
Johnson see Johnston
Johnson,Abner 53
Johnson,Ada C.28
Johnson,Adda P. 54
Johnson,Albert 53
Johnson,Almeda 66
Johnson,Amasetta(x)36
Johnson,Ammasetta 28
Johnson,Anna P. 54
Johnson,Armilda 66
Johnson,Bell 53
Johnson,Benjamin 53
Johnson,Bennett 28
Johnson,Bradley 63
Johnson,Daniel 53
Johnson,David 79
Johnson,Eliza 53
Johnson,Eliza V.50
Johnson,Elizabeth 67
Johnson,Emily 53
Johnson,Emily F. 63
Johnson,Emma 54
Johnson,Emogene 50
Johnson,Evaline 67
Johnson,Florence 50
Johnson,Fredrick 54
Johnson,George H.50
Johnston,Henry(x)22
*Johnson,Irvin 42

Johnson,Irvin 67
*Johnson,Isom 66
Johnson,Jackson 63
*Johnson,James 50
Johnson,James E. 54
Johnson,Jefferson 66
Johnson,Jenetta(x)36
*Johnson,John 67
*Johnson,John L.54
Johnson,John W.63
Johnson,Joseph 67
*Johnson,Joseph 63
*Johnson,Joseph 79
Johnson,Joseph R.63
Johnson,Libba 54
Johnson,Lucinda 67
Johnson,Lucy 63
Johnson,Lucy A.63
Johnson,Mahaley 66
Johnson,Malissey 79
Johnson,Marcelles 54
Johnson,Marietta 66
Johnson,Marion 67
Johnson,Martha 42
Johnson,Martha 53
Johnson,Martha 79
Johnson,Martha C. 54
Johnson,Mary 50
Johnson,Mary E. 54
Johnson,Mary E.42
Johnson,Mary J. 54
Johnson,Melvena 79
*Johnson,Merritt 67
Johnson,Minnie L.50
Johnson,Nary 79
Johnson,Rachel 79
Johnson,Robert 53
Johnson,Robert 63
Johnson,Rody 67
Johnson,Samuel 53
*Johnson,Samuel 53
Johnson,Sarah J. 54
Johnson,Sarah J.(x)36
Johnson,Spicy 67
Johnson,Stephen 54
Johnson,Susan J.63
Johnson,Susan L. 54
Johnson,Thomas 53
Johnson,Thomas R.63
*Johnson,Warren M.28
Johnson,William 50
*Johnson,William 54
*Johnson,William 66
Johnson,Zerilda 66

Johnston see Johnson
Johnston,Agnes(x)20
Johnston,Amanda A 60
Johnston,America 76
Johnston,Andrew 73
Johnston,Anjalina 76
Johnston,Bettie A.76
Johnston,Charles R.7
Johnston,Clemintine 7
*Johnston,Columbus 60
Johnston,Edward P.73
Johnston,Eliza J.73
Johnston,Emily F.76
Johnston,Everman 60
Johnston,Frank 54
Johnston,Harry W. 54
Johnston,James L.7
Johnston,James M.76
Johnston,Jane 73
*Johnston,Lewis 73
Johnston,Martha 7
Johnston,Martha J. 60
Johnston,Nancy(x)22
*Johnston,Napoleon 54
Johnston,Sarah 54
Johnston,Sarah 73
Johnston,Sarah 76
Johnston,Sina 76
Johnston,Sirnea 76
Johnston,Squire 73
*Johnston,Wesley 76
*Johnston,William 73
*Johnston,Wilson 7
Jones,Robert J.(x)43
Jorden,Abreham 25
Jorden,Alkendrew 23
Jorden,Carena F.23
Jordan,Charles R.62
Jorden,Christopher(x23
Jordan,Cintha 72
Jordan,Edward 72
Jorden,Eliza F.23
Jorden,Emily C.23
Jorden,Esther 25
Jorden,Harriet 23
Jorden,Harriet 25
Jorden,Henry C.23
Jorden,Henry N. 25
Jordan,Ida 72
Jorden,James 23
Jordan,Jeremiah 72
Jordan,Jeremiah(x)72
Jorden,John 25
Jordan,John H.62

*Jorden,John L.23
*Jordan,John P.72
Jordan,John W.72
Jordan,Joseph 72
Jordan,Lafayette 72
Jorden,Lora L.23
Jordan,Margaret 72
Jordan,Marshall 62
Jordan,Martha E. 62
Jourdon,Matilda(x)63
Jorden,Moris F.25
*Jordan,Peter G.62
Jordan,Potary F.62
Jourden,Rosa(x)18
Jorden,Sarah 23
Jordan,Sarah E. 62
*Jorden,Thomas 23
*Jorden,William 25
Joseph,Alford L.46
Joseph,Charles W.46
Joseph,Emma R.46
Joseph,Ezra S.46
Joseph,Francis M.46
Joseph,Hellen M. 46
Joseph,James L.46
*Joseph,John 46
Joseph,Nathaniel 46
Joseph,Sarah M. 46
Joseph,William E.46
Joy,Anna 11
Joy,Josafine 11
Joy,Nancy 11
Joy,Sarah(x)6
*Joy,Thomas 11
Judy,Mary(x)51
Justice,Jennetta(x)14
Kaysar see Keyser
Keaton,Albert 28
Keaton,Almeda 28
Keaton,Amanda 28
*Keaton,Calvary 28
Keaton,Emily 28
Keaton,Henry 28
Keaton,Jefferson 28
Keaton,John 28
Keaton,Leelie 29
Keaton,Lucinda 28
Keaton,Mary E. 28
*Keaton,Preston 28
*Keaton,Rilen 28
Keaton,Rosall 29
Keaton,Sarah F.28
Keaton,William 28

Keenan,Andrew 15
*Keenan,Andrew J.48
Keenan,Frances 43
Keenan,Henry P.15
Keenan,John C.15
Keenan,Kate E. 15
Keenan,Mary A. 15
Keenan,Missouri 15
*Keenan,Patrick H.15
Keenan,Rebecca 48
Keenan,Sallie 48
*Keenan,Samuel 43
Keenan,Sanford 48
Keheff,William(x)19
Kelf,Charles(x)16
Keller,Adaline 31
Keller,Adam 3
*Keller,Adam 31
*Keller,Albert 31
Keller,Allice 3
Keller,Edward 31
Keller,Elizabeth 3
Keller,Elizabeth 31.
Keller,Henry 31
Keller,Jasper 3
Keller,Jefferson 31.
Keller,John 31
Keller,Lucretia 31
Keller,Matta 31
Keller,Nancy 31
Keller,Nancy E.3
*Keller,Samuel 3
Keller,Thomas 31
Keller,Virginia 31
Keller,William S.3
Kelly,Martin(x)49
Kelly,Mary(x)7
Kelly,Stephen(x)7
Kennedy,Patrick(x)9.
Keyser,Addie F.63
Keyser,Albert 70
Keyser,Alphius 63
Keyser,Annie 70
Keyser,Charles 70
Keyser,Charlott 63
*Keyser,David 70
Keyser,Dora 70
Keyser,Eliza 70
Keyser,Eliza F.70
Keyser,Elizabeth 70)
Keyser,Ely B.63
*Keyser,Ephram 70
Keyser,Fannie 63
Keyser,Fannie 70

Keyser,Gallitin 70
*Keyser,George 63
Keyser,George 70
Keyser,Hughy 70
Keyser,John 70
Keyser,John 70
Keyser,John B.63
Kayer,John B.(x)63
Keyser,Mary M.63
Keyser,Oscar 70
Keyser,Patrick H.70
Keyser,Susan A. 63
Keyser,Thomas 70
Keyser,Vetera F.70
Keyser,Vila A. 70
Keyser,William 70
Killgore,Bennett 24
Killgore,Charles 24
Killgore,Eliza N.26
Killgore,Galiten 24
Killgore,George S.26
Killgore,James M.26
Killgore,John E.24
Killgore,John W.26
Killgore,Joseph C.24
Killgore,Mary F.26
Killgore,Mary J.24
Killgore,Netta 24
Killgore,Rachael 26
Killgore,Rufus C.26
Killgore,Sarah 26
*Killgore,Thomas W.24
*Killgore,William 26
Kimble,Lara(x)53
King,George 70
King,Martha J.70
*King,Mary 70
King,William 70
Kinght,Harriet 75
*Kinser,John L.54
Kinser,Mary J.54
Kinser,William 54
Kirk,Emerine 64
Kirk,Fannie 64
Kirk,James 64
*Kirk,Jemima 64
Kirk,Sallie 64
Kirk,William 64
Kline,Jacob A.16
*Kline,Thomas B.16
Knapp,Catherine 80
Knapp,David 80
Knapp,Elizabeth 80
*Knapp,Henry 80

Knapp, Ira 80
Knapp, Lymon 80
Knapp, Samuel 80
Knapp, William 80
Knibb, Rachel 60
*Knibb, Wilford 60
Knight-Nite
Knight, Abigal (x)72
*Knight, Abner 76
Knight, Abner 78
*Knight, Abner P.76
Nite, Adelade 2
Knight, Alsindra 76
Nite, Allen 40
Nite, Alvin S.2
Knight, Amacetta 7
*Knight, Anselum 78
Knight, Caroline 76
Knight, Eliza E. 78
Knight, Eliza F.76
Knight, Eliza(x)72
Nite, Elizabeth 2
Knight, Fannie(x)7
Knight, George 76
*Knight, George 76
Knight, Henrietta 7
*Knight, Henry 7
Knight, Henry L.75
Knight, Henry M.76
Knight, James 76
Nite, Jane 40
Knight, Jefferson 78
*Knight, John 76
Knight, John 78
Knight, John H.76
Nite, John L.2
Knight, Julia 78
Knight, Laffyett 7
Knight, Lafyette 76
Knight, Laura E. 76
Knight, Leelie 78
*Knight, Lenard 78
Knight, Lucy A. 7
Knight, Margaret 7
Knight, Margaret 76
Knight, Martha 76
Knight, Martha A. 78
Knight, Mary 76
Knight, Mary J.78
Nite, Mary 2
*Nite, Mathew 2
Knight, Matilda 78
Knight, Missouri E. 78
Nite, Nancy 2

Nite, Nancy A.2
Knight, Parthena 76
Knight, Phillip S.76
Knight, Rosa B.75
Knight, Sarah E. 78
Knight, Sarah M.7
Knight, Sarah S.75
Knight, Verena J.75
Knight, Virginia 76
Knight, Walter 76
*Nite, Wayne
*Nite, William 40
Knight, William 76
*Knight, William 75
Knight, William 78
Knop, Sarah(x)78
Kyle, Catherine A.8
Kyle, James J.8
Kyle, John E.8
Kyle, Margaret 8
Kyle, Peter 8
*Kyle, Peter 8
*Kyle, Tennessey 14
Lacy, Cristina(x)79
*Lacy, David 79
Lacy, Eustatia 79
Lacy, George(x79
Lacy, John P.(x)79
Lacy, Mary(x)79
Lafter, Elizabeth(x)18
Lafter, Malina J.(x)18
Lafter, Morgan(x)18
*Laidley, Albert 15
Laidley, Alberta 15
Laidley, Anna L.47
Laidley, Charles 47
*Laidley, George S.45
*Laidley, James H.26
*Laidley, John 47
Laidley, John B.15
Laidley, Laura A.26
Laidleu, Mary L.47
Laidley, Mary S.(x)52
Laidley, Mary V.45
Laidley, Sarah E.47
Laidley, Ulisses(x)52
Laidley, Vesta 15
Lallance, Anna 16
*Lallance, Charles N.16
Lallance, Harry H.16
Lallance, Martha E. 16
LallanceHenrietta 16
Lane, Albert 79
Lane, Ann(x)57

*Lane, Charles 79
Lane, Frances (x)57
Lane, Mary J.79
Lane, Mary(x)57
Lane, Thomas(x)57
Lane, Varena 79
*Lapole, John 74
Lapole, Rebecca 74
*Lapool, John 80
Lapool, Margaret 80
Lapool, Pedilla A. 80
Lapool, Zerilda 80
Latta, Philena(x)52
Latta, William(x)52
*Lawhorn, George W.59
Lawhorn, Mary E.59
Lawhorn, Pheba P.59
*Lawson, John 45
Lawson, Luemma 45
Laywell, Cristina 3
*Laywell, James 3
Lecky, Ana B.43
Lecky, Columbia (x)42
Lecky, Henry 42(x)42
Lecky, Susan 43
*Lecky, William 43
Legg, Adison 81
Legg, Allen 25
Legg, Charles W.81
Legg, Daniel 81
Legg, Elias 81
Legg, Elizabeth 25
Legg, James A. 81
Legg, James(x)25
Legg, John H.81
Legg, Martha L.81
Legg, Mary E. 81
Legg, Rebecca 81
Legg, Sallie A. 81
*Legg, Thomas 25
Legg, Thomas 81
Legg, Violetta(x)25
*Legg, Willis 81
*Legrand, James 38
Legrand, Mary 38
Legrand, Robert 38
Legrand, William 38
Leist, Catherine 13
Leist, Flora 131
Leist, Nannie 13
Leist, Phillip 13
*Leist, Vallentine 13
Leist, Walton 13
Lemaster, John(x)12

Lenard,Anna B.80
Lenard,Emma 80
Lenard,Frank M.80
Lenard,Franklin 12
Lenard,Harvey S.12
Lenard,Hester 12
*Lenard,John 12
Lenard,John F.80
Lenard,Margaret 80
Lenard,Mary E.58
*Lenard,Reuben E.80
*Lenard,Rufus 58
Lenard,Wiliam 80
*Lesage,Francis 75
Lesage,Francis J.75
*Lesage,Julius 76
Lesage,Juluis C.75
Lesage,Lvesa S.75
Lesage,Mary F. 75
Lesage,Mary M.75
Lesage,Mary M.76
Lesage,Zelia J.75
Letulle,Josephine 43
Letulle,Leanera 43
Letulle,Lewis P.43
*Letulle,Nancy 43
Letulle,Sarah 43
Linkfield,Alice(x)77
Linkfield,Riley(x)78
*Lloyd,John E. 15
Lloyd,Urania 15
Long,Adaline 28
Long,Bettie A.28
Long,Emily J.28
Long,James S.28
Long,Sarah B.28
*Long,William 28
Love,Allen 71
Love,Alphonso 19
Love,Ann A. 71
Love,Chalres 19
Love,Charles 71
Love,Cintha 19
Love,Cintha A. 19
Love,Conwelsa 71
*Love,Daniel 19
Love,James 71
Love,John 71
Love,Leonades 71
Love,Mary H. 19
*Love,Peter E.71
Love,Shelby J.19
Love,Thomas 71
Lovejoy,John(x)43

Low,George W.(x)49
Lucas,Adaline(x)18
Lucas,Cintha(x)11
Lucas,David 65
Lucas,Edward 65
Lucas,Fannie(x)44
*Lucas,George 60
Lucas,Georgie 51
Lucas,Hamit(x)45
Lucas,Helina 66
Lucas,Irvin 65
*Lucas,John W.51
Lucas,John(x)65
Lucas,Marion(x)67
Lucas,Palina 66
Lucas,Parke 65
Lucas,Pheba J.60
Lucas,Rebecca 65
Lucas,Rebecca 65
Lucas,Sarah 51
*Lucas,Vinson 65
*Lucas,William 66
Lunsford,Calvary 58
Lunsford,Eldrage 58
Lunsford,Elijah 58
Lunsford,Emily 58
Lunsford,Hughy 21
Lunsford,James F.21
Lunsford,John 21
Lunsford,John H.58
*Lunsford,Joshua 21
Lunsford,Lewis(x)26
Lunsford,Mary 58
Lunsford,Mary E.21
Lunsford,Nancy 58
Lunsford,Nora E.58
Lunsford,Peter 21
*Lunsford,Richard 58
Lunsford,Sallie 21
Lusher,Henry J.16
Lusher,James M.(x)11
*Lusher,Johnston 16
Lusher,Lucy 16
Lusher,Lucy F.16
Lusher,Mary E.(x)15
Lusher,Mary E.16
Lusher,Mathew E.(x)11
Lusher,Tolaver(x)11
Lusher,Winfield S. 16
Luster,Ellen(x)27
Lytes,Howard 23
*Lytes,Isaac 23
Lytes,Joseph 23
Lytes,Mary E. 23

Lytes,Matilda 23
Lytes,Sarah J.23
Maghee,Harriet(x)10
Maghee,Lucinda(x)10
Maghee,Mary B.(x)10
Magnus,Johanetta(x)45
*Malcum,Edward 25
Malcum,Francis 25
Malcum,Margaret 25
Malcum,Mary V.25
Malcum,Virginia 25
Malcum,Wilard 25
Mann,Catherine(x)10
Markins,Elizabeth(x)70
Markins,John(x)70
Marmaduke,James(x)44
Marre,Amanda 37
Marre,Daniel 37
Marre,Edward 37
*Marre,Joseph 37
Marre,Louisa 37
Marre,nancy 37
Marre,Wesley 37
Marshall,Allen(x)19
*Marshall,Lewis 12
Marshall,Lucy 12
Martin-Marten
Marten,Amanda 39
*Martin,Andrew 15
Marten,Benjamin 39
Marten,Butler 69
Marten,Charles 39
Marten,Clementine 39
Martin,Earnest 15
Martin,Eliza 15
Marten,Ella 39
Martin,Emaline 15
Martin,Emily 69
Martin,Fannie 15
*Martin,George 15
Marten,George 39
Martin,Grace 69
Marten,Harriet 39
Martin,Ida 15
*Martin,James 32
Martin,John 15
*Martin,John B.69
Marten,John F.39
Marten,Josephine 39
Martin,Nancy 32
Martin,Olivia 32
Martin,Sallie 32
Martin,William 15

*Marten,William 39
Mathena,Mary(x)78
Mather,Augusta G.13
Mather,Carrie B.44
Mather,Emma 44
Mather,George H.13
Mather,Jacob 2
Mather,James A.2
*Mather,John 2
*Mather,John N.4
Mather,Mahala 2
Mather,Nancy 2
*Mather,Oscar W.13
Mather,Sarah A.2
Mather,Sidney 13
Mather,Sumner 13
Mather,Valcolon W.13
Mattson,Avel G.(x)16
Maupin,Ada R.(x)20
Maupin,Albert 52
Maupin,Allen F.44
*Maupin,America 44
*Maupin,Beverly 51
Maupin,Chapman 51
*Maupin,Chapman 52
Maupin,Cintha 51
Maupin,Fannie C.52
Maupin,Ira J.44
Maupin,Julia A.51
Maupin,Lucy 51
Maupin,Lucy M.52
Maupin,Mary A.52
Maupin,Matilda 52
Maupin,Sarah A.44
Maupin,Shelby 52
Maupin,Virginia D.51
Maupin,William 52
Mayse,America 54
Mayse,Eliza 54
Mayse,Emily 54
Mayse,John 54
Mayse,Malissa 54
Mayse,Mary A. 54
*Mayse,Parker 54
Mayse,Sarah 54
McCallister-McCo-tor
McCallister,Ada 30
McCollister,Albert 29
*McCollister,Alexander 29
McCollistor,America 29
McCallister,Annie 30
McCallister,Betavia 61
*McCallister,Boniah 30
*McCallister,Corydin 61

McCallister,Eliza S.30
McCollister,Eliza 27
McCollister,Elizabeth 27
McCollistor,Elizabeth 29
McCallister,Emma 30
McCollister,Evaline 29
McCallister,George 30
McCollister,Hamilton 27
McCallister,Harriet 30
McCallister,Hellen 29
McCollister,Isaac H.61
McCollistor,Isabel 29
McCollister,James 29
McCollister,John 27
*McCallister,John 61
McCallister,John H.30
McCallister,Joseph 30
McCollister,Joseph 29
McCollister,Lafyette 29
McCollister,Letha 29
McCollister,Louisa 29
McCallister,Malinda 61
McCollistor,Manuel 29
McCallister,Mariah 61
McCallister,Martha J.30
McCollister,Martin 29
McCollistor,Mary A.29
McCollister,Mary E. 29
McCollister,Nancy 27
*McCollister,Olevia 27
McCollister,Patrick 27
*McCollister,Preston 29
McCallister,Preston 61
McCallister,Sarah A.61
McCallister,Susannah 61
McCollister,William 27
McCollistor,Wilmothe 29
McCartie,Francis(x)3
*McCartie,John L.3
*McClary,Alexander 19
McClary,Catherine 19
McClary,Charles L.19
McClary,Ida M.30
McClary,Isaac W. 19
*McClary,John J.30
McClary,Joseph A. 19
McClary,Lucretia 19
McClary,Mary 30
McClary,Mary L.19
McClasky,Alexander 82
McClasky,Emily 82
*McClasky,Floyd 82
McClasky,Hamilton 82
McClasky,James W.82

McClasky,John H.82
McClasky,Mareom 82
*McClasky,Nancy 82
McClasky,Nancy J.82
McClasky,Robert 82
McClasky,Sarah T.82
McClasky,Thomas 82
McCollister,Albert 29
McCollister,Alexander 29*
McCollister,Hamilton 27
McCollister,Hellen 29
McCollister,William 27
McCollistor,America 29
McCollistor,Elizabeth 29
McCollistor,Isabel 29
McCollistor,Manuel 29
McCollistor,Mary A. 29
McCollistor,Preston 29*
McCollistor,Wilmothe 29
McComas,Albert 64
McComas,Alexander 9
McComas,Andrea 81
*McComas,David 64
McComas,Elisha(x)80
McComas,Eliza 9
McComas,Ellen 80
McComas,Emily 64
McComas,George 17
McComas,George C.81
McComas,James J.64
*McComas,Jefferson 17
McComas,Job 81
*McComas,John 81
*McComas,John 9
McComas,John(x)80
McComas,June 17
McComas,Kate R.9
McComas,Lelia F.9
McComas,Lucinda 81
McComas,Margaret 17
McComas,Martha 17
McComas,Martha 17
McComas,Oliver P.(x)9
McComas,Pulina(x)58
McComas,Rebecca(x)51
McComas,Roxey L.9
McComas,Sarah 64
McComas,Thomas J.81
McComas,Walter 64
McComas,William 81
*McComas,William 80
McComas.Agnus 9
McConnell,Albert 39
McConnell,Clarona 39

McConnell,Eliza 39
McConnell,George 39
McConnell,James K.39
McConnell,Lerona 39
McConnell,Mary A.39
McConnell,Roddy(x)52
*McConnell,William 39
McCorkle,Arena 31
McCorkle,Arthur 18
McCorkle,Benjamin 31
McCorkle,Effie M.18
*McCorkle,Ellen S.18
McCorkle,George 18
McCorkle,Ida S. 18
*McCorkle,James 31
McCorkle,Jefferson 31
McCorkle,Lee Jackson 31
McCorkle,Oliva V.31
McCorkle,Phebe(x)44
McCorkle,Sarah 31
McCoy,Catherine 29
McCoy,Charles L.29
*McCoy,Elizabeth 29
McCoy,Emily 29
*McCoy,John L.62
*McCoy,Lawrence 29
McCoy,Mildred 62
McCoy,Rachel F.62
McCoy,Rutha 29
McCoy,Semantha 29
McCoy,William 62
McCoy,William H.29
McCulloch,Bob C.54
McCulloch,Emma F.54
McCulloch,Fannie M.54
McCulloch,Frank R.54
McCulloch,Georgie L.54
*McCulloch,Patrick 54
McCune,Bailey 7
*McCune,Benjamin 7
McCune,Charles 7
McCune,Frank 7
McCune,George 7
McCune,Henry 7
McCune,John 7
McCune,Julia 7
McCune,Lawrence 7
McCune,Mary E. 7
McCune,Salem 7
McCune,Sarah 7
McDermont,Elvira 11
McDermont,George M.11
McDermont,George R.(x)11
*McDermont,James 11

McDermont,Leslie 11
McDermont,Mary(x)11
McDowell,John (x)49
McDowney,Charles 20
McDowney,Henry 20
*McDowney,James 20
McDowney,James B. 20
McDowney,Mary 20
McDowney,William C.20
McElavy,Alich 33
McElavy,Barbary 33
*McElavy,David 33
McElavy,Mary 33
*McGhee,Benjamin 58
McGhee,Eugenia 58
McGhee,George(x)58
McGhee,Milda C.58
*McGinnis,Achilles 56
McGinnis,Allice B.55
McGinnis,Amanda(x)56
*McGinnis,Allen 47
McGinnis,Benjamin 56
*McGinnis,Benjamin D.44
McGinnis,Cora E. 55
McGinnis,Eliza 14
McGinnis,Eva 44
McGinnis,Flavius 56
McGinnis,Grant 56
McGinnis,Jennie 47
McGinnis,Lucien 56
McGinnis,Maggie 47
McGinnis,Minnie 56
McGinnis,Miranne 56
McGinnis,Sarah 44
McGinnis,Sarah E.47
*McGinnis,William 55
McGown,James(x19
*McKendree,Aaron F.63
McKendree,Catherine 63
McKendree,Emma M.63
McKendree,Lydia 63
McKendree,Mary S.63
McKendree,William P.63
*McKindy,Azel 79
McKindy,Baze 79
McKindy,Benjmain 79
McKindy,Cora B.79
McKindy,Elmore S.79
McKindy,George L.79
McKindy,Ida J.79
McKindy,Lurania 79
McKindy,Mary 79
McKindy,Olive P.79
McKinney,Estaline 27

McKinney,George 27
McKinney,Sallie 27
*McKinney,William 27
McMahon,George(x)9
McMahon,Wayne(x)43
McNeely,Mary(x)23
McVickers,Archebald 36
*McVickers,Archibald 53
McVickers,Harriet 53
*McVickers,Hilvery 36
McVickers,James 36
McVickers,James 53
McVickers,James F.53
*McVickers,John 53
McVickers,Malinda 36
McVickers,Mary 36
McVickers,Matilda 53
McVickers,Nancy 36
McVickers,Permelia 53
McVickers,Vianna 36
McWharter,Calferna 82
McWharter,Consentine 82
McWharter,Edna P.82
McWharter,Elizabeth 82
*McWharter,James 82
McWharter,James H.82
McWharter,Mahaley F.82
McWharter,Mariettta 82
Meadows,Meadowrs,Medows
Meadows,America 31
Meadows,Anna B.31
*Meadowrs,Balester 71
Medows,Drucilla 82
Meadows,Henry 31
Medows,Henry J.83
Medows,Hezekiah 82
*Meadows,James 31
Medows,James J.82
Meadows,John A.31
*Meadowrs,John O.71
Medows,Laurinda J.83
Meadowrs,Mandora 71
Medows,Margaret 82
Medows,Mary A.83
Meadowrs,Mirem 71
Meadowrs,Nannie 71
*Medows,Ranson 82
Meadowrs,Rebecca F.71
Meadowrs,Salena 71
Medows,Sarah 82
Medows,Sarah E.83
Meadows,Sylvester 82
Meadows,Thomas 31
*Medows,William 82

Mealing see Meeling

Mechesly, Agnis 19
Mechesly, Elizabeth 19
Mechesly, Ellen 19
*Mechesly, John 19
Mechesly, Susanna 19
*Medler, Bruno 57
Medler, Eliza J.57
Medler, Emma E. 57
Medler, Ernest 57
Medler, Fannie 57
Medler, Henrietta 57
Medler, Henry C.57
*Medler, John 57
Medler, John G.57
Medler, Julius 57
Meeling, Catherine 6
*Meeling, Charles F.6
*Mealing, Charles 6
Mealing, Elizabeth 6
Mee(a)ling, John 6
Mealing, Matilda 6
Meiller, Dwies(x)33
Merkl, George(x)83
Merrett, Cassie 11
Merrett, Debera 14
Merrett, Emma 11
Merrett, Frances 16
Merrett, George 16
*Merrett, John 16
*Merrett, Joseph 11
Merrett, Lucy 16
Merrett, Martha 11
Merrett, Mary 11
*Merrett, Melchi 11
Merrett, Olevy 11
Merrett, Sarah 16
Merrett, Susan 16
Merrett, Tennessey 14
Merrett, Thadeus 14
Merrett, Thomas 11
Merrett, Thomas 16
Merrett, Virginia 16
Merrett, Walter 14
*Merrett, William 14
Merrett, Willie 11
Merrimen, Frances 78
Merrimen, Hester 78
Merrimen, Mathew 78
Merrimen, Nellie 78
*Merrimen, Thomas 78
Messinger, Marion(x)52
*Meyers, Charles 30
Meyers, Ellen 30

Meyers, Julia 30
Meyers, Mary A.30
Meyers, Milton 30
Michael, Daniel 79
Michael, David 79
Michael, Elizabeth 79
Michael, Elizabeth(x)79
Michael, John 79
Michael, Malissey J.79
Michael, Mary M.(x)79
Michael, Olive 79
Michael, Sarah 79
Michael, Ulysses 79
*Michael, William 79
Michael, Wilson 79
Midkiff, America 64
Midkiff, Eliza A.62
Midkiff, Elizabeth 62
Midkiff, Emily E.62
*Midkiff, Gordon 62
Midkiff, Harvey 62
Midkiff, Henry C.64
Midkiff, John T.64
Midkiff, Julia M.64
Midkiff, Lewis E.64
Midkiff, Rachel S.62
Midkiff, Roland W.64
Midkiff, Sarah 62
Midkiff, Solomon 62
*Midkiff, Solomon 64
Midkiff, Veturi 62
Midkiff, William A.62
Miller, Abigal 56
Miller, Alexander 17
Miller, Alvin N, 27
Miller, Anna 13
Miller, Arrova 74
*Miller, Carolina 74
Miller, Charles 74
Miller, Charles H.13
Miller, Charles(x)15
Miller, Claudius 17
Miller, Cornelia 27
Meiller, Dwies(x)33
Miller, Eliza 13
Miller, Eliza 17
Miller, Evvie V. 17
Miller, Frances 17
Miller, Frank 13
Miller, Fredrick 64
Miller, Fredrick S.17
*Miller, George 13
*Miller, George F.15
Miller, George M.15

Miller, George R. 17
Miller, George(x)49
Miller, Hannah 15
*Miller, Henry 27
Miller, Henry 64
*Miller, Henry 56
Miller, Isabel 74
Miller, Jacob 64
Miller, James W.64
*Miller, Jessey 64
*Miller, John 14
*Miller, John G. 71
Miller, John O.14
Miller, John W. 13
Miller, Joseph 13
Miller, Leanina 74
Miller, Levna A. 17
Miller, Lewis T.27
Miller, Lucinda 64
Miller, Manerva 27
Miller, Marcelles(x)15
Miller, Mary 13
Miller, Mary 15
Miller, Mary M.14
Miller, Maxium 14
Miller, Palina(x)24
Miller, Rose A.74
Miller, Sarah 27
Miller, Sigman(x)17
Miller, Susan 56
Miller, Susan(x)15
Miller, William 14
Miller, William 15
*Miller, William C.13
Mitchell, Arthur P.53
*Mitchell, Elisah T.53
Mitchell, Elisha S.53
*Mitchell, Elizabeth 43
Mitchell, Elizabeth 53
Mitchell, Ella 43
Mitchell, Fannie E.53
Mitchell, Isaac H.53
Mitchell, Martah V.53
Mitchell, Nancy 43
Mitchell, Samuel H.53
Mitchell, William 43
Mobley, Isaac 77
*Mobley, James 77
Mobley, Margaret 75
Mobley, Margaret 77
Mobley, Mason 77
Mobley, Rachel 75
Mobley, Rachel 77
Mobley, Thomas J.77

*Mobley, William 75
*Montgomery, Alexander 71
Montgomery, Joanna 71
Mooney, Edward(x)19
Mooney, Elizabeth(x)19
Mooney, James W.(x)16
Moore, Anna(x)79
Moore, Edith C.79
Moore, George 15
Moore, John 79
Moore, Julia A. 79
*Moore, Mary 15
Moore, Roda J.79
Moore, Sarah 79
*Moore, William 79
Mores see Morris
Mores, Anna(x)39
Mores, Cratin(x)39
Mores, Edward 39
*Mores, Eton 41
Mores, George 41
Mores, George M.39
*Mores, Henry 39
Mores, Lucy 41
Mores, Mary E.39
Mores, Robert(x)39
Mores, William(x)39
Morgan, John(x)16
Morgan, John(x)7
Morris, Albert 21
Morris, Ann 5
*Morris, Benjamin 5
*Morris, Benjamin 73
Morris, Buregard 26
Morris, Charles 21
Morris, Charles 5
*Morris, Charles K.12
Morris, Charles R.12
Morris, Edna E.12
Morris, Eliza(x)13
Morris, Ellen L.12
Morris, Emily 12
Morris, Ester 12
Morris, Eugene 26
Morris, Fannie 21
Morris, Fannie 26
Morris, Ferdenan 26
*Morris, George 57
Morris, Hellen 26
Morris, Hellen J.27
Morris, Henry 12
Morris, Iva V.12
*Morris, James R.26
Morris, James T.27

Morris, John A.12
*Morris, Joseph W.21
Morris, Joseph W.27
Morris, Julia A.63
Morris, Louisa 12
Morris, Lucretia 63
Morris, Lucy 63
Morris, Mahaley 5
Morris, Malon S.63
Morris, Margaret 57
Morris, Martha 12
Morris, Mary 5
Morris, Mary E.12
Morris, Mary(x)26
Morris, Moses 5
Morris, Nancy 57
Morris, Nancy A.57
Morris, Peggy 57
Morris, Rose(x)12
Morris, Sallie 26
Morris, Sallie 57
*Morris, Samuel 12
Morris, Sarah A.27
Morris, Walter 26
Morris, William 5
Morrison, Anis 61
Morrison, Annie 61
Morrison, Calvary 70
Morrison, Calvin 61
Morrison, Charles 3
Morrisn, Catherine 70
Morrison, David(x)20
Morrison, Eliza 61
Morrison, Elizabeth 3
Morrison, Eugenia 3
*Morrison, Frances 67
Morrison, Franklin 3
Morrison, Harrison, 61
*Morrison, Henry 67
Morrison, James 70
Morrison, James A.60
*Morrison, John E.70
Morrison, John T.70
Morrison, Leander 61
Morrison, Malinda 3
Morrison, Martha A. 70
Morrison, Marion W.60
Morrison, Mary 67
Morrison, Mary E.70
Morrison, Mary M.60
Morrison, Nancy 70
*Morrison, Nancy B.70
Morrison, Nannie W.3
Morrison, Napoleon B.70

*Morrison, Patrick 3
Morrison, Patrick H.3
Morrison, Sarah 60
Morrison, Telitha 67
Morrison, Thomas J.60
Morrison, Thomas W.3
*Morrison, Thompson 61
Morrison, Virnilla(x)68
Morrison, Wesley 60*
Morrison, William 70
Morrison, William 3
Morrison, William 60
Morton, Caroline 77
Morton, Helena 77
*Morton, John 77
Moses, Martha(x)49
Moses, Massie(x)49
*Moss, Randolph 14
Mossgrove, Mariah 43
Mossgrove, Thomas 43*
Mullen, Mary 20
*Mullen, Michael 20
Murphy, Allice M.20
Murphy, Ella E.20
*Murphy, Francis 20
Murphy, James M.20
Murphy, Julia 20
Murphy, Mary N.20
Murphy, Paul 20
Murrey, Thomas(x)19
*Neal, Abreham 43
Neal, Adison G.23
*Neal, Andrew 23
Neal, Charles H.23
Neal, Eliza A.23
Neal, George 23
Neal, John M.23
Neal, Malinda 23
Neal, Salina 43
*Nelson, Allen E.9
*Nelson, Anderson 12
Nelson, Catherine 9
Nelson, Henry E.9
Nelson, Isabel 9
Nelson, James W.9
Nelson, Jane 12
Nelson, Sarah A.9
*Newberger, Harriet 15
Newcomb, Edgar J.48
*Newcomb, George 34
Newcomb, Labon T.48
Newcomb, Lemuel P.34
Newcomb, Louisa 34
Newcomb, Margaret 48

*Newcomb, William 48
*Newman, Adison 24
Newman, Albert G.24
Neuman, Albert G.75
*Newman, Alexander 73
Newman, Amanda 24
Neuman, Carolina 75
Newman, Dora D.10
Newman, Elizabeth 73
Newman, Emily 73
Newman, Emily E.10
Newman, Emma 24
Newman, Frances 10
Newman, Harvey(x)76
Newman, Hettie F.24
Newman, Isabel 10
Newman, James 73
Newman, James S.10
Neuman, Lucinda 75
Neuman, Mariah 75
Neuman, Mary 75
Neuman, Pernellia 35
*Newman, Meltin 24
*Newman, Morris 10
Newman, Robert M.10
Newman, Sarah 10
Newman, Serena 10
Newman, Ulysses 10
Neuman, Viola G.75
*Neuman, Warren 35
Newman, William 10
*Neuman, William 75
*Newman, Winston 10
Newman, Winston S.10
Nicely, Adaline 69
Nicely, Albert 68
Nicely, Andrew 69
Nicely, Anna J.26
Nicely, Charles 5
Nicely, Charles R.26
*Nicely, Dudley 5
Nicely, Elizabeth 26
Nicely, Elizabeth 68
Nicely, Emily 68
Nicely, George 69
Nicely, Henry 68
Nicely, Hughey 69
Nicely, James 68
*Nicely, James H.69
Nicely, John 5
Nicely, Joshua 69
Nicely, Louisa 68
Nicely, Margaret 69
Nicely, Martha 26

Nicely, Mary 5
Nicely, Mary L.26
Nicely, Morgan 26
Nicely, Nancy 26
Nicely, Palina 26
Nicely, Robert 26
*Nicely, Roland 26
Nicely, Sarah 5
Nicely, Sarah 68
Nicely, Susan 5
Nicely, Thomas 69
Nicely, William 26
Nicely, William 5
Nicely, William 68
Nicely, Zach 5
Nicely, Zacheriah 26
Nicholas, Sela(x)42
Nipps, George(x)72
*Nipps, Jacob 70
Nipps, Juriah 70
Nipps, Morris(x)8
Noel, Rodrick(x)57
Noell, Arthur 39
Noell, James 39
*Noell, Larkin 39
Noell, Polley 39
Noell, Queen V. 39
Norris, Richard(x)50
Nucel, Cora(49)
Nucel, James(x)49
Nucel, Sallie(x)49
Oley, Alberta 38
Oley, Eliza C.38
Oley, Elizabeth 38
Oley, Emma 38
Oley, John 38
Oley, Julius 38
Oley, Luticia 38
Oley, Martha 38
Oliver, Ann(x)76
Oliver, Nancy(x)76
Oliver, Rachel(x)76
Ong, Ernest M.44
Ong, Isaac B.44
Ong, Joseph(x)16
Ong, Margaret(x)16
*Ong, Susan 44
*Osborn, Aaron 59
Osborn, Jemima 59
Osborn, John T. 59
Osborn, Sarah C. 59
Owens, Edward 33
Owens, Elizabeth 33
Owens, James 33

*Owens, James M.33
Owens, John L.33
Owens, Martha 33
Owens, Mary A. 33
Owens, Mary B.33
*Owens, Salinda 33
Parish, Elizabeth 23
*Parish, James 23
Parish, Julia 23
Parish, Julia A. 23
Parish, Malard 23
Parson, Edward 4
*Parson, John H.4
Parson, Julia 4
Parson, Lorenzo D.4
Patton, Emma M.2
*Patton, Erastus 2
Patton, Sabina 2
*Paulees, Ernest 75
Paulees, Henrietta 75
Paulees, Henry 75
Paulees, Lvesa 75
*Payne, Charles 28
Payne, Ella 28
Payne, Henry(x)7
Payne, Sarah 28
Payne, Sidney 28
Payne, William 28
Payton see Peyton
Pease, Josaphine(x)47
Pennybacker, Albert 51
Pennybacker, Braefton 51
Pennybacker, Fannie 51
Pennybacker, Florida 51
*Pennybacker, James 51
*Pennybacker, John M.53
Pennybacker, Lucy 51
Pennybacker, Mason S.53
Pennybacker, Minnie M.53
Pennybacker, Mollie L.53
Pennybacker, Sallie H.53
Pennybacker, Tena L.53
Pennybacker, William 51
Pennybacker, Wm.(x)53
Perry, Addie 73
Perry, Affie J.62
Perry, Albert 74
Perry, America 62
Perry, Anna E.62
Perry, Anna E.63
Perry, Annie 73
Perry, Bailey S.62
Perry, Barbery 63
*Perry, Benjamin 62

Perry,Brevatta 62	Peters,Rachel 77	Peyton,William K.61
Perry,Charles J.62	Peters,Richard H.45	Phillips,Robert(x)34
Perry,Cintha 62	Peters,Stonewall 45	Phinetta,Patrick(x)19
Perry,Cintha 63	Peters,Violet V. 45	Pinnell,Alma L. 14
Perry,David 1.62	Pettit,Charles 64	Pinnell,Clara L.14
*Perry,Elijah 62	Pettit,Ellen 53	Pinnell,Estetta 14
Perry,Eliza J.74	Pettit,Fannie 53	Pinnell,Mary E.14
Perry,Emily J.62	Pettit,Frances 53	Pinnell,Mary V. 14
Perry,Emily V.62	Pettit,George 53	Pinnell,Perry 14
Perry,Harrison 73	*Pettit,Hugh 53	*Pinnell,Perry G.14
Perry,henry 73	Pettit,James 53	Pinnell,Thomas N.14
Perry,Ida A. 63	Pettit,John 64	Pinnell,Witten H.14
perry,Ira S. 62	*Pettit,John 64	Plybon,Cintha V.33
Perry,Jackson 62	Pettit,Mary A. 53	Plybon,Eliza 41
Perry,James 63	Pettit,Nodiah 53	Plybon,Eliza E.33
*Perry,James E.63	Pettit,Robert 53	Plybon,Elizabeth 33
Perry,James F.62	Pettit,Sarah C.64	Plybon,Elizabeth 41
Perry,Jenetta 63	*Pettit,William 53	Plybon,Emily 32
Perry,John H.74	Pettit,William 64	Plybon,Irene 32
*Perry,John J.63	*Peyton,Alexander 22	Plybon,Isaac N.33
Perry,John L.8	Peyton,Allen 22	*Plybon,Jacob 41
Perry,John W.62	Peyton,Alvin 58	Plybon,Jacob M.32
Perry,John(x)74	Peyton,Alzira 22	*Plybon,James 32
Perry,Joseph 63	*Payton,Archibald 58	Plybon,James L.32
Perry,Joshua M.63	*Peyton,Elisha 58	*Plybon,John 32
Perry,Julia A. 62	Peyton,Elizabeth 60	*Plybon,John C.33
Perry,Lucinda 73	Payton,Emma 58	Plybon,Lewis G. 32
Perry,Lucy 74	Peyton,Emma M.60	Plybon,Lucinda 32
Perry,Lucy(x)74	Peyton,Evazetta 60	Plybon,Mary 41
Perry,Manerva 63	Peyton,Fianna 22	Plybon,Sheriden 32
*Perry,Mary A.	Peyton,Francis(x)9	Plybon,Sherman 32
Perry,Mary C.62	Peyton,Franklin 60	Plybon,Simeon 33
Perry,Mary C.63	*Peyton,Harrison 60	Plybon,Victoria 33
Perry,Mary E. 62	Peyton,Isabel 22	Plybon,William 32
*Perry,Melcher A.8	Peyton,John 58	Poague,Anna 53
Perry,Nancy 74	Peyton,Judy A.(x)58	Poague,Bayless 53
Perry,Rachel 74	Payton,Kirby 58	Pouge,Bertie E.(x)54
Perry,Randolph 62	Peyton,Luvada 22	Poague,Edgar 53
Perry,Rebecca 8	Peyton,Marietta 60	Poague,George H.53
*Perry,Richard 73	Peyton,Martha J.61	*Poague,James H.53
Perry,Sarah J.62	Peyton,Mary E.22	Pouge,Marcel A.(x)54
*Perry,Silas 62	Payton,Mary F. 58	Poague,Robert C.53
Perry,Susa 74	Peyton,Mary J.(x)58	Poague,Sallie K.53
*Perry,Thomas 63	Peyton,Milla 58	Poague,Sarah A. 53
Perry,Virginia 74	Peyton,Palina 22	*Poar,Alford 18
Perry,William 62	Peyton,Perlina 61	Poar,Allen(x)18
*Perry,William 74	Peyton,Rosco V.61	Poar,Elias(x)18
Perry,William M.63	Payton,Sarah C.58	Poar,Frank M.18
Peters,Franklin 77	Peyton,Sofia (x)9	Poar,Mary J. 18
Peters,John L.45	Payton,Susan 58	Poindexter,Charles 46
*Peters,John L.77	Peyton,Thomas(x)9	*Poindexter,James 46
Peters,John T.77	Peyton,Viola M.22	Poindexter,Nannie 46
*Peters,Lewis 45	Peyton,William 22	Pollard,Frances 44
Peters,Mary V. 45	Peyton,William 58	Pollard,George E. 44

Pollard,Ida C. 44
*Pollard,John 44
Porter,Adaline 64
*Porter,Alexander 69
Porter,Alonzo(x)36
Porter,America V.69
Porter,Catherine 69
Porter,Elijah 69
Porter,Elisha(x)70
Porter,Eliza 69
Porter,Elizabeth 67
Porter,Frank 67
Porter,Harriet 69
Porter,Jacob g.64
Porter,James H.64
*Porter,James S.69
*Porter,Jerurhel 64
Porter,John 67
*Porter,John 69
Porter,John J.64
Porter,Julia A.64
Porter,Letha 67
Porter,Louisa C.64
Porter,Malinda 67
Porter,Margaret 69
Porter,Martha 69
Porter,Mary A.69
Porter,Mary(x)70
Porter,Milley 67
Porter,nancy A.64
Porter,Patrick H.69
Porter,polley 67
Porter,Robert 69
*Porter,Samuel 67
Porter,Sarah 67
Porter,Sarah 69
Porter,Sarah J.64
Porter,Susan A.69
Porter,William 69
Poteet,Albert 13
Poteet,America 40
*Poteet,Clements 40
Poteet,Fannie 13
Poteet,George 40
*Poteet,Henry C.13
Poteet,James(x)8
Poteet,John 49
Poteet,Maggie A.13
Poteet,Martha 49
*Poteet,Skelton 49
Price,Clarence(x)15
Price,Frances(x)9
Price,Joseph(x)9
Prichard,Sarah(x)4

Prise,Albert (x)3
Prise,Emma 5
Prise,George(x)13
*Prise,John 5
Prise,John O.5
*Prise,Joseph 46
Prise,Minerva 46
Prise,Minnie 12
Prise,Rochy(x)13
*Prise,Sophia 12
Prise,William 5
Pulley,David 73
*Pulley,John 8
Pulley,Julia 73
Pulley,Malissa 8
Pulley,Mary 73
Pulley,Mary 8
Pulley,Rebecca 73
*Pulley,William 73
Quinn,Margaret(x)51
Qwalk,Dorcas 52
*Qwalk,Joseph 52
Qwalk,Kate 52
Qwalk,Sarah E. 52
Qwalk,William 52
Qwalk,Willie 52
Radfort,Peter(x)55
Rariden,Ammazilla 80
Rariden,Henry 80
*Rariden,John 80
Rariden,Melvina 80
Rariden,Sarah 80
Ratcliff,Allice 37
Ratcliff,Ephram 37
Ratcliff,George 37
Ratcliff,John 37
Ratcliff,Matlida 37
Ratcliff,Squire 37
*Ratcliff,Virginia 37
Ratcliff,William 37
Ray,Albert 33
Ray,Alonzo 33
Ray,Anna H.34
*Ray,Benjamin 34
Ray,Catherine 33
*Ray,Cathorine 29
Ray,Cato 34
Ray,Cornetta 35
Ray,Elijah 34
Ray,Emily 33
Ray,Georgie 33
*Ray,Isiah 33
Ray,Isriel 33
*Ray,James F.35

Ray,Jefferson 33
Ray,Jennie 29
Ray,Joseph 34
Ray,Lemuel 33
*Ray,Lucy 34
Ray,Lycetta 33
Ray,Marcillaus 33
Ray,Marion 33
Ray,Mary 34
Ray,Mary E. 33
Ray,Millard 34
Ray,Oley 34
Ray,Sarah F.33
Ray,Sarah R.34
Ray,Sophia 35
Ray,Ulysses 29
Ray,Virginia 33
*Ray,William 33
*Ray,William E.35
*Rece,Abia 20
Reece,Albert S.23
Reece,Alice L.(x)21
*Reece,Allen W.24
Reece,Andrew 55
Reece,Charles 24
Reece,Dianna 8
*Reece,Edmond C.21
Reece,Ella 20
Reece,Emma V.55
Reece,Frankie S. 20
*Reece,James T.24
*Reece,James 24
Reece,James A.(x)21
Reece,Jennie L.21
*Reece,John B.8
*Reece,John C.55
*Reece,John M.25
*Reece,Joseph A.20
Reece,Leanora 20
Reece,Lewis 55
Reece,Lizzie H. 20
Reece,Louisa 24
Reece,Margaret 55
Reece,Martha E.24
Reece,Mary 25
Reece,Mary C.24
Reece,Mary E.8
Reece,Medora S.20
Reece,Mirem 25
Reece,Permilla 20
Reece,Rebecca 24
Reece,Rebecca A.24
Reece,Sophia 21
Reece,Thomas 24

Reece, Walter 24
*Reece, Warren P.20
Reed, Charles 80
Reed, Charles L. 44
Reed, Ida 44
Reed, John 44
Reed, John H.80
Reed, Margret 80
*Reed, Mary A. 44
Reed, Sarah C.80
Reed, Vinson 44
*Reed, William 80
Retherford, Eliot(x)63
*Reynolds, Archibald 62
Runnels, Benjamin 24
Runnels, Cassie 24
Runnels, Charles T.24
Runnels, Elijah 24
Runnels, Elizabeth 22
Runnels, Frances 24
Runnels, George 24
*Runnels, Griffin 22
*Reynolds, Hardon 72
*Runnels, John D.24
Runnels, John E.24
Runnels, Joseph 24
Reynolds, Mary 72
Reynolds, Solomon(x)38
Reynolds, Susan H.62
Reynolds, Twintna 72
Richards, Ann 49
*Richards, Hezekiah 49
Ricketts, Charles 40
Ricketts, Edwin 40
Ricketts, Ella 40
Ricketts, Girard 40
*Ricketts, Virginia 40
*Rider, Charles W. 45
Rider, Elizabeth 45
Rider, Isadore 54
*Rider, John 54
Rider, Martha 45
Rider, Mary J.45
Rider, Sarah 45
*Riggs, Albert 80
Riggs, Amanda 35
Riggs, Celila A.(x)80
Riggs, Effe 35
Riggs, Greenville 35
Riggs, Hatty 35
Riggs, James 35
*Riggs, James 35
Riggs, Larrah 35
Riggs, Mary 35

Riggs, Nancy 35
Riggs, Thomas J.(x)80
Riggs, Vida 80
Riggs, Virginia 80
*Roberts, Absolum 42
Roberts, America 62
Roberts, Arther B.70
Roberts, Benjamin 35
*Roberts, Elizabeth 27
Roberts, Ellie 70
Roberts, Emma J. 43
Roberts, George A. 35
*Roberts, Harrison 62
Roberts, James H. 35
*Roberts, James L. 43
Roberts, James M. 43
Roberts, Jaunetta 35
Roberts, Jeremiah 35
Roberts, John 35
Roberts, John 62
Roberts, John W. 43
Roberts, John(x)41
Roberts, Lincoln 70
Roberts, Lubecia 42
Roberts, Lutrecia 42
Roberts, Mary E. 42
Roberts, Mary E.68
Roberts, Nancy A.36
*Roberts, Neuman 36
*Roberts, Patterson 35
*Roberts, Rebecca 68
Roberts, Richard J.70
Roberts, Salcia 35
Roberts, Sanford(x)41
Roberts, Sarah L. 43
Roberts, Selvana 35
Roberts, Susan 62
Roberts, Susan(x)41
Roberts, Viola E. 42
Roberts, William 43
Roffe, Ann 12
Roffe, Augusta 12
Roffe, Callie D. 60
Roffe, Charles 12
*Roffe, Charles L.12
Roffe, Charles P.60
Roffe, Effie A. 60
Roffe, Ida 12
*Roffe, James H.64
*Roffe, Joseph W. 60
Roffe, Kate 12
Roffe, Mary 64
Roffe, Mary E.12
Roffe, Rebecca 60

Roffe, Susan 12
Roffe, Virginia 60
Roffe, William 64
Rogers, Amanda 70
Rogers, Bascom 70
Rogers, Charles M.49
Rogers, Cintha 70
Rogers, Emmetta 49
*Rogers, Fenton 70
*Rogers, George 57
Rogers, Isabel 57
Rogers, Jahive 57
Rogers, James 49
Rogers, Kate V.49
Rogers, Nancy 57
Rogers, Nannie 49
Rogers, Rodie 57
Rogers, Susie L.49
Rogers, Thomas 57
Rogers, Wilburn B.70
*Rogers, William 57
*Rogers, William C.49
Rogers, Wilson 57
Ronoe, Adelia 19
*Ronoe, Daniel 19
Ronoe, Henird 19
Ronoe, John 19
Ronoe, Margaret 19
Ronoe, Michael 19
Rose, Anderson(x)79
Rose, Charles H.56
*Rose, Cintha 72
Rose, Eliza 57
Rose, Elizabeth 56
Rose, Elizabeth 64
*Rose, Enoch 56
Rose, George 64
Rose, Hugh 64
Rose, John H.64
Rose, John T.57
Rose, Malinda 72
Rose, Mary R. 72
Rose, Nancy 64
*Rose, Robert 64
Rose, Sarah C.72
Rose, Virginia 72
Rose, Walter 64
Ross, Amacetta 37
Ross, Cela J. 37
*Ross, David P.37
Ross, George 37
Ross, Isaac 37
Ross, Jane 37
Ross, William D. 37

Rouse,Charles 75
Rouse,Drucilla 75
Rouse,Eliza 75
Rouse,Frances 75
*Rouse,Richard 75
Rouse,Samuel(x)75
Rouse,Spencer(x)75
Rousey,Andrew O.62
*Rousey,Archibald 62
Rousey,Dicy 62
*Rousey,James 21
Rousey,James S.(x)21
Rousey,John 21
*Rousey,John J.63
Rousey,Mary 21
Rousey,Sarah 63
*Ruatin,David 36
Ruatin,Eliza 36
Ruatin,Jesse S.36
Ruatin,Marion 36
Ruffner,Elizabeth(x)71
Runnels see Reynolds
*Russell,Albert G.46
Russell,Allice 45
Russell,Charles A.56
Russell,Dollie 45
Russell,Edward T.46
Russell,Georgie 56
Russell,James C.52
Russell,John L.52
Russell,Laura J.46
*Russell,Malissa 56
Russell,Mary M.46
Russell,Nannie 56
Russell,Olaver E.56
Russell,Olivia M.46
Russell,Robert E.56
*Russell,St.Mark 45
Russell,Susan 52
*Russell,William H.52
Salmon,Albert E.13
Salmon,Catherine(x)11
Salmon,Edward B.13
Salmon,Joel K.13
Salmon,Lucy 13
Salmon,Lucy(x)11
Salmon,Martha 13
Salmon,Mary L. 13
Samuels,Ceres B. 13
Samuels,Fannie 14
*Samuels,Henry J.13
Samuels,John E. 14
*Samuels,Laffayett 14
Samuels,Mary E.(x)13

Samuels,Mary E.14
Samuels,Minnie 14
Samuels,Nettie D.13
Samuels,Rebecca A.13
Samuels,Verona 14
Samuels,Willie R. 14
Sanders,Catherine 41
*Sanders,Francis 41
Sanders,John H. 41
Sanders,Malinda 41
Sanders,Margaret 41
Sanders,Robert L. 41
Sanders,William F. 41
Sandridge,Allice 8
Sandridge,Amacetta 8
*Sandridge,Benjamin 8
Sandridge,John 8
Sandridge,Lucy 8
Sandridge,Sarah E. 8
Sandridge,Virginia 8
*Savage,George 69
Savage,Judy 69
Savage,Manerva 69
Scarberry,William(x)77
Schankes,Lucy(x)43
Schlagal,Henry 74
*Schlagal,John 74
Schlagal,Mary 74
Schmidt,Antonio(x)13
Schmidt,Ludwick(x)13
Scott,Abbia 43
Scott,Charles(x)43
Scott,Delphine 15
Scott,Harvey 15
*Scott,Harvey M. 15
Scott,James 43
Scott,Mary J. 43
Scott,Sanford W. 43*
Scott,William H.43
*Seamonds,Aaron 36
Seamonds,Agnis G.71
Seamonds,Albert G.10
*Seamonds,Andrew 10
Seamonds,Charles W.10
Seamonds,Delia 36
Seamonds,Frank P.10
Seamonds,Helena 10
Seamonds,Henrietta 10
Seamonds,James A.37
Seamonds,James D.10
Seamonds,John L.10
Seamonds,Mary 10

Seamonds,Nancy(x)8
Seamonds,Nathaniel 36
Seamonds,Paton(x)8
Seamonds,Randolph 10
Seamonds,Richard 36
*Seamonds,Robert 37
*Seamonds,Sampson 71
Seamonds,Sarah J.10
Seamonds,Susan 10
*Seamonds,William 10
Seamonds,William(x)8
Seashols,Ematine 27
*Seashols,John 27
Seashols,Lucretia 27
Sedam,Abraham (x)13
Sedinger,Agnes 45
Sedinger,Henry L.45
*Sedinger,James D.45
*Serange,George 47
Serange,Rebecca 47
Sexton,Ann 9
Sexton,Frank 9
Sexton,Henry B.9
Sexton,Horatio H.9
*Sexton,John 9
Sexton,John A. 9
Sexton,Mary 9
Sexton,William 9
Shankley,Annie(x)61
Shaver,Clore E.(x)41
Shaver,Daniel(x)41
Shaver,Emogene(x)41
*Shaver,John 41
Shaver,Luell 41
Shaver,Mary M. 41
*Sheff,Andrew 80
Sheff,Carolina(x)15
Sheff,Catherine 80
Sheff,Lerrie(x)81
Sheff,Olevia 11
*Sheff,William P.11
Sheff,William(x)21
Shelton,Albert 14
Shelton,America 14
Shelton,Anthony(x)14
Shelton,Charles 13
*Shelton,Chas.50
Shelton,Eliza 13
Shelton,Emma 14
Shelton,Fannie 14
Shelton,Frank 14
Shelton,Gains 14
Shelton,Henry W.50
*Shelton,James 14

Shelton,Margaret(x)14
Shelton,Martha(x)64
Shelton,Mary 14
Shelton,Mary M.(x)50
Shelton,Mary Y.11
Shelton,Mattie 14
Shelton,Nancy G.50
Shelton,Robert 14
Shelton,Susan 50
Shelton,Susie(x)50
*Shelton,Thomas 13
*Shelton,Walter 11
Shelton,William(x)50
Shelton,Willie 14
Sheppard,Charles 7
Sheppard,Elizabeth 7
Sheppard,George 7
*Sheppard,James 7
Sheppard,William 7
*Sheratz,Canaro 68
Sheratz,Nancy 68
Shinburg,George 47
Shinburg,John 47
Shinburg,Mary E.47
*Shipe,Charles 14
Shipe,Ellen 14
Shipe,Hellen 14
Shipe,Mary E. 14
Shipe,Robert A. 14
Shipe,William A.14
Shoemaker,Joseph(x)82
Shultz,Charles 42
*Shultz,Jacob 42
Shultz,James E. 42
Shultz,Mary 42
Shultz,Rosey 47
Shultz,William 47
*Shumaker,Charles 71
Shumaker,Conwelsa 71
Shumaker,Elizabeth 71
Shumaker,James 71
Shumaker,Lucy(x)63
Shumaker,Nancy(x)63
Shumaker,Robert 71
Shumaker,Sarah M.71
Shy,Abigal 38
Shy,Albina 39
*Shy,Benjamin 53
Shy,Clarona 39
Shy,Dudley
Shy,Edgar F.53
Shy,Edna 41
Shy,Edward(x)2
Shy,Elizabeth(x)2

Shy,Frank 39
Shy,Franklin 38
Shy,Georgia E. 41
Shy,Gerard 39
Shy,Harvey W.41
Shy,Jackson 39
Shy,Jefferson 41
Shy,Josephine 41
Shy,Marcellus
Shy,Mary 53
Shy,Mary E.53
Shy,Melvina 39
Shy,Richard E.53
Shy,Robert 39
Shy,Waldo J.41
Shy,William 39
Sidebottom,Elizabeth 29
Sidebottom,George 29
*Sidebottom,John C.29
Sides,Vincent 49
*Simmon,Conwesla 71
Simmon,Elizabeth 71
Simmonds,Fannie 36
Simmonds,John W. 36
*Simmonds,Joseph 36
Simmonds,Lucy E.36
Simmonds,Lussa J.36
Simon,Bena 16
Simon,Catherine 16
*Simon,Fredrick 16
Simon,Henry 16
Sirus,Emma(x)15
Sites,Carolina 61
Sites,Cintha V.61
Sites,Emily 61
*Sites,Godfrey 61
Sites,Martha E. 61
Sites,Mary A. 61
Sites,Susan 61
Sites,Thomas J.61
Skitter,Anna(x)45
Smallridge,Ellen E.9
*Smallridge,James 9
Smick,Albert 74
Smick,James B.74
Smick,Mary 74
*Smick,Phillip 74
Smick,Sarah 74
Smick,Semantha 74
Smith,Abraham 47
Smith,Albert S.83
Smith,Allen 2
Smith,Amanda 70
*Smith,Ambros 70

Smith,Amie 83
Smith,Anjaline 4
Smith,Ann 2
Smith,Ann 52
smith,Anna A.70
Smith,Anna L.27
*Smith,Austin 47
Smith,Barlery(x)23
Smith,Bennett 28
Smith,Burrel 4
smith,Catherine 23
*Smith,Charles 28
*Smith,Charles 49
Smith,Charles 57
Smith,Charles F.49
Smith,Collins(x)72
*Smith,Daniel 23
Smith,Daniel G.54
*Smith,David F.70
Smith,David(x)20
*Smith,Dudly D.47
Smith,Dudly J.47
*Smith,Edward A.45
Smith,Edward S. 45
Smith,Ela C.4
Smith,Elijah 23
Smith,Eliza(x)24
Smith,Eliza(x)82
*Smith,Elizabeth 4
Smith,Elizabeth 49
Smith,Elizabeth(x)82
Smith,Ellen(x)72
Smith,Ellinor(x)20
Smith,Ellison 2
Smith,Eloner 47
Smith,Elvery(x)63
Smith,Ezra W.54
Smith,Fanney J.54
Smith,Frances(x)83
Smith,Francis 52
*Smith,Frank 83
Smith,Fredrick(x)19
Smith,Georgie 70
*Smith,Gorham 82
Smith,Grant 70
Smith,Granville(x)72
*Smith,Henry 52
Smith,Henry S.47
Smith,Isadora(x)23
Smith,Jacob F.4
Smith,James 4
Smith,James M.54
Smith,James R.81
Smith,James(x)24

Smith,James(x)82	Smith,Vetria 71	*Spurlock,Thomas D.77
Smith,Jefferson 4	Smith,Virginia 54	Spurlock,William M.74
Smith,John 23	Smith,Virginia(x)23	Spurlock,William 78
Smith,John 52	Smith,Walter L.70	Stark,Charena 38
Smith,John H.54	Smith,WilLiam 49	Stark,Emily 38
Smith,John w. 81	*Smith,William 27	Stark,Emily 38
*Smith,Joseph 81	Smith,William 54	Stark,Fannie 38
Smith,Joseph S. 81	Smith,William 82	Stark,George 38
Smith,Josia G.45	Smith,William J.81	Stark,James 38
Smith,Julia 28	Smith,William(x)2	*Stark,John 38
Smith,Julia A.81	Smith,William(x)20	Stark,Lerona 38
Smith,Leander(x)83	Smith,William(x)24	Stark,Mary V. 38
Smith,Lee 27	Spears,Albertia 52	Steel,Emma E. 59
Smith,Lucy 71	Spears,Hulda J.(x)52	Steel,Everett E. 59
Smith,Lucy A. 47	Spears,Margaret(x)52	Steel,Lyda L.59
Smith,Luella 47	Spears,Mary J.51	Steel,Mary E.59
Smith,Mahala 2	*Spears,William 51	Steel,Mary M.59
Smith,Malinda 27	Spencer,Anna E.72	*Steel,Samuel E.59
Smith,Marenda 4	*Spencer,James 72	Steel,Wilmont L.59
Smith,Margaret(x)63	Spencer,Mary 72	Stentson,Anthony 15
Smith,Martha(x)18	*Spicer,Henry 41	Stentson,Henry 15
Smith,Mary 81	Spicer,Lee 41	Stentson,Laura 15
Smith,Mary 82	Spicer,Lucella 41	Stephenson,Addison 32
Smith,Mary A. 47	Spicer,Medora 41	Stephenson,Allen 32
Smith,Mary E. 49	Spicer,Nicholas 41	Stephenson,Allin B.49
Smith,Mary E.44	Spurlock,Abner 78	Stephenson,Amanda 32
Smith,Mary F. 81	Spurlock,Andrew 74	Stephenson,Amanda 40
Smith,Mary G. 71	Spurlock,Anetta M.78	Stephenson,Amasetta 42
Smith,Mary G.71	Spurlock,Catherine 74	Stephenson,Anna 42
Smith,Mary J.54	Spurlock,Charles J.77	Stephenson,Charles 34
Smith,Mary P. 45	Spurlock,Daniel A. 77	Stephenson,Charles 40
Smith,Mary(x)24	Spurlock,David 77	Stephenson,Charles 42
Smith,Mary(x)55	Spurlock,Elizabeth 77	Stephenson,Edna 49
Smith,Mary(x)83	*Spurlock,Harvey 77	Stephenson,Elby 32
Smith,Matilda(x)83	Spurlock,Ira J.74	Stephenson,Ella M.35
Smith,Missouri(x)83	Spurlock,James H.77	Stephenson,Ellena J.49
Smith,Olive F.70	Spurlock,Jane A. 78	Stephenson,Etna C.40
*Smith,Percival 57	Spurlock,Jesse 77	Stephenson,Evaline 32
*Smith,Persivel 44	Spurlock,Jesse(x)77	*Steveson,Everman 20
*Smith,Ralph 2	Spurlock,John E.74	Stephenson,Fredrick 49
Smith,Randolph 70	Spurlock,Joseph(x)48	Stephenson,Georgianna 34
Smith,Robert 49	Spurlock,Levery W.77	Stephenson,Georgie F.32
Smith,Robert 52	Spurlock,Lillie B.74	*Stephenson,Henry 49
Smith,Roda 2	Spurlock,Lonora S.74	Stephenson,Hutaka 42
*Smith,Samuel 54	Spurlock,Lora A.74	Stephenson,Jefferson 42
Smith,Sarah 52	Spurlock,Margaret 78	Stephenson,John L.49
Smith,Sarah A. 49	Spurlock,Margret 78	Stephenson,John M. 40
Smith,Sarah E.70	Spurlock,Mary E. 77	Stephenson,John W.42
Smith,Sarah M.81	Spurlock,Nancy E. 78	*Stephenson,Joseph 40
Smith,Sarah(x)20	Spurlock,Sarah A. 78	Stephenson,Jospeh M.40
Smith,Sigman 71	*Spurlock,Simeon 78	*Stephenson,Lafyett 42
Smith,Talethia 2	*Spurlock,Stephen 78	Stephenson,Lucian 32
Smith,Tamsey 57	Spurlock,Susan 78	Stephenson,Lucy 40
Smith,Telitha 70	*Spurlock,Thomas 74	Stephenson,Manera 32

Stephenson,Mark(x)35	*Stroops,William 11	Suter,James P.(x)82
Stephenson,Martha 32	Sturgeon,Mary A. 11	Swan,Anzonetta 60
*Stephenson,Mary 34	*Sturgeon,Robert 11	*Swan,Ballard 60
Stevenson,Mary C.20	*Sullivan,Alonzo 36	*Swan,Benjamin 16
Stephenson,Mary E.32	Sullivan,Alonzo C. 35	Swan,Benjamin(x)60
Stephenson,McHerston 32	Sullivan,Alven 35	Swan,Beverly 58
Stephenson,Medora 34	Sullavin,Amanda 32	*Swan,Calvary 59
Stephenson,Nancy 42	Sullavin,Andrew 32	Swan,Catherine(x)60
Stephenson,Preston 42	*Sullavin,Anna 32	Swan,Charlotte 16
Stephenson,Robert 40	Sulliven,Bridget 21	Swan,Cintha A.69
*Stephenson,Samuel 32	Sullivan,Catherine 35	Swan,Daniel W. 59
Stephenson,Sidney 32	Sullivan,Daniel C. 35	Swan,Edith 59
Stephenson,Sidney A.34	Sullavin,David 32	Swan,Elizabeth 60
Stephenson,St.Luke 40	Sullavin,Ellen 32	Swan,Elizabeth 68
Stephenson,Stonwall J.49	Sullaven,Elizabeth 37	Swan,Emeretta 60
Stephenson,Susan 40	Sullivan,Elizabeth 35	Swan,Emily J. 16
Stephenson,Sylvester J.32	Sullivan,Emma 35	Swan,Emily J.59
Stephenson,Thomas 34	Sullivan,George 35	Swan,Enoch A.68
Stephenson,Thomas(58)	Sullavin,Harriet 32	Swan,Francis M.16
Stephenson,Vinson W.42	*Sullivan,Henry 35	Swan,Franklin 59
Stephenson,Willam P.34	Sullivan,Henry M.35	Swan,Garrett J.59
*Stephenson,William 32	*Sullavin,Jacob 32	Swan,George W.58
Stephenson,William 40	*Sullaven,James 37	Swan,Georgie 69
Stevenson,William H.20	Sulliven,James 21	*Swan,Henly C.60
Stephenson,Willie A. 49	*Sulliven,Jerry 21	*Swan,Hezekiah)60
Stephenson,Wm.E.32	Sulliven,John 21	*Swan,Isiah 58
Stewart,Allice 53	Sullavin,John 32	Swan,Isiah 60
Stewart,Charles(x)14	Sulliven,Julia 21	Swan,James H.69
Stewart,Columbia 53	Sullavin,John 32	Swan,Jasper 68
Stewart,Daniel E. 48	Sullivan,Malissey 35	*Swan,John K.68
Stewart,Edward(x)14	Sullivan,Martha S.	*Swan,John R.69
Stewart,Ella F.50	Sulliven,Mary 21	Swan,John T.59
Stewart,Emma 50	Sullivan,Mary J. 35	Swan,Joseph E.58
Stewart,Fletcher 48	Sullivan,Sarah E.	Swan,Joseph W.69
Stewart,Hamilton 48	Sullavin,Parvilla 32	Swan,Leanna 60
Stewart,Harriet(x)14	Sullavin,William 32	*Swan,Leven C.69
Stewart,Henry H.53	Summers,Edgar 23	Swan,Lizzie K. 16
Stewart,Isaac F.53	*Summers,George 23	Swan,Louisa J. 16
*Stewart,James 53	Summers,Julia 23	*Swan,Manville 69
Stewart,James B.53	Summers,Lyra 23	Swan,Martha 60
Stewart,Joseph 53	Summers,Margaret 23	Swan,Martha A.(x)57
*Stewart,Mariah 48	Summers,Mathew 23	Swan,Maru A. 60
Stewart,Martha 50	Summers,Sarah 23	Swan,Mary A. 59
Stewart,Mary F. 50	*Summers,Sylvester 23	Swan,McHerston 68
Stewart,Mary(x)14	Summers,Thomas 23	Swan,Mollie 69
*Stewart,Robert 50	Summerson,Ada 9	Swan,Nancy 60
Stewart,Sarah 53	Summerson,Birdie 9	Swan,Nancy 68
Stewart,Sarah B.48	*Summerson,Charles 9	Swan,Nettie 16
Stewart,Viola 48	Summerson,Emma 9	Swan,Patrick H.60
Stowater,Cristina 83	Summerson,George 9	Swan,Rachel 58
*Stowater,Frank 83	Summerson,Netta 9	Swan,Rezin 68
Stratton,Cezar(x)51	Summerson,Richard 9	Swan,Richard 59
Stroops,John H.11	*Sunderlin,Charlotte 26	Swan,Sarah 59
Stroops,Sarah F.11	Sunderlin,John H.26	Swan,Shelby J.69
	Sunderlin,William 26	

Swan, Susan A.69
Swan, Walter E.60
Swan, William J.68
Switzer, Clymer 18
*Switzer, Ellen 18
Switzer, Rufus 18
Switzer, Vara 18
Switzer, Virginia 18
Tacket, Minerva(x)38
Tasson, Cintha A.29
*Tasson, John 30
Tasson, Mary 29
Tasson, Ona A.29
Tasson, Rebecca H.29
Taylor, Edward(x)41
*Taylor, Gabriel 55
Taylor, George 75
Taylor, Henry 75
*Taylor, Henry M.51
Taylor, Henry P.51
*Taylor, Isaac 75
Taylor, Isabella55
Taylor, James W.51
Taylor, Lotta B.51
Taylor, Mary 75
Taylor, Mary C.51
Taylor, Melcina 75
Taylor, Rody 75
Taylor, Sarah E. 51
Taylor, William R.51
Telgner, Agnis 83
*Telgner, Emile
Telgner, Julia 83
Telgner, Teressey 83
Templeton, Adison H.83
Templeton, Bennett V.81
Templeton, Charles 81
Templeton, Charles H.83
Templeton, Claressey E.81
Templeton, Elizabeth 83
Templeton, Esom T.83
Templeton, Francis J.81
*Templeton, Harvey 83
Templeton, Isaac 83
*Templeton, Jesse A. 81
Templeton, John L.81
Templeton, John L.83
Templeton, Julia 81
Templeton, Lucinda 83
Templeton, Mary A.83
Templeton, Mary J.81
Templeton, Minisota 83
*Templeton, Ransom 83
Templeton, Sarah A. 81

Templeton, Thomas 81
Templeton, William 81
Templeton, William 83
Thacker, America(x)47
Thacker, Benjamin 35
Thacker, Clarissey(x)35
Thacker, Elizabeth 35
*Thacker, Gerard 35
Thacker, Louisa 35
Thacker, William(x)47
*Thackston, Benjamin 15
Thackston, Eugenia 15
Thackston, James A. 15
Thackston, Kate K. 15
Thackston, Mary W. 15
Thackston, William C. 15
Thomas, Burton 22
Thomas, Cora 23
Thomas, Fannie 18
Thomas, Flora 23
Thomas, Henry 22
Thomas, Jane 22
Thomas, Julia A.18
Thomas, Mary S.18
Thomas, Matha A.18
*Thomas, Nelson C.18
Thomas, Nora 23
*Thomas, Samuel 22
Thomas, Samuel 23
Thomas, Viola 23
Thomas, William 18
Thompson, Almeda(x)11
Thompson, Elizabeth 42
Thompson, Elizabeth 58
Thompson, Emily S. 61
Thompson, Frances(x)27
Thompson, Frances 54
*Thompson, Gilbert 37
*Thompson, Henry 42
Thompson, Isaac 11*
Thompson, James 37
Thompson, James(x)11
Thompson, James N.58
*Thompson, John L.61
Thompson, Lawson 58
Thompson, Lucinda 37
Thompson, Lucy(x)45
Thompson, Lucy C.37
Thompson, Martha C.58
Thompson, Martha J.58
Thompson, Mary(x)45
Thompson, Mary L.54
Thompson, Ora 37
Thompson, Richard 37

Thompson, Samuel(x)45
Thompson, Sarah 11
Thompson, Sarah J.37
Thompson, Stanhope 58
*Thompson, Thomas 54
Thompson, Virginia 54
Thompson, Walter 61
Thompson, William 37
*Thompson, William 58
Thompson, William 61
Thornburg, Barbery 38
Thornburg, Bentin 38
Thornburg, Caroline(x)4
Thornburg, Charles(x)4
Thornburg, Charles 55
Thornburg, Claudius 3
*Thornburg, David 46
Thornburg, David B.46
Thornburg, Elizabeth(x)4
Thornburg, Emily H.3
Thornburg, George E.13
Thornburg, Georgie 14
Thornburg, Gerturde 3
*Thornburg, Hezakiah 38
Thornburg, James L.3
*Thornburg, James M.55
Thornburg, Joanna 46
Thornburg, John M.3
*Thornburg, John W.14
*Thornburg, John W.3
Thornburg, Joseph 49
Thornburg, Maggie 13
Thornburg, Mariah 49
Thornburg, Mary A.55
Thornburg, Mary F.49
Thornburg, Mary L.13
Thornburg, Mary S.13
Thornburg, Mary S.3
*Thornburg, Miller 49
*Thornburg, Moses 13
*Thornburg, Moses 4
Thornburg, Moses M.46
Thornburg, Nannie A.13
Thornburg, Nannie(x)42
Thornburg, Rachel 46
Thornburg, Sarah 14
Thornburg, Sarah W.(x)4
*Thornburg, Thomas 13
Thornburg, Thomas 38
Thornburg, Thomas H.13
Thornburg, Victoria 55
Thornburg, Virginia 55

Thornburg,Walter 38
Thornburg,Willie F.3
Tiche,Martin(x)19
Toney,Edith 74
Toney,Elena E.74
Toney,Elizabeth 74
*Toney,Joel 74
Toney,Joel A. 74
Toney,John(x)69
Toney,John 74
Toney,Lucinda 74
Toney,Thomas L.74
Toney,William 74
Tooley,Cintha A.68
*Tooley,Tandy 68
Toppings,Albertie 56
Topping,Andrew(x)37
Topping,Cassus 31
Topping,Catherine 31
Toppings,Charles A.56
Toppings,Colvia 56
Toppings,Elinda(x)31
Toppings,Emma 56
Topping,Fenton 31
Topping,Fermanda 31
Toppings,Henry 56
*Toppings,John 56
Toppings,Lenard 56
*Topping,Levi 31
Toppings,Lucy 56
Topping,Medley 31
Topping,Nancy 31
Toppings,Susan 56
Topping,Virgel 31
Topping,Virginia 56
Topping,William T.56
Townson,Amanda 38
Townson,Hagan 38
*Townson,William 38
Trippeet,Caleb 79
Trippeet,Jane 79
*Trippeet,Jesse G. 79
Trippeet,William 79
Tucker,Aber S.47
*Tucker,Elijah 51
*Tucker,Francis M.55
*Tucker,Fulton 47
Tucker,Georgie 47
Tucker,Lucy 55
Tucker,Malissa 46
Tucker,Virginia 51
Tucker,Willard 55
*Tucker,William 46
Tucker,William M.55

Turley,Anna 10
Turley,Douglas 10
Turley,Eliza 10
Turley,Eliza A.10
Turley,Fannie 10
*Turley,Jonathan 10
Turley,Mary D.10
Turley,Sofia 10
Turner,Alice(x)15
Turner,Allice 31
Tuner,America 84
Turner,Andrew 84
Turner,Columbia(x)36
Turner,Henry B.31
Turner,Joseph 84
Turner,Leander 42
*Turner,Lenard 84
Turner,Lucy 84
Turner,Lymon 42
Turner,Mary(x)36
Turner,Mary 84
Turner,Mary J.42
*Turner,Nathaniel 31
Turner,Susan 42
*Turner,Thomas 42
Tuner,Victor A.42
Turner,Zerilda 31
Upton,John(x)56
Upton,Missouri(x)56
*Venatta,Jackson 48
Vanatta,John J. 41
Vanatta,Lucy 41
Venatta,Mary J.48
Vanatta,Robert 41
*Vanatta,William 41
Vance,Elizabeth(x)44
Venath,Amanda 65
Venath,Delpha 65
Venath,George O.65
*Venath,Irvin 65
Vess,Cintha A.(x)59
Vess,Filande 11
Vess,Huldy 12
Vess,Jacob(x)58
Vess,James 12
Vass,John(x)56
Vess,John(x)59
Vess,Mary E. 11
Vess,Mary J.11
*Vess,Mathew 11
Vess,Missouri 12
Vess,Oliver 12
Vess,Salie 12
Vess,William 11

Viney,Jupiter(x)51
Viney,Leah(x)51
viney,Virginia(x)51
*Vinson,Bennett 25
Vinson,Charles 25
Vinson,Gracy 25
Vinson,Mary F. 25
Vinson,William 25
Waldin,Thomas(x)69
Walker,Adelia 4
Walker,Anna M.4
Walker,Charles(x)49
Walker,Elisha C.4
Walker,Eliza H.(x)54
Walker,Elizabeth 4
Walker,Franklin 4
*Walker,Harvey 4
Walker,Henry W.4
Walker,James A.4
*Walker,Leland 15
Walker,Martha V.4
Walker,Richard E.4
Walker,Sarah J.4
Walker,Sidney 4
(Wall),James O.53
*Wall,John 18
Wall,Zernah 18
Wallace,Ada 22
Wallace,Edna 21
Wallace,Emily 21
Wallace,Emily 80
Wallace,Georgia 21
Wallace,Harriet 22
*Wallace,Henry 21
*Wallace,Hughy 22
Wallace,Ida 22
Wallace,Isaac 21
Wallace,Jennetta 21
*Wallace,Jessey 22
Wallace,Laura 80
Wallace,Letta 22
Wallace,Luvena 21
Wallace,Malinda 80
Wallace,Margaret 22
Wallace,Tabitha 22
*Wallace,Thona 22
*Wallace,Tolaver 80
Wallace,Uriah 22
Walters,Catherine 64
Walters,Dora G.64
Walters,Francis 64
Walters,James L.64
Walters,Rachel 64
Walters,Rebecca 64

Walters,Ulysses G.64
*Walters,William 64
*Ward,Adaline 44
Ward,Charles 50
*Ward,David Y.49
Ward,Eliza 50
Ward,Elizabeth 50
Ward,Fannie 50
Ward,Henry 50
Ward,James 50
Ward,Joanna 50
*Ward,John 50
Ward,Mortica(x)42
Ward,Phillip 50
Ward,William 44
Ward,William 50
Warren,Anna(x)41
Warren,Bluford(x)41
Warren,Elizabeth(x)41
Warren,Sarah(x)41
*Warring,Clement 51
Warring,Elizabeth 51
Warring,Rebecca 51
Warring,Susan P.51
*Watters,George 23
Watters,Jane 23
Watters,Mary 23
Watton,Emma(x)43
*Waugh,Charley 6
Waugh,Hiram 6
Waugh,Lemary 6
Waugh,Nancy 6
Waugh,Patrick 6
Waugh,Susan S.6
Webb,Arabella 51
Webb,Enoch G.51
Webb,George(x)60
Webb,James D.51
*Webb,Theodore 51
Webb,Willie C.51
Weed,Aldie 46
Weed,Bula 46
Weed,Dora F.46
Weed,Flora 46
Weed,Gennie 46
Weed,Howerd 46
*Weed,Isaac 46
Weed,Sarah 46
Weekly,Alcinda 79
Weekly,Amanda 79
*Weekly,Elias 78

Weekly,Henry 79
*Weekly,James 79
Weekly,Joseph 79
Weekly,Phebe 79
Weekly,Sarah 78
Weeman,Henry E.33
Weeman,Omillian H.33
*Weeman,Otto 33
Well,Angela 79
Well,George 79
Well,Emadelia 79
Well,Elizabeth 79
*Well,Jesse 79
Well,Lenard 79
Wellington,Albina F.48
Wellington,Charlott(x)48
Wellington,Elizabeth 48
Wellington,John 48
Wellington,Mary L.48
Wellington,Nathaniel 48
Wellington,Taylor 48
*Wellington,Nodiah 48
Wentz,Alexander 39
Wentz,Anthony 39
Wentz,Arnetta 6
Wentz,Cora 39
*Wentz,Elizabeth 10
Wentz,Henry C.39
Wentz,Jenetta 6
Wentz,John 6
*Wentz,John P.39
Wentz,John T.(x)57
Wentz,John W.39
*Wentz,Lewis M.6
Wentz,Louisa 39
Wentz,Matilda 39
Wentz,Mary E.39
Wentz,Morris 39
Wentz,Nora E.39
Wentz,Sarah E.6
Wentz,William 10
*Wentz,William 39
*Wheeler,Adison 20
Wheeler,Edna J. 20
Wheeler,James 21
Wheeler,Jefferson 21
Wheeler,John M.21
Wheeler,Joseph 20
Wheeler,Margaret(x)68
Wheeler,Robert J. 20
Wheeler,Sarah 20
Wheeler,William 20
Wheeler,William(x)68
*White,Albert G.45

White,Anna R.46
White,Atta A.45
White,Catherine 82
White,Dave 29
White,Drucilla E.46
White,Emily 18
White,Eugenia 46
White,James G.45
*White,James H.82
*White,John H.46
White,John H.82
White,Lucy 29
White,Lucy 82
White,Martha M.46
White,Mary 18
White,Mary 29
White,Mary L.45
White,Mary V.46
White,Nimrod 82
White,Octava 29
*White,Peter 18
White,Sallie M.45
White,Sarah J.82
White,Susan 45
White,William 82
*White,Zacheriah 29
Willey,Arametta 6
Wiley,Anna 26
Wiley,Elizabeth 26
Wiley,Frances 26
Wiley,Henry 26
Wiley,James 26
Wiley,Jesse 26
*Willey,Joseph L.6
Wiley,Lucinda 26
Wiley,Martha 26
*Wiley,Robert 26
*Wiley,William 26
Willey,William F.6
Wilks,Albert 33
Wilks,Alexander 33
Wilks,America 39
Wilks,America 33
Wilks,Barbery 33
Wilks,Barbery 39
*Wilks,Burwell 33
Wilks,Henry 33
*Wilks,James 39
Wilks,Josephine 39
Wilks,Levila 39
Wilks,Mary(x)80
Williams,Andrew 57
*Williams,Arthur 54
Williams,Charles E.57

Williams,Ellen(x)52	Wilson,Lorustus 59	Wolcott,Clara A. 54
Williams,George(x)75	Wilson,Maggie 8	Wolcott,Cora A.54
Williams,Harriet 54	Wilson,Malinda 8	Wolcott,Missouri 55
Williams,Herndon J.54	Wilson,Margaret 59	Wolf,Emily 55
Williams,James A.57	Wilson,Martha 59	Wolf,James M.55
Williams,John(x)61	Wilson,Mary A. 8	Wolf,Julia E.55
Williams,John A.(x)37	Wilson,Mary S.18	Wolf,Martha J.55
*Williams,John E.54	Wilson,Mary V.9	Wolf,Mary E.55
*Williams,John L.56	Wilson,Olliver 50	*Wolf,Reuben D.55
Williams,John W.57	Wilson,Sarah A.42	Wolf,Sannova 55
Williams,Joseph H.57	Wilson,Susan 81	Wolford,Amanda 42
Williams,Levery(x)56	*Wilson,Thomas 50	Wolford,Cintha 42
Williams,Lillie 57	Wilson,Thomas 59	Wolford,David 42
Williams,Lilley B.37	Wilson,Thurston 50	*Wolford,James 42
Williams,Lora E.54	Wilson,Virginia 50	Wolford,Jennie 42
Williams,Lucinda(x)37	Wilson,William(x)42	Wolford,William 42
Williams,Margaret 56	Wilson,William(x)76	Womeldroff,Anna E.45
Williams,Martha 57	*Wingo,Abner W. 52	Womeldroff,Augustes 45
Williams,Mary 38	Wingo,Charles B.52	Womeldroff,Daniel(x)44
Williams,Mary E.57	Wingo,Henry L.52	Womeldroff,Harriet E.45
Williams,Mary M.54	Wingo,John T.52	Womeldroff,Henry C.45
Williams,Nancy L.56	Wingo,Samuel 52	*Womeldroff,James 45
Williams,Phillip D.54	Wingo,Sarah L.52	Womeldroff,Jennie L.45
Williams,Robert E.57	Winters,Alice R.76	Womeldroff,Robert E.45
Williams,Ruth C.54	Winters,Charles 77	Womeldroff,Virginia(x)44
*Williams,Samuel 38	Winters,Esther(x)76	Wood,Anetta 6
Williams,Samuel L.57	*Winters,George 77	*Wood,George H.6*
*Williams,Samuel P.57	*Winters,Hannah 8	Wood,Fannie 42
Williams,Sarah E.38	Winters,Henry J.76	*Wood,Horatio H.42
*Wilson,Acy L.8	Winters,Henry V.76	Wood,Laura 42
Wilson,Albert 50	Winters,Laura 76	Wood,Lucy 6
Wilson,Alexander 59	*Winters,Lemuel 76	Wood,Margaret 42
Wilson,Alice E.81	Winters,Mary E. 77	Wood,Mary E. 42
Wilson,Ammacetta 18	Winters,William F.76	Wood,Millroy 6
*Wilson,Ann V.9	Winters,Telitha 8	Wood,Susan 6
Wilson,Anna J.59	Wise,Cerus J.58	Wood,William 42
Wilson,Benjamin 59	*Wise,John 58	Woodard,Adaline 28
Wilson,Charles(x)76	Wise,Hardin 58	Woodard,Anjaline 27
Wilson,Ella 50	Wise,Hester A.58	Woodard,Elizabeth 28
Wilson,Ellen 8	Wise,Jacob H.58	Woodard,Frances 75
Wilson,Ellen 50	Wise,John 58	Woodard,Harriet 28
Wilson,Ellen E.50	Wise,John B.58	Woodard,Henrietta(x)26
Wilson,George W.59	Wise,Joseph L.58	*Woodard,Hezekiah 27
Wilson,Georgiana 50	Wise,Margaret 58	Woodard,John W.27
Wilson,Hettie 8	Wise,Nancy(x)58	Woodard,John(x)26
*Wilson,James 42	Witcher,Anna 14	Woodard,Madison,28*
*Wilson,James 59	*Witcher,John S.47	Woodard,Martha 75
Wilson,James A.50	Witcher,John T.47	Woodard,Mary 27
Wilson,Jemy 50	Witcher,Mahaly F.47	Woodard,Sarah 27
Wilson,John 42	*Witcher,Stephen 14	*Woodard,William 75
*Wilson,John T.18	Witcher,T.Sheriden 47	Woodrum,Anna 55
*Wilson,Lemuel 81	Witcher,Valera 47	Woodrum,Catherine 55
Wilson,Leonades 81	Witcher,William V.47	Woodrum,Cora 55
	*Wolcott,Bryon A.54	Woodrum,Elizabeth 55

Woodrum,Harriet 55
*Woodrum,Ira 55
Woodrum,John 55
Woodrum,Lena 55
Woodrum,Lewis 55
Woodrum,Robert 55
Woodrum,Sarah(x)44
Woodrum,Sarah 55
Woods,Bridget 20
Woods,Ellen 20
Woods,Elsly 278
Woods,James 20
Woods,Luanna 27
*Woods,Lyda 27
Woods,Margaret 27
Woods,Mary 20
Woods,Mary F.27
*Woods,William 20
Woodyard,Abraham 10
*Woodyard,Amos 10
Woodyard,Barthena 10
Woodyard,Charles 10
Woodyard,Eliza 10
Woodyard,George M.10
Woodyard,James F.10
Woodyard,Jasper 10
Woodyard,John W.10
Woodyard,Manly 10
Woodyard,Rebecca 10
Woodyard,Susan 10
Woodyard,William 10
Woolwine,Charles 19
*Woolwine,Henry 19
Woolwine,Mary 19
Woolwine,Nancy 19
Woolwine,William 19
Worden,Charles M.44
Worden,George 44
Worden,Hatta B.44
Worden,Ida 44
*Worden,William 44
*Workman,Ambrose 2
Workman,James N.2
Workman,John E.2
Workman,Lizzie V.2
Workman,Susan 2
Wray,George 72
*Wray,Henry 72
Wray,Nancy 72
Wray,Rody(x)72
Wray,Wilson 72
Wright,Ada 43
Wright,Albert 56
Wright,Albert N.55

*Wright,Bazel 55
Wright,Benjamin 55
Wright,Cora L.55
Wright,Edward E.43
*Wright,Edward D.56
Wright,Elizabeth 56
Wright,Ethel 56
Wright,Fannie 45
Wright,Flora 55
Wright,Florida 55
Wright,Harriet E.56
*Wright,Henry 52
Wright,Henry H.56
Wright,James 55
*Wright,James H.45
Wright,James H.56
Wright,Lucy 56
Wright,Luticia 52
Wright,Mary E. 56
Wright,Pheba 55
*Wright,Richard 56
Wright,Sallie 43
Wright,Sarah E.56
Wright,Thomas M.55
*Wright,William O.43
*Wyett,Davis 57
Wyett,Douglas 40
Wyett,Joseph 40
*Wyett,Ralph 40
Wyett,Rhoda 40
Wyett,Sarah 40
Yates,Adaline 81
Yates,Clarke S.61
Yates,Ezra W.81
Yates,Elizabeth(x)18
Yates,Frances 61
Yates,Jacob 81
Yates,James 81
Yates,James M.61
*Yates,John T.18
Yates,John W.(x)3
Yates,John W.61
Yates,John W.81
Yates,Julia 81
Yates,Lucretia 81
Yates,Nancy 61
*Yates,Peter A. 61
Yates,Rebecca 81
Yates,Sarah A. 61
Yates,Sarah E.(x)3
Yates,Sarah E. 61
Yates,Silas 61
Yates,Virgel 61

Yates,William M.
Yates,William P.(x)18
Yates,William 81

www.ingramcontent.com/pod-product-compliance
Lightning Source LLC
Chambersburg PA
CBHW080616270326
41928CB00016B/3082